S0-AGD-885

SALLY M. WEAVER is a member of the Department of Anthropology at the University of Waterloo.

The Trudeau government's White Paper on Indian policy issued in 1969 was a shock to members of the general public as well as the Indian population. Proposing to terminate all special rights, including the Indian Act, reserves, and treaties, it was diametrically opposed to what the Indians had been led to believe: that their rights would be honoured and that they would participate in shaping the policies that determined their future.

This book looks inside the federal government in the early Trudeau years to see how that White Paper was formulated. The author examines ideologies held by major policy makers in the face of concepts of public participation and public servant activism – two approaches to policy making closely coupled in Ottawa during the period. She reveals how the policy was developed behind closed doors by a number of conflicting bureaucracies, in spite of the efforts of those who recommended Indian participation. The result was Indian militancy and mistrust, the very condition the government hoped to dispel.

The White Paper was shelved in 1970, but it left a powerful legacy. It continues to have an impact on government-Indian relations, as the Indians judge current policies and action on the basis of their memories. The author evaluates this impact and its implications for future governments with an eye to avoiding past errors.

This book contributes to a greater understanding of government policy making. It demonstrates that personal aspirations and histories, individual philosophies, and political craftsmanship can dominate reason and logic in policy formulation.

STUDIES IN THE STRUCTURE OF POWER:

DECISION-MAKING IN CANADA
editor JACK GROVE

SALLY M. WEAVER

Making
Canadian
Indian Policy

The Hidden
Agenda
1968-70

UNIVERSITY OF TORONTO PRESS
Toronto Buffalo London

© University of Toronto Press 1981
Toronto Buffalo London

Printed in Canada

ISBN 0-8020-5504-4 (cloth)
     0-8020-6403-5 (paper)

*E
92
W4*

Canadian Cataloguing in Publication Data

Weaver, Sally M., 1940–
  Making Canadian Indian policy

  (Studies in the structure of power, decision-making
  in Canada ; 9)
  Bibliography: p.
  Includes index.
  ISBN 0-8020-5504-4 bd. ISBN 0-8020-6403-5 pa.

  1. Canada. Dept. of Indian Affairs and Northern Develop-
  ment. White paper on Indian policy, 1969. 2. Indians,
  Treatment of – Canada. 3. Indians of North America –
  Canada – Government relations. I. Title. II. Series.

E92.W42   323.1′197′071   C80-094754-1

To David

329354

Contents

Preface

This book began out of my curiosity about the way the White Paper on Indian policy was developed. My interest in the policy was fostered by my previous research experience with the Six Nations Iroquois on the Grand River Reserve in southern Ontario beginning in 1963. For a period of almost three years (1967–70), I attended most of the band council meetings, which both gave me an insight into Indian administration on a local level and also sparked my interest in the workings and policies of the Department of Indian Affairs and Northern Development (DIAND), the branch of the federal government entrusted with administering Canada's Indian population.

I can readily recall the radio announcement of the White Paper in June 1969 when I was having lunch at Bobby's Grill in Ohsweken, the village on the reserve. The question most people were asking, including myself, was 'What does it mean?' The radio announcement had been too brief for much of an understanding of what was being proposed by the federal government. I recall thinking that the proposal sounded like the termination policy the United States had adopted in 1954, and rejecting the notion that the Canadian government could have made the same mistake. The American policy of terminating special rights for Indians had proven so destructive to Indian communities that it was withdrawn in 1961.

The most immediate stimulus to write this book was a request in the fall of 1975 from Dr Jan Loubser, director of the Social Science Research Council, to give a paper on the role of social science in the formulation of the White Paper at the council's conference on Social Science and Public Policy.[1] Shortly after the conference I decided to study the total government process of policy formulation, the major concern of this book. As the research progressed the volume of material I was able to gather proved to be so extensive that the originally intended article evolved into a book.

The information on which this book is based comes from three sources; 51 interviews with 33 individuals who were involved in shaping the policy, government documents and reports, and published materials. Because this is not a study of Indian organizations, I did not interview Indian leaders, but I used their published accounts of the period in question and I corresponded with many of them to clarify or confirm certain issues.

From the winter of 1976 to early 1977 I conducted interviews in Ottawa, Vancouver, Victoria, and Toronto with most of the civil servants who played a major role in formulating the White Paper, as well as with the two ministers then responsible for Indian Affairs. Unfortunately, the major figure in the Prime Minister's Office, Jim Davey, died an accidental death before the research was begun.

None of the civil servants interviewed hold the same government positions at the time of writing that they held in 1968–69. Some have retired, one was fired, and others have left the government service voluntarily to pursue careers elsewhere. Confidentiality was a condition of most interviews, or portions of them, and consequently the sources of information are not acknowledged. In the few cases where individuals are named, I have not sought their endorsement of my analysis; the interpretation of their roles is my own. In all other instances where the analysis required singling out individuals, I have used pseudonyms, as indicated in the text. Personalities, however, were very important factors in the policy-making process and, when possible, I have described the personal styles of individuals according to either their own descriptions or those of others.

In addition to interviews, much information was obtained from government file materials. Collectively, these records provided me with specific information on most of the formal arguments presented during the policy-making process. Interviews provided necessary data on the unofficial arguments and events, as well as clarification of the contents of the documents and their use. The interviews also allowed me to decide whether the documents' contents were, in fact, the substance of the arguments or whether they were, in addition, 'strategy statements' designed to elicit responses other than the contents might suggest. Although all documents could be considered forms of strategy, there was a considerable degree of variation in this type of usage, as I indicate in the book. Collectively, the interviews and the file materials allowed me to construct a detailed picture of how the White Paper on Indian policy was developed.

Determining the use of favoured concepts and phrases during the policy process proved to be an important part of the research. It became apparent that the policy-makers did not share the same meanings for some of the terms they frequently used. Terms such as 'non-discrimination,' 'equality,' 'aboriginal rights,' and especially 'policy' were used in different ways by different people. For some, 'policy' meant a formal substantive statement prepared in secret within government; for others it meant a process of negotiation between government and Indians that produced a mutually agreed-upon position for future action. As the policy process continued, terms reflecting certain values became loaded, such as 'special rights,' so that they were dropped and replaced by others – 'transitional rights' in this case.

In both the documentation and the interviews it was evident that individuals often talked past each other because of their different constructions of reality – their own world view, values, ideology, and professional training. For some, the term 'development,' for instance, meant economic development (capital, jobs, resource development, managerial skills), while for those with social work training and community development experience it meant broadscale social development, fostering skill in such areas as education, leadership, work, and communication. The professional backgrounds of the policy-makers – be it in administration, law, social work, sociology, community development and adult education, physics, computer science, or economics – provided them with a particular frame of reference through which they viewed the problem and sought the solution. Although senior civil servants are theoretically 'generalists,' able to synthesize many different kinds of information and perspectives, their backgrounds understandably led to varied interpretations of events and to the systematic exclusion of certain types of information: a proposal considered sound by one official was described as 'a bunch of sociological crap' by another; what made good sense to one person was considered 'an absurdly legalistic interpretation' by another; graphs and flow charts prepared by one official for cabinet's edification were considered 'useless drawings' or 'pretty pictures' by another, and so on. There is no reason whatever to expect civil servants to be less immune to cognitive frameworks they derive from their professional training and experience than other professionals – including academics – but the myth of the 'generalist' persists.

One final point is worth noting. Almost all of the persons interviewed were displeased with the final shape of the White Paper. Most of them felt that the policy objective of 'equality' was ultimately correct, but they believed it would have been acceptable, or more acceptable, to Indians had the policy-making process developed in a different way. *Post facto* rationalizations by these policy-makers cannot be ruled out as a distorting factor in the information I received. In many cases emotional neutrality did not characterize the policy-makers as they recalled the events of the period, although many of them obviously attempted to back away from the events, and even their own behaviour, by commenting in a detached fashion on why they had held certain beliefs and how they had tried to bring about acceptance of these beliefs by others. The interviews provided an opportunity for them to explain what they felt should have happened and why it did not. The extensive documentation I had of the period provided me with one basis of checking *post facto* rationalizations.

It is important to underscore at the outset that the process of policy-making is a complex one, involving formal structural features of the bureaucracy and the cabinet; a certain dynamic created by a mix of personalities, personal career motivations, and career histories; and varying degrees of conformity to roles as well as certain attempts to develop new rules and roles. The period during which Indian policy was developed saw structural change within government and considerable anticipation that far-reaching reforms might be effected under the new administration in many policy fields. It would be impossible to replay this period and totally reconstruct the intricate web of persons, ideas and ground rules that shaped Indian policy, but incomplete attempts are perhaps not without some utility. The reader must be the judge of this.

It is hoped that this book will not only be relevant for those interested in policy-making processes at the federal level, but that it will have some lasting utility for policy-makers who deal with Canadian Indians and other unorganized minority groups. The 1968–69 policy-making exercise elicited discussion within government about many ideological stances on 'special' and 'normal' status for Indians. These same arguments exist today and can be expected to arise whenever Indian policy and the Indian Act are being revised because they reflect the underlying liberal-democratic values of Canadian society. In my own opinion there will always be a liberal ideology in Canadian politics that will guide attempts to eliminate special status for Indians. Ironically, this is the same force that will bring to public attention, as it did in the 1960s, the injustices and inequities of the treatment of Indians. The implication of this for Indians is that if they want to retain special status, they will have to counteract this force by fully rationalizing their own position with each change in the political climate. This book demonstrates that an accurate rationalization of Indian positions cannot be done within government by ministers and civil servants whose liberal ideology and personal ambitions distort the Indian viewpoint.

In addition, I hope my work will contribute to a corporate memory in government about Indian policy. In my experience I have found both minsters and civil servants unaware of past policies and the implications of these policies for both the client and the government. When ministers and civil servants leave the portfolio, they often take with them their individual experiences. As a result, the collective experience is not synthesized and lessons from even the recent past remain unlearned. Thus, policies promoted as innovative often arouse a strong sense of *déjà vu* in Indians and longstanding government employees. I hope this book will foster a corporate memory, not in the simplistic sense of separating the old from the new, but in the genuine belief that the White Paper experience can provide constructive lessons for both the government and Indians in the future.

As for my own biases, my own myth of neutrality – to the extent that I can consciously understand them – I do not believe that meaningful socio-cultural change can occur without the direct participation of, and compromise by, the persons and communities undergoing change. This position is nothing more than a basic tenet of applied anthropology. The values that guide change must be acceptable to groups that experience change. Since policy-making is basically an exercise in the selection of values to guide future behaviour, it follows in the case of Indian policy that Indians must engage in the policy-making exercise in a meaningful and informed way. Realistically, difficult compromises and trade-offs will be required, but unless these adjustments result from a joint effort on the part of Indians and government, Indians will reject them, discrediting government efforts. I do not believe there are easy solutions to complex problems, or that readily known solutions are at hand. But I do think that honest, direct discussion is the initial step – not the development of policies behind a wall of secrecy and promises of participation that are belied by government action.

ACKNOWLEDGMENTS

I am very grateful to the many people who helped me with this book while holding none of them responsible for my errors: Drs Alan Cairns and Ken Kernaghan for reading early drafts of the manuscript and suggesting many valuable revisions; Professor Douglas Sanders for his detailed help with Indian law and for his patience in demystifying the legal profession's writings for me; Mr George Manuel, past president of the National Indian Brotherhood, for his painstaking comments on certain parts of the manuscript; Mr Dave Courchene, past president of the Manitoba Indian Brotherhood, and Mr Walter Deiter, past president of the Federation of Saskatchewan Indians, for their helpful replies to my letters; Dr Stewart Raby and Mrs K. Lamb for the use of the collections in the Indian Claims Commission library; Dr Audrey Doerr for her guidance into the political science literature and the use of her valuable doctoral dissertation; Professor Victor Valentine for his support of my work and discussion of events in the early 1960s; Mr Arthur Kroeger, deputy minister of Indian and Northern Affairs, for granting me permission to interview DIAND personnel; Elizabeth Kriegler, Mr Kroeger's special assistant, for directing me through the bureaucratic maze to the proper sources of information; and Mr John Leslie of the Treaties and Historic Research Centre, DIAND, for responding to my many inquiries with his unfailing sense of humour.

I owe a particular debt of gratitude to the many civil servants who tolerated my repeated interviews and at times extended gracious hospitality to me in their homes. The book would have been impossible without the willingness of civil servants to recall the events of the period for me. I am also grateful to several of them who reviewed the manuscript, or parts of it, and made valuable corrections and comments. Contrary to popular opinion, I found these officials to be dedicated and articulate people, many of whom were deeply committed to producing a good Indian policy that would alter significantly the unacceptable conditions of native people. Furthermore, some were far more innovative in their approach to Indian policy than the politicians were willing to accept, particularly in the area of Indian participation.

Several people helped in preparing various versions of the manuscript: Judii Rempel and Barbara Faulkner, secretaries in the Department of Anthropology, University of Waterloo; Vic Neglia, Patty Weber, and Nancy Sadler in the Faculty of Arts Computing Office; and Lindsay Dorney, my patient editor and friend. I owe these people, and especially R.I.K. Davidson, Social Science editor of the University of Toronto Press, and Sonia Kuryliw Paine, the copy editor, my sincere thanks for their untiring efforts to get the manuscript into shape for me. Financial support for my research came from the Canada Council Sub-Committee, and the Research Grants Committee of the University of Waterloo and I gratefully acknowledge their assistance.

I am particularly indebted to my mother for her valuable help on the manuscript, and to my husband, David, for his consistent support of my work. Helpful husbands who take time from their own academic careers are an invaluable resource to a professional woman.

This book has been published with the help of a grant from the Social Science Federation of Canada, using funds provided by the Social Sciences and Humanities Research Council of Canada, and from the Publications Fund of University of Toronto Press.

Sally M. Weaver
Cambridge, Ontario
July 1978

Jim Davey (Program Secretary, PMO), Pierre Trudeau (Prime Minister), and Marc Lalonde (Principal Secretary, PMO) at a business session in Stratford, Ontario, in August 1968 (Dick Wallace of the *London Free Press*)

An Indian Act consultation meeting at Sudbury, Ontario, in August 1968
(DIAND Photo Division)

right The National Indian Act consultation meeting in Ottawa, April-May 1969. L to R: Isaac Beaulieu (Conference Secretary), Jean Chrétien (Minister), and George Manuel (Conference Chairman)

left Robert K. Andras (Minister without Portfolio, assigned to Indian Affairs, July 1968 to May 1969)

left An Indian Act consultation meeting, this time at Chilliwack, BC, in November 1968 (DIAND Photo Division)

Jean Chrétien and Pierre Trudeau at the presentation of the Red Paper in Ottawa,
4 June 1970

MAKING CANADIAN
INDIAN POLICY

Introduction

In 1969 the federal government came forward with a White Paper on Indian policy which Indians rejected and the government subsequently withdrew. Public controversy concerning the policy was widespread, but much of it centred on the secretive fashion in which the policy was prepared. Despite government commitments to Indians that they would participate in the process, the production of the White Paper had many earmarks of political deception. For its critics, the policy was, at best, a perversion of 'consultative democracy' and, at worst, a case of duplicity.

To date there has been no recounting of how the White Paper was developed within the federal government. This book attempts to fill this void by providing one microcosm of policy-making during the first Trudeau administration. In a more general vein, it offers some insight into how the government attempted to apply the notion of participatory democracy in policy-making to an unorganized and disadvantaged minority. Still broader, it tries to show how the policy-makers attempted to work with the basic political values in our society and apply them to a minority group.

OVERVIEW OF THE POLICY

In some respects the recent history of Canadian Indian policy is a familiar feature of Canada's social and political landscape. It is now well known that after a year of consultations with Indians on the revision of the Indian Act – a process that the minister called 'an attempt at consultative democracy' – the federal government released its White Paper in June 1969 that proposed a global termination of all special treatment of Indians, including the Indian Act. The Act had been heavily criticized by Indians themselves; they also recognized that it enshrined some of their charter rights, which had been granted, or promised, them prior to Confederation in 1867. The new policy was an abrupt departure from the traditional practice of dealing with Indians, even though the implicit long range goal of terminating the special treatment of Indians had been a part of government policies since the 1830s. In 1947, for example, during the Special Joint Committee hearings on the Indian Act, termination had been explicitly proposed by Diamond Jenness, then Dominion Anthropologist, in his 'Plan for Liquidating Canada's Indian Problem in 25 Years' (Jenness 1947: 310-11). In 1969 this implicit policy theme was finally brought into the open and scheduled for immediate implementation.

The White Paper argued that 'equality,' or 'non-discrimination' as it was often phrased, was the key ingredient in a solution to the problems of Indians, and that special rights had been the major cause of their problems (DIAND 1969). The goal of equality was to be achieved by terminating the special legislation and bureaucracy that had developed over the past century to deal with Indians, and by transferring to the provinces the responsibility for administering services to Indians. Henceforth Indians would receive the same services from the same sources as other Canadians after a transitional period in which enriched programs of economic development were to be offered. The large Indian Affairs bureaucracy would be dismantled within five years, and the federal government was to retain trusteeship functions only for Indian lands which would be administered through an Indian Lands Act. By implication, the result of the policy would see Indians with 'Indian problems' become provincial citizens with regular citizens' problems. The policy was essentially one of 'formal equality,' to use Cairns' phrase from the Hawthorn Report (1966), but the question remained as to whether it would foster equality of opportunity for this disadvantaged minority. Cairns had argued three years previously that such a policy would not: 'The equal treatment in law and services of a people who at the present time do not have equal competitive capacities will not suffice for the attainment of substantive socioeconomic equality' (Hawthorn 1966: 392).

Predictably, the policy caused shock and alarm among Indians. Even though they were an unorganized minority, they responded with a clearcut rejection of the White Paper: 'the MacDonald-Chrétien doctrine,' as Cardinal labelled it after DIAND's deputy minister and minister, respectively (Cardinal 1969: 1). Throughout the Indian Act consultation meetings (July 1968 to May 1969), Indians had expressed a wide range of opinions on how the Act should be revised, and some Indian spokesmen even called for its removal. Although there was little of the consensus on the Act's revisions that the government had hoped for, an unmistakable consensus on certain priorities emerged among Indians and these priorities were evident in the government's verbatim reports of the consultation meetings (DIAND 1968–69): Indians wanted their special rights honoured and their historical grievances, particularly over lands and treaties, recognized and dealt with in an equitable fashion. Equally important, they wanted direct and meaningful participation in the making of policies that affected their future.

When the policy was released, it was obvious that none of these priorities had been acceptable to the government. The ministers themselves had actively raised expectations among Indians that their views would be listened to, but the policy in both substance and preparation indicated otherwise; it had been prepared within government and without Indian participation. The attempt at consultative democracy miscarried and the government's efforts were discredited. Among Indians, the policy invited a retrenching of distrust which was, ironically, the very condition the government had hoped to remove.

Indians responded to the policy with a resounding nationalism unparalleled in Canadian history. Their spokesmen rallied to the moment by preparing their own counter-proposals[1] and by renewing their efforts to build provincial and national organizations through which they could lobby for their own policies. With the press and other sectors of the public supporting the Indian indictment of the policy, the government came under heavy pressure to set the White Paper aside.

The ambiguity with which the policy was delivered to the public compounded the problem of its reception. It was unclear whether the policy was simply a proposal or a firm policy signifying government commitment. Statements by Chrétien and certain actions by the department only reinforced the confusion. Eventually, after the first counter-proposal, the Red Paper prepared by the Indian Chiefs of Alberta (1970), Trudeau publicly said the government would not press the implementation of the White Paper.[2] By spring 1971, the policy was formally withdrawn by Chrétien[3] although some Indian spokesmen today claim, and some civil servants privately concur, that termination remains the unofficial policy of the government and is still being implemented.[4]

Social scientists, especially anthropologists, were shocked by the White Paper. They could not believe the government's intention of embarking on a policy that had proven so destructive to Indian communities in the United States during the 1950s.[5] Paradoxically, the American termination policy had subverted its own intended goal of equality (Brophy and Aberle 1966: 188-9). The fear and insecurity it brought to tribal communities were so great that nativism was the reaction – a process of cultural reaffirmation which often arises when cultural systems are severely threatened. Instead of seeking equality, Indian communities reasserted their cultural uniqueness, emphasizing their social distance from the dominant society. 'Termination psychosis' continued to dominate Indian-government relations, making administration very difficult (Josephy 1971).

Closer to home was the government's disregard of the recommendations in the Hawthorn Report (1966, 1967), itself a government-commissioned national survey on Canadian Indians. Working between 1963 and 1967, Hawthorn and his co-researchers had produced a lengthy report on the current conditions of Indians in Canada. The team had rejected termination as a policy option (1966: 8), arguing instead for a 'citizens plus' status for Indians, which they did not view as a deterrent to delivering proper provincial services to Indians. They also recommended the role of advocate-ombudsman for the Indian Affairs Branch because many Indian bands lacked the social, economic, and political skills of self-defence. As well, the team refuted the usual constitutional argument that Indians were the exclusive responsibility of the federal government, thereby leaving the way open for the provinces to deliver programs to Indians (see also Lysyk 1967). In their view the thrust of policy should be middle range, with programs emphasizing development on a broad socio-economic scale in order to reverse Indian poverty and dependency on the government (1966: 386-403). They urged the government to recognize the increasing social problems among Indians in cities, but this recommendation, too, was disregarded in the new policy.

Although social scientists had no proven solutions to the complex problems of Indian administration and marginality, the Hawthorn Report and the Brophy and Aberle study, among others, argued that the answer lay in broadscale social development programs, and in changing public attitudes, not in simplistic legal solutions and rapid legislative action.

Both these studies provided guidelines for Canadian policy-makers in assessing the possible impact of various policy alternatives. Furthermore, the policy-making approach espoused by the new Trudeau government at that time called for rigorous policy research which, theoretically, would have required evaluations of policy experiences in other countries as well as at home. When the White Paper was released, however, it became apparent that the Hawthorn Report and the Brophy and Aberle study were either unknown to the policy-makers or disregarded by them.

A combination of all these factors led social scientists to respond to the new policy with considerable incredulity. That the White Paper would backlash on the policy-makers was no surprise.

MAKING INDIAN POLICY

Indian policy was developed within the upper reaches of the federal government, under tight secrecy common to the policy-making process. The policy-makers were ministers, their advisers and senior civil servants, and although the policy-making group included almost fifty people during the peak period, less than twenty played a major part in shaping the policy. The process lasted a full year, beginning in summer 1968 and ending in June 1969, just a week before the White Paper was released.

Ideally, Indian policy was to be developed according to a new more rational approach to policy making which Trudeau and his policy advisers in the Prime Minister's Office (henceforth, PMO) were then establishing in government.[6] Policies were to be more deliberately and systematically planned, from the initial identification of the problem which the policy was to address, through the selection of policy objectives or goals, to the weighing of the alternative ways of achieving these goals. The implications of each alternative were to be carefully examined in the hope of minimizing undesirable consequences, especially those that would create new problems for the government or the public. Ministers and civil servants were encouraged by the PMO to be far-sighted in their thinking and to consider fundamental changes in policy, rather than limiting their horizons to mere incremental changes. In general, Trudeau's approach was intended to improve government's capacity to develop effective policies by undertaking rigorous policy reviews and by engaging in a far-reaching examination of the issues.

Serious efforts were made by the PMO to develop Indian policy along the lines of the new approach. Beginning in summer 1968 and ending in spring 1969, each season witnessed the gradual progression of Indian policy through the planned stages, from the initial problem identification to the final choice of language in the policy statement. However, despite conformity to this general plan, the overall process of formulation was not characterized by reason and equanimity.

From the outset the development of Indian policy was a tangled and tortured process. Policy-makers became preoccupied with their own internal conflicts, and efforts to straighten out the confusions and hostilities frequently failed. Although the procedures in rationalizing the policy were relatively similar to those elsewhere in government at that time, Indian policy was considerably more contentious.[7]

Studies of policy-making demonstrate that the process often involves heated exchanges and conflicting values. In Lindblom's experience, policies are often fought out rather than thought out (1968: 19). This aptly describes the making of Indian policy. What made Indian policy a particularly quarrelsome issue was the fact it tried to cope with the notion of public participation.

THE QUESTION OF PARTICIPATION

During the late 1960s Indian spokesmen frequently blamed senior officials in DIAND for ineffective policies (e.g. Cardinal 1969a). In the opinion of Indian critics the bureaucracy had played an excessively influential role in policy matters, but the future lay in opening up the process to Indians themselves. This demand reflected a more widespread concern in many sectors of society which saw big government and powerful bureaucracies as impediments to the responsiveness and accountability of government to the people.

Opening up policy process to the public had great appeal during the federal election of 1968, when Trudeau promised 'to make Government more accessible to people, to give our citizens a sense of full participation in the affairs of Government ...'[8] 'Participatory democracy' became the catch phrase, although the meaning of participation was never publicly explained by Trudeau (Doerr 1973: 98). Paradoxically, in terms of its ultimate fate, the White Paper on Indian policy can be seen as an extension of this concept in several ways.

During the 1960s local citizen-participation movements sprang up across the country with the intention of eradicating the problems of urban blight and poverty (Lotz 1977). Grass roots activism was a common feature of Canadian society, especially in urban areas and on university campuses. With the public demanding a more powerful role in shaping government policies, the policy-making process itself came under greater public scrutiny (Aucoin 1971).

But grass roots activism in Canada was not confined to the public. During the mid-1960s the federal government adopted the idea of citizen participation with the most striking examples being the Company of Young Canadians, the Challenge for Change Program, and New Start Program (Draper 1971). Less dramatic were the Agricultural Rehabilitation Development Act (ARDA) programs designed to reduce rural poverty and regional economic disparity. Within the Department of Indian Affairs, the community development program was such an example. More pertinent to Indians was the film *Encounter with Saul Alinsky – Rama Reserve* made jointly by the National Film Board and the Company of Young Canadians in 1967. As a professional organizer of underprivileged groups, Alinsky spent a good part of the film suggesting to Indian discussants how they might focus Indian concerns and more effectively exert pressure on government to support their goals. Finding the native discussants reluctant to consider his activist approach, Alinsky ends the film by stating that Indians are 'the God damnest best ally the government has' if they seek to opt out of society and yet expect politicians to take an interest in their well-being. The clear messages of the film were that Indians must organize if they wanted change, and they must mobilize public support if their efforts were to succeed.

Federal involvement in the citizen participation movement usually occurred whenever the government dealt with unorganized sectors of the public that were unable to articulate their needs and bring them to the government in a focused fashion (Kernaghan 1976). Ministers sometimes promoted policies that were designed to enhance public participation, civil servants were consequently called upon to act as facilitators in focusing public opinion so government could respond more effectively. Under these conditions, bureaucratic involvement in the political process increased and some civil servants, whether encouraged by the administration or inspired by their own personal philosophies, began to act as agents of social change, a role traditionally assigned to ministers (Kernaghan 1976: 439). But the activism of civil servants was not always appreciated by other officials or ministers, especially when their efforts to organize the public succeeded in raising demands for change which were directed back to the government in a forceful fashion (Bregha 1971). In many instances, the government sponsors, faced with a rejection of their traditional policies by an agitated public, reacted by closing down the programs rather than changing their policies (Dimock 1971). The community development program in Indian Affairs was a classic example of this problem with government-sponsored intervention (described in Chapter 1).

The question of public participation and Indian policy-making did not rest with bureaucratic involvement alone. Individual ministers who encouraged public participation often had to wrestle with the uncomfortable results of raising public expectations when they presented their policy recommendations to the cabinet. A minister could personally seek greater public involvement in policy-making, but in the end he had to convince the cabinet of the wisdom of this approach. Decision-making rested with the collective cabinet, not with individual ministers, and a minister could run the risk of cabinet rejecting his ideas, as apparently happened with Hellyer's Task Force on housing (Axworthy 1971). In the case of Indian policy, ministerial activism became a contentious issue because there was no agreement between the two ministers assigned to Indian Affairs on the nature and extent of Indian participation in the policy-making process. In the end, Indian policy would test the Trudeau government's commitment to public participation, particularly when it came to the question of how much the government would acquiesce to Indian demands.

An early connection between citizen participation and Indian policy was established in 1967 when the government decided to hold systematic consultation meetings with Indians to discuss revisions to the Indian Act. Although the idea was started by the Pearson government, the Trudeau administration supported it and Indians were encouraged to contribute. Statements by the ministers to Indians during the consultation meetings (July 1968 to May 1969) raised certain expectations about the nature of the new policy, including the amount of influence Indians should and could have in the policy process itself. The consultation procedure itself led Indians to believe that the government's policy in 1968 was a 'positional policy,' to use Aucoin's term (1971: 25): a policy designed to give Indians a position in the general structure of decision-making. Aucoin comments on the nature of public concern with policy-making (1971: 25): 'A good deal of policy activity by individuals and groups is related not so much to securing (at least in the short run) an allocation of desired values but rather the attainment of desired positions vis-à-vis other individuals or groups. What is sought is a share of the coercive abilities of the government.' As Indian policy took shape, the question of Indian participation in the process became one of the most contentious issues among policy-makers. As they struggled with the notion, its meaning took various forms as did the implications of these meanings for Indians and the government.

The theme of participation wove its way through many aspects of Indian policy, including the decision to release the policy as a White Paper rather than draft legislation for parliamentary debate. The policy-making process ostensibly began with consultation meetings with Indians; its development within government focused on debates as to the importance of participation (at what stage and with what effect); and its delivery as a White Paper was intended to further the process of participation. Participation was said to have taken place, but in fact, it did not occur; Indians were not party to the deliberations that produced the White Paper.

The ultimate failure to include Indians raises the basic question of how the demands of the Indians at the consultation meetings were perceived by the policy-makers inside government. It also requires us to understand how 'the Indian problem' was defined by the policy-makers and the public, for defining the problem that a policy is to solve is the first and the most crucial step in policy-making.

CHAPTER ONE   The 'Problem'

Like many social problems, 'the Indian problem' existed for decades before it was shaped into a political issue of sufficient strength to attract government attention (e.g. Jenness 1942; Loram and McIlwraith 1943). Public understanding of Indians and Indian policy was predictably limited since general knowledge of the conditions of Indians was at best fragmentary, and Indian Affairs had rarely been a topic of legislative reform until after the Second World War. Even though the hearings of the Special Joint Committee of the Senate and House of Commons (1946–48) had sparked some public interest in the Indian Act revisions of 1951,[1] there were no effective lobbying groups among Indians or whites at that time to mould Indian issues and exert pressure on the government for continued reform.

This situation began to change in 1959 when a Joint Committee of the Senate and House of Commons was appointed to examine Indian administration. The committee's report (1961) recognized 'the winds of change' in Indian affairs, and although its approach was largely incremental, recommending various measures to accelerate the process of Indian integration, it triggered a series of program innovations. At the same time, its hearings (1959–61) aroused moderate public concern, which was sustained and given focus by public interest groups, the most prominent being the Toronto-based Indian-Eskimo Association. Although there were native people on its executive, it was largely a white liberal group whose aims were to raise public consciousness about the substandard conditions in Indian communities and to advocate changes in government priorities and policies.

Thus, while the Indian Affairs Branch was searching for ways to improve its programs and lessen Indian dependence on government, public opinion was slowly diverging from the cautious approach taken by the Joint Committee. By the late 1960s the public was generally critical of most government efforts relating to Indians. In 1968, when the Trudeau government took over, 'the Indian problem' was a disjointed mixture of the public's appreciation of Indian issues and the results of Indian Affairs' innovative efforts of the mid-1960s. In broad terms, the White Paper was as much a response to the government's own record in Indian administration as it was a reaction to public opinion.

Many events shaped the Indian problem in the 1960s, each casting a different light on Indians. The centennial celebrations fostered a national curiosity about the past, and in one sense the Indian problem took shape within the framework of historical reassessment. As Canadian identity strengthened, and as news of the civil rights movement in the United States dominated the press, liberal-minded people developed a concern for minority groups and their rights to cultural and linguistic expression. Equally powerful was the anti-poverty movement which focused public attention on the economic disparity between Indians and the general population. Thus Indians were 'rediscovered,' to use George Manuel's phrase, but the rediscovery was not a particularly rewarding exercise for many Canadians. Nor was it always welcome by Indians. The Indian pavilion at Expo '67, for instance, was organized by white officials, with Indians being confined to advisory roles much like they were in the larger political system (Manuel and Posluns 1974: 172). As the citizen participation movement took hold, it focused public attention on the political marginality of Indians, bringing to light yet another aspect of the Indian problem.

But above all, the political climate of the time was dominated by the question of national unity. The basic issue was how national unity could be maintained in the face of Quebec's demands for greater autonomy within Confederation and the more dramatic expression of secessionist desires by militant Quebeckers. As pressures from Quebec for special status within the federal system increased, 'special' and 'separate' became loaded words in the national political vocabulary. Many Quebeckers feared the loss of their language and culture and some argued that a separate political state was the only way to safeguard them.

To address the cultural expression of this problem, the Royal Commission on Bilingualism and Biculturalism, which had been established in 1963 by Prime Minister Pearson, continued to examine the position of Francophones in Canadian society with a view to recommending how

TABLE 1 Indian population by province

	1959*	1969[†]	1978[‡]
Prince Edward Island	343	432	508
Nova Scotia	3,561	4,524	5,625
New Brunswick	3,183	4,280	5,256
Quebec	20,453	26,985	32,217
Ontario	42,677	54,072	65,966
Manitoba	23,658	34,422	44,642
Saskatchewan	23,280	35,072	46,189
Alberta	19,286	28,343	36,293
British Columbia	36,186	46,955	55,650
Yukon	1,868	2,661	2,810
Northwest Territories	4,598	6,277	7,593
Total	179,093	244,023	302,749

* Department of Citizenship and Immigration, *Annual Report for 1959/60*, Table 1, p. 89.
† *The Canadian Indian: Statistics* (Ottawa: DIAND, 1973), p. 8.
‡ Source: data compiled by the Program Coordination and Analysis Division, DIAND.

'equal partnership between the two founding races' could be established (Innis 1973: 185). Much of the public debate about the French fact focused on whether there should be 'special rights' for Quebeckers and for Francophones elsewhere in Canada. This issue of special rights was not unrelated to the Indian problem.

To many Canadians the Official Languages Act of 1969, which was publicly debated and prepared at the same time Indian policy was being developed, was seen to given special rights to Francophones in that it gave both French and English equal status as official languages of parliament and the federal government. Not unexpectedly, some Indian spokesmen, primarily from the western provinces, would argue that Indians were in fact the original founding race and that their special rights were at least as valid as those of the French. The political fact, however, was that Quebec's secession would destroy Confederation. Indians, as Trudeau himself had noted (1968: 31), comprised only one per cent of the population and did not pose the same threat (see Table 1).

The French and the Indians shared not only the desire for special rights, but also a fate of being social and cultural unknowns to most of the Canadian population. Given the persistent though unsuccessful pressures on them to assimilate, their respective political demands to safeguard their cultural traditions are neither unexpected nor unreasonable responses.

In many respects both the French and Indians had remained separate from the rest of Canadian society, in part illustrating what John Porter called 'the vertical mosaic' of Canadian society (1965). Porter had recently alerted Canadians to the fact that their society was characterized not by a melting pot, which minimized ethnic differences, but rather by forces that tended to maintain these differences. Not surprisingly, Porter's study showed that the French were under-represented in most elite groups in society and that Indians held the bottom position in the occupational scale (1965: Ch. 3).

Consequently, as efforts to cope with national unity, ethnic diversity, and poverty gained momentum in the 1960s, Indians became more visible to the public and were placed all too obviously among the most disadvantaged minorities in society (Harding 1965; Borovoy 1966). As the public, and particularly the press, became better informed of Indian poverty and alienation, a collective sense of guilt about the historical treatment of Indians emerged and the federal government came under heavy criticism. Its caretaker role had been performed improperly, or too well, depending on the point of view of the various critics – church groups, academics, civil rights advocates, or journalists. The press, increasingly sympathetic to the Indian cause, carried stories of the government's indifference or disregard for the circumstances of the Indians (Bowles et al. 1972). The key censorious concept became 'paternalism,' which was seen as a force denying Indians the freedom to develop as they wanted and discouraging any initiatives they undertook. Public sympathy for the Indian cause was unquestionably enhanced by the civil rights and anti-poverty movements in the United States and by the emerging nationalism of decolonizing third-world countries. The youth movement and activism on campuses in Canada lent further support. With the exception of a few, MPs, who for years had remained both silent and uninformed about the conditions of Canada's Indians, began to ask questions in the House of Commons, sometimes demanding legislative reform and insisting that Indians be allowed to participate in the process.

Until 1960 substantive published information on Indians in Canada was largely confined to anthropological materials, most of which had limited public appeal and distribution. Because Indian traditions and history were rarely taught in schools,[2] the cultural and linguistic diversity of native people was not commonly known by the public, who tended to see Indians as a homogeneous ethnic group (see Maps 1 and 2). Moreover, the term 'Indians' incorrectly implies a collectivity: that Indians act together in an organized fashion, or, at the very least, that they are aware of the conditions and concerns of other Indians in different regions of

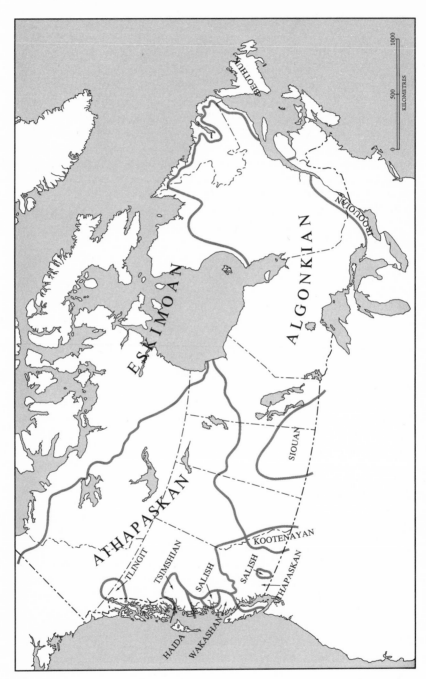

MAP 1 Major Canadian Indian linguistic groups (*source:* Abler and Weaver 1974: xiv)

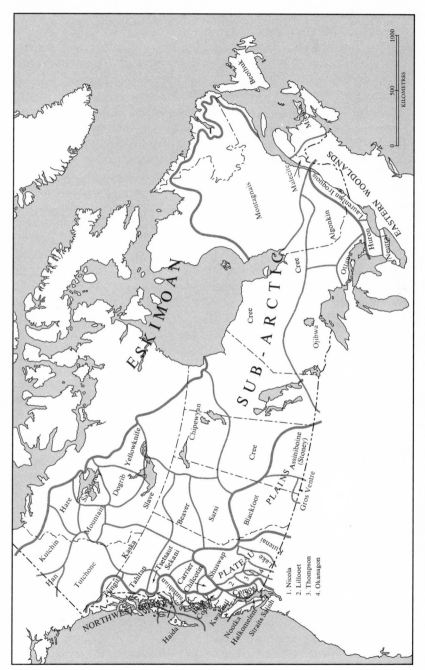

MAP 2 Canadian Indian tribes and culture areas (*source:* Abler and Weaver 1974: xv)

Canada. Although the public image of Indians was improving (Haycock 1971), textbooks were still 'teaching prejudice' (McDiarmid and Pratt 1971). Furthermore, the history of Canadian Indian administration remained largely undocumented, and conventional policy research or policy-relevant data by government personnel and academics on Indians were almost non-existent (Weaver 1976: 53-5).

Given these factors, it is not surprising that one of the major developments in the early 1960s was the collection of current information on Indians as a basis for new programs and policies. The most systematic effort by the public to foster research and produce information came from the Indian-Eskimo Association as it organized conferences and symposia, and prepared briefs to the government on economic development, hunting and trapping rights, housing, and community development.[3] Its most effective research effort was the first scholarly study, in 1966, of the legal aspects of Indian rights and treaties. This produced *Native Rights in Canada* (1970), the first book to synthesize Canadian Indian law, written by Douglas Sanders and later revised by Peter Cumming and Neil Mickenberg (1972). From these studies, as well as others commissioned by the government, a clearer sense of the Indian problem developed. Much of this information benefited the uninformed non-Indian, for many Indian spokesmen and communities felt their problems were well known. Eventually, as the decade passed, various reports became a useful resource for Indian spokesmen, allowing them to document the nature of the problems facing Indians and to demonstrate the need for change.

Much of the public criticism of government action or inaction during the 1960s focused on the paternalistic administration and the Indian Act which created this special bureaucracy. The Act, historically designed to protect Indian lands, enables the federal government to administer the affairs of Indians through its provisions on land-holding and land transfer, on taxation, local government, education, wills and estates, and band membership. Some of the special rights which Indians highly prize derive from the Act – more accurately from its central purpose of protecting Indian lands by limiting their occupation and use to legal-status Indians, or those who can trace descent through the patrilineal line back to 1874, when the Act was first consolidated. The provisions in the Act apply only to status Indians, not to Metis and non-status Indians who are of Indian ancestry but, through intermarriage with whites or by signing away their land rights (as the Metis did), have lost their right to legal status.

Special rights under the Act, although not as clearly prescribed as Indians have at times asserted, include (1) the right of a status Indian to reside on the reserve that is assigned to his/her band, (2) freedom from estate taxes on reserve lands, (3) freedom from land taxes on reserve lands, (4) freedom from income taxes on income earned on a reserve, and (5) the right to vote in band council elections (Sanders 1972: 89-90). Contrary to some Indian opinion, the Act is not the basis for most of the special federal programs developed for Indians over the years, such as medical care, housing, welfare, and economic development. Some treaties have special provisions for these kinds of services, but even non-treaty Indians often consider these services a basic right and a federal responsibility. Regarding medical services the federal government has provided them for such a long time in some areas, albeit inadequately, that Indians have come to regard them as rights even in the absence of treaty provisions (e.g. Weaver 1972).

Although the purpose of the Indian Act was not generally understood by the public, and by many Indians as well, the Act soon became a symbol of discrimination, a piece of racist legislation (e.g. Currie 1968: Canadian Welfare 1967). Both Indians and whites increasingly criticized it, and by extension the Indian administration which had been created by the Act, as a dehumanizing instrument (e.g. Staats 1964; Dunning 1959, 1962, 1964). To civil libertarians who espoused the Indian cause, the Indian Act became a public embarrassment and a source of confusion (e.g. McGilp 1963: 306). Especially to liberal-minded politicians, such as Minister of Indian Affairs Arthur Laing (1966–68), it was seen as restricting freedom of choice and individuality, which other Canadians enjoyed.[4] In keeping with the rhetoric of the urban anti-poverty movement, reserves were frequently characterized by the press and vocal university students as 'ghettos' on which Indians were forced to live, and the very notion of segregation in the reserve system became increasingly offensive (e.g. Melling 1966, Thompson 1965).

The press and the urban white public rarely discerned the century-old ambiguity that Indians have felt about the Indian Act – their resentment of its constraints and yet their dependence on it for the special rights it provided, especially that of protecting their lands. The rhetoric of the period was largely negative toward the Act but positive toward the treaties, mainly because the most articulate Indian spokesmen came from the prairies where treaty rights, including the highly valued hunting and trapping rights, were the central issue in Indian politics. Thus, although only half of Canada's legal-status Indians had treaties with the Crown, symbolically Indian rights were seen to reside in established treaties – or in those that had been promised them. Legally, the bulk of their rights derived from the Act (Hawthorn 1966: 248-9) but this fact, too, was not fully comprehended by the press and the public.

Public sentiment for improving the conditions of Indians had begun to grow in the mid-1960s and although the public still lacked a basic knowledge about Indians, it was more curious and concerned. There had been a general awakening to the Indian problem as there had been within government itself.

REFORM EFFORTS WITHIN GOVERNMENT

By late 1963 senior civil servants in the Indian Affairs Branch, then a part of the Department of Citizenship and Immigration, had become discouraged with the limited effectiveness and outreach of their programs.[5] The report of the Joint Committee of the Senate and House of Commons (1961) had recommended that the branch speed up the process of integrating Indians into the wider society, but branch officials felt their programs were not doing this. As one official recalled: 'We were at a dead end; nothing more was happening. We needed some feedback on where to go from here.' There was a strong desire to assess the effectiveness of current programs, and with the resulting information design new ones which would provide provincially based services to Indians and lessen their dependence on the federal government. Thus from 1963 to 1967, Indian Affairs carried out a variety of programs designed to improve its services, and to collect information on current and future needs of Indians. These were: 1/The Hawthorn Report; 2/community development programs; 3/transfer of certain programs to the provinces; 4/grants to bands for self-administration; 5/Indian advisory boards; 6/research on the administration of justice to Indians; 7/experimental relocation programs; 8/draft legislation for an Indian Claims Commission.

THE HAWTHORN REPORT

Policy-relevant research both inside and outside government was meagre, but the branch's own capacity to undertake such research was limited. The desire by officials to have it done auspiciously coincided with external political pressure on the government; the result was the Hawthorn Report.

In January 1963 a delegation from the national executive of the IODE (Independent Order of the Daughters of the Empire) presented Minister of Indian Affairs Richard Bell with a brief, urging the branch to do a three- to five-year study to determine how Indians could achieve equality of opportunity with other Canadians.[6] Senior officials supported the idea, finding it more timely than the IODE probably realized, and under the initiative of Colonel H.M. Jones, who was about to retire as director of the branch (1953–63), they managed to convince their minister to commission the first full-scale national survey of the conditions of Indians in Canada.

Some years earlier, Harry Hawthorn, together with Cyril Belshaw and Stuart Jamieson (1958), had completed a study on the Indians of British Columbia that officials in the branch found useful. They approached Hawthorn to consider doing the national survey, and although initially reluctant to take up the task, Hawthorn eventually agreed. After preparing the terms of reference with branch officials, he organized a team of fifty-two social scientists, who completed the survey by 1966. Branch officials were eager for the results of the work almost as soon as the survey began, and senior researchers on the Hawthorn team recall having to become more cautious in their coffee break conversations lest the officials interpret their interim findings and hunches as final judgments.[7] The rapport was good between the team and the senior officials who went to great lengths to accommodate the researchers (Weaver 1976).

The first volume of the Hawthorn Report, *A Survey of the Contemporary Indians of Canada* (1966–67), was the most relevant for Indian policy because it dealt with the role of the Indian Affairs Branch and spelled out the philosophy of special status for Canadian Indians, which Hawthorn and Cairns called 'citizens plus' (1966: 396-8). The thrust of the report was on the concept of choice; Indians should have a greater choice of lifestyle, whether it meant staying in their own communities or leaving them. But in either case, 'Indians can and should retain the special privileges of their status while enjoying full participation as provincial and federal citizens' (p. 7). Questions of assimilation were viewed as decisions that neither the government nor anyone else could effectively take on behalf of Indians. Given this approach, the government's objectives should be to improve its development programs on all fronts and to ensure that the provinces delivered services to their Indian citizens. The federal government was to protect their special status and 'act as a national conscience to see that social and economic equality is achieved between Indians and Whites' (p. 13). To monitor all developments, an Indian Progress Agency was proposed, an independent public body to review programs and report annually on the condition of Indians. The report, in analysing the branch's programs and assessing the general conditions of Indians, documented the magnitude and complexity of the Indian problem as no other report had yet, or since, attempted.

In general, the Hawthorn Report demonstrated that Indians suffered from poverty, underemployment, and unemployment (pp. 21-198). Dr

Stuart Jamieson, the senior economist and author of the section on economic development, found that Indians in 1965 had per capita gainful earnings of $300 compared with the national average of $1,400 (p. 45). He estimated that any serious attempt to mount adequate development programs and instil viable economic skills in the Indian labour force would cost hundreds of millions of dollars (p. 14). Though it would be costly to mount these programs, the consequences of not doing so would cost even more in welfare payments and the human condition.

The second major focus of the report was on the jurisdictional and constitutional issues surrounding Indian administration. The senior researcher, Dr Alan Cairns, a political scientist and specialist on Canadian federalism, with Professor Kenneth Lysyk, a legal scholar specializing in constitutional law, sought to untangle some of the complexities. They argued that the BNA Act mandate for Indians did not exclude provincial participation in Indian administration (p. 235). Rather, the mandate was 'permissive,' meaning that provinces should be expected and encouraged to extend services to Indians on reserves. This interpretation was particularly vital, for it was under provincial, not federal, jurisdiction that the welfare programs were assigned according to the division of powers in the Canadian constitution (pp. 208, 250-4), and these were the services which Indians needed and had a right to expect as citizens. Among their many other recommendations, they emphasized the need for Indian Affairs to abandon its 'parochial' and 'isolationist' tradition, and develop 'diplomatic' relations with the provinces if it expected them to extend services to Indians (pp. 209-10).

Volume II of the Hawthorn Report dealt with education and local government. It revealed, among other things, the high drop-out rates among Indian school children and the weaknesses of the band councils on the reserves. Although it contained many useful recommendations, it was less relevant for general Indian policy, and its delayed publication until 1969 meant that it was not the subject of public debate during the policymaking period (1968–69).

The Hawthorn Report was the most comprehensive study of the current conditions of Indians. Its 151 specific recommendations substantiated many aspects of the Indian problem and provided Indian Affairs officials with a detailed blueprint for revising their programs. Volume I, which had the greatest policy relevance, also had the greatest impact on the public because it was leaked to the *Globe and Mail* and favourably reviewed by George Mortimore.[8] Because Indian spokesmen concurred with its philosophy of 'citizens plus' status, they used the report in framing their response to the White Paper (Indian Chiefs of Alberta 1970).

TABLE 2 Ministers of Indian Affairs, 1958–80

Government	Prime minister	Minister	Department	Date of office	Tenure
Progressive Conservative	J. Diefenbaker	E.D. Fulton	Citizenship and Immigration	21 June 1957 to 11 May 1958	11 months
		E.L. Fairclough		12 May 1958 to 8 August 1962	4 years
		R. Bell		9 August 1962 to 22 April 1963	8 months
Liberal	L.B. Pearson	G. Favreau		22 April 1963 to 2 February 1964	10 months
		R. Tremblay		3 February 1964 to 14 February 1965	1 year
		J.R. Nicholson		15 February 1965 to 17 December 1965	10 months
		J. Marchand	Northern Affairs and National Resources	18 December 1965 to 30 September 1966	9 months
		A. Laing	Indian Affairs and Northern Development*	1 October 1966 to 5 July 1968	20 months
	P.E. Trudeau	J. Chrétien		6 July 1968 to 10 August 1974	6 years
		R. Andras, minister without portfolio		6 July 1968 to 5 May 1969	11 months
		J. Buchanan		10 August 1974 to 14 September 1976	2 years
		W. Allmand		14 September 1976 to 16 September 1977	1 year
		H. Faulkner		16 September 1977 to 4 June 1979	22 months
Progressive Conservative	J. Clark	J. Epp		4 June 1979 to 3 March 1980	9 months
Liberal	P.E. Trudeau	J. Munro		3 March 1980 to present	

* DIAND became referred to as the Department of Indian and Northern Affairs in 1973 as part of the federal identity program, although the official title of the department has not been altered by statute.

Although the Hawthorn Report documented the conditions of Indians, it did not indict the Indian Affairs bureaucracy, as some civil servants and social scientists later wished it had. For social scientists like R.W. Dunning, the report did not challenge the paternalistic role of Indian Affairs sufficiently. Dunning's criticism was the strongest in this regard, and although he considered the research sound and many of its recommendations well taken, he argued that its philosophy was 'worthy of 1867' because it did not question the monopoly of the branch in Indian management (1967: 52). Like others, Dunning had anticipated more far-reaching recommendations for change in Indian administration.

However, at the time the Hawthorn team was preparing its recommendations, the community development program had just been launched and senior officials were actively searching for new directions. Hawthorn felt this was encouraging and that it demonstrated a willingness to implement change.[9] Through his numerous recommendations, Hawthorn left little doubt that extensive change was needed throughout the system, but he had not recommended the dissolution of the branch or its programs 'at any near point in time' (1966: 8). The researchers had considered dissolution as a possible course of action, but rejected it (pp. 8, 387-400).

The Hawthorn Report had more impact on programming than on policy. Branch officials, however, did attempt to use some of its recommendations in 1968 to substantiate their earliest policy proposals for the White Paper. Like most programs in Indian Affairs in the 1960s the Hawthorn Report suffered the fate of a rapid succession of no less than seven ministers (see Table 2) from the time it was initially discussed in late 1963 until the second volume was published in the spring of 1969. Without ministerial support, chances of implementing the report were limited; indeed, Minister of Indian Affairs Arthur Laing, who received the final drafts of both volumes, was even reluctant to release the report to the public. There was the further problem of senior officials wanting the findings at the time the study started. This impatience, although not unusual in government-contracted research, is especially strong when senior officials have ministerial support to revise their programs but lack a clear sense of direction for these changes. Indeed, the events of the period threatened to outstrip the pace of the research; the branch had already made changes while the report was being prepared, and some programs were even terminated before the report became public in 1967.

NEW PROGRAMS IN THE BRANCH

From 1963 to 1967, during the years the Hawthorn Report was being prepared and awaiting release, many new programs were simultaneously

TABLE 3 Indian Affairs Branch expenditures – on specific programs
(in millions of dollars; percentage in parentheses)

	1956–57	1958–59	1960–61	1962–63	1964–65	1966–67	1968–69
Education	14.8	22.3	27.7	29.0	35.7	52.2	81.6
	(62.2)	(61.2)	(59.8)	(56.8)	(55.1)	(50.3)	(49.2)
Welfare	4.2	7.8	10.4	12.3	16.7		65.5
	(17.9)	(21.2)	(22.3)	(24.2)	(25.7)	46.6	(39.5)
Economic	–	–	1.1	2.3	2.4	(44.8)	9.3
development	–	–	(2.4)	(4.5)	(3.8)		(5.6)
Total expenditures of the branch	23.7	36.4	46.4	51.0	64.8	103.9	165.8

Source: Annual reports of the Indian Affairs Branch.

mounted by the branch as it sought new directions for improving the conditions of Indians. The purpose of all these measures was to reduce Indian dependence on the branch by encouraging local initiative in Indian communities and by convincing the provinces to deliver social services to Indians within their boundaries. Next to education, welfare was the branch's largest expenditure (see Table 3), and yet both these services were constitutionally the responsibility of the provinces. During these years the Pearson government began promoting 'consultative federalism' through cost-sharing programs that were intended to spur the provinces into improving certain services. Beginning with the national medicare program in 1963, this general federal initiative provided a supportive context, if not a major stimulus, for changes within the Indian administration.

Branch officials grew increasingly alarmed at the prospects of coping with the general expansion of the welfare state in the early 1960s, because it threatened to outstrip their expertise and their realistic budget expectations, and because it required 'duplication' of services for Indians. In 1945 similar concerns had led to the transfer of medical services from the branch to the Department of National Health and Welfare, whose expenditures on Indians by 1963 amounted to $27 million (Graham-Cumming 1967: 128). The second move to transfer services had begun even before 1960, when the branch started to integrate Indian children in provincial schools and fund the program through cost-sharing agreements with the provinces. Throughout the post-war period the branch's devolution policy in education resulted in increasing the proportion of Indian children attending provincial schools from 5.6 per cent in 1949 to 59 per cent in 1968/69.[10]

By 1963 'the Indian problem' was seen not only in the context of administrative problems and federal-provincial relations, but increasingly

TABLE 4 Statistical profile of Indian poverty 1963*

Item	National	Indian
1. Average per capita salaries and wages	$3,500†	$1,600
2. Access to credit and loans per person (including farm improvement and housing)	$255	$1
3. Total per capita investment in housing	$90	$21
4. General assistance and welfare per capita (combining federal, provincial, and municipal payments and including farm assistance and mother's allowance)	$10	$70
5. Percentage of the population receiving general assistance	3.5	36
6. Percentage of houses with septic tank or sewer services	92	9
7. Percentage of houses with running water	92	13
8. Percentage of houses with indoor bath	84	7
9. Percentage of houses with electricity	99	44
10. Average age of death:		
for females	64.1	34.71
for males — including deaths in year one of infancy	60.5	33.31
for females	–	48
for males — excluding deaths in year one of infancy	–	46

* Source: W. Rudnicki, 'The Big Picture: Indian Affairs Branch Statement for Federal-Provincial Conference on Poverty, November 1965.'
† This figure derives from 1964 data.

in terms of poverty. The war on poverty, however, would not be mounted until 1965, by Prime Minister Pearson, and even then it would not impress certain officials, such as Executive Director of the Canadian Welfare Council Reuben Baetz, who referred to it as 'a paper war' with 'paper tanks' (1967: 5).

By 1964 branch officials and the Hawthorn team had begun to pull together some disturbing comparisons between Indians and the general Canadian population on a range of services. Equally upsetting comparisons were coming from the Department of National Health and Welfare on the causes and rates of Indian deaths,[11] especially the discovery that Indians were dying of diseases which were not only curable but preventable.

When Jamieson in the Hawthorn team uncovered the extent of poverty among Indians, it was clear that their economic deprivation was of major proportions. A variety of indicators comparing the standard of living of Indians with national averages showed that Indians were unquestionably a disadvantaged and 'high cost general assistance group.' The most forceful attempt to dramatize this poverty profile was made by Walter Rudnicki, a senior branch official in 1965, and his statistical package was frequently cited by the press in an effort to encapsulate the Indian problem for the public.[12] The poverty profile (see Table 4) revealed that besides being poor, Indians were marginal to the many services that other citizens received, they were over-consumers of welfare services, and housed in substandard dwellings.

The combination of these factors led branch officials in early 1964 to mount several new programs. Two of them, the devolution of branch programs to the provinces and community development, were conceived of as a 'package' and were intended to develop Indian initiative and self-determination.[13] Another program, in which grants were transferred directly to the band councils for expenditure and accounting, was also linked to Indian self-management, but it was not implemented until 1965.

COMMUNITY DEVELOPMENT AND
DEVOLUTION TO THE PROVINCES

The devolution program began in late 1963, foreshadowing the White Paper policy as much as indicating the trend in Indian Affairs policy since the early 1960s.

In keeping with Pearson's 'consultative federalism,' Indian administration became a topic of discussion in late 1963 at a federal-provincial conference on financial affairs.[14] This was the first time in Canadian history that the Indian problem was put on the agenda with the result that a Federal-Provincial Relations Division was established within the branch to promote shared-cost agreements with the provinces. The following spring the cabinet approved a policy for a community development program together with plans to promote the extension of provincial welfare services to Indians.[15] The objectives of both programs were related: through the community development process Indians would become more self-reliant, and through the transfer of federal services to the provinces, Indians would receive services from the same sources as other Canadians, thereby reducing dependence upon the Indian Affairs Branch. The minister of Indian Affairs convened a special federal-provincial conference in the fall of 1964 to discuss transferring services on a 'function by function' basis to the provinces, beginning with welfare programs.[16] A landmark, the conference signalled the serious intent of the federal government to pursue the gradual transfer of the rest of its programs to the provinces.[17] The net effect of the conference, however, proved to be more a gain in principle than in practice. With the exception of Ontario, most provinces continued to argue that Indians were a federal responsibility, according to the BNA Act, and because of this position the branch had limited success in establishing federal-provincial agreements in welfare programs.

The second major undertaking by the branch, community development, began in 1964 under the initiative and direction of Walter Rudnicki, then chief of the Social Programs Division. Community development was being encouraged in other federal departments at that time, although self-help at the grass-roots level had been pioneered with native people in Manitoba during the 1950s under the direction of Jean Lagasse (Lagasse 1961). The Indian Affairs program of community development, however, was the most extensive yet mounted at the federal level (Lloyd 1967), predating the most controversial program, the Company of Young Canadians.

In 1964 the branch, reorganizing to align some of its personnel with the new policy of community development, employed certain specialists, among them Dr Farrell Toombs from the University of Toronto, to train community development workers through 'sensitivity training.' Both headquarters and field officers were familiarized with the philosophy and techniques of community development work. By 1966 the branch had made agreements with several provinces and community workers were on reserves with programs already in motion.[18]

The community development program had significant potential for reducing bureaucratic involvement in Indian communities, but following a short period of high expectation about what it could achieve, the program rapidly became controversial within the branch. The young and enthusiastic community development workers, who were committed to changing the traditional ways of Indian Affairs management, inevitably clashed with the authoritarian Indian agents on the reserves. The purpose of these workers was to inspire self-determination and confidence in the communities, at the same time lessening their dependence on branch superintendents. Some bands achieved a sense of self-determination which predictably led the superintendents to view the workers as disruptive forces. When the communities became organized, they pressed the agents to give up their control, and often bypassed them in seeking outside sources of assistance.[19] Superintendents resented the threat to, or the loss of, their authority, and their dissatisfaction rebounded up the bureaucratic hierarchy to senior officials who were quickly becoming disenchanted with the program. One official, who had opposed the program from its inception, claimed it 'was the stupidest thing we ever did.' Rudnicki, who had initiated the program and tried to save it from termination, was transferred to a different part of the branch.[20]

It was soon evident that some branch officials had not understood that Indian self-determination would probably bring with it a vehement rejection of the branch and its representatives at the local level. Finding the publicity discomforting and the turmoil between superintendents and community workers apparently unresolvable, the branch recast the program in 1968 to focus on leadership training for band councillors. Like many sponsoring agencies in government, the branch had terminated the program when it encountered unexpected agitation from the communities (Dimock 1971).

Although the training workshops for senior officials were designed to redirect their thinking, necessary changes had not been made in the lower levels of the bureaucracy to accommodate the program, so that the confrontation of officials at the local level recoiled on the bureaucratic hierarchy. Vic Valentine, then chief of economic development in the branch, recalled a marked lack of support for the program among the regional and field superintendents, despite official sanction of the policy by senior officials in Ottawa. Resistance to change had concentrated at the mid-range level in the bureaucracy, the same locus of resistance that the Hawthorn team had encountered.[21] Efforts of workers to change the system 'from below,' as George Manuel has recounted from his own experience as a community development officer, proved extremely frustrating (Manuel and Posluns 1974: 128-55).

In the end, the top officials reaffirmed the traditions of the bureaucracy rather than the activism of the community development workers. Although community development programs were referred to in later branch publications, these programs did not have the same purpose and were not operated by the same personnel who had mounted the original programs in 1964. Rudnicki left Indian Affairs in 1966 to take a position in the Privy Council Office, the central bureaucratic agency advising the cabinet, where he played an important role in the evolution of the White Paper. After this experience the branch's position on community development was referred to as 'evolutionary,' leaving implicit its disapproval of revolutionary change.

The community development program in Indian Affairs epitomized the grass-roots activism of the 1960s, and its termination would substantiate one more aspect of the Indian problem: the branch's reluctance to lessen its bureaucratic grasp of Indian Affairs at the local level.

INDIAN ADVISORY BOARDS

In 1965, while the community development program was getting under way, Indian advisory boards at the national and regional levels were established by the branch, and these would also have important implications for the White Paper. The advisory boards, composed of band-appointed representatives, reflected the notion of Indian participation at the regional and national levels rather than at the local level as the community development program was designed to do.

The National Indian Advisory Board and the regional advisory councils met frequently in 1966 and early 1967 with the main purpose of discussing the revisions to the Indian Act that the branch had been preparing.[22] The branch wanted to proceed quickly with the amendments, which were then expected to go before Parliament at the next session, possibly in the late spring of 1967.

But that spring a new topic was raised for the National Advisory Board's consideration. The government introduced a new system that required officials to undertake long-range planning which began with an identification of the goals of their respective administrative units against which plans and budgets were to be developed and ultimately evaluated. Branch officials wanted the views of the National Advisory Board on the long-term objectives of the branch so that they could proceed with their planning.[23] The National Board members, however, did not agree with branch officials that their meeting was the ideal place to begin such discussions. Instead they criticized the government's failure to communicate with Indian communities, and repeatedly suggested that the local level, not the National Advisory Board, was the place to begin determining national goals for Indians.[24]

It became obvious that the National Board members were uncomfortable in their role as advisers. The question was raised repeatedly whether they were expected to speak their own opinions or those of their constituent communities, and, as Cardinal has noted (1969: 103-4), there was a decided unease about this representativeness. Several members spoke of the difficulty in contacting the communities in their regions, and their inability, without further funds, travel, and organization, to know what these communities wished in terms of Indian Act revisions or long-range planning.

In the end, the National Advisory Board's decision on long-range objectives for the branch was to refer the matter to the regional advisory boards. But the message was clear: the planning process should begin at the local level, reflect local needs, respect local initiatives, and represent the desires of Indians in general. To accommodate this grass-roots approach, local band councils should be given broader powers and resources to undertake the job of planning and governing.

Most of the discussion at the advisory group meetings at both regional and national levels was devoted to revisions of the Indian Act. Although a proposed version of the Act had been drafted by branch officials for the purposes of discussion and focusing debate,[25] as George Manuel, co-chairman of the National Advisory Board later noted, the delegates recommended only minor revisions to the Act (Manuel and Posluns 1974: 163-7).

Looking back on the experience, Manuel credited the failure of the advisory system to two factors: the government's disregard for their recommendations and the competition in the western provinces from resurgent Indian organizations.[26] Increasing disenchantment with the limited advisory role continued to grow, and Harold Cardinal, then in the process of rebuilding the Indian Association of Alberta, led the rejection of advisory boards as a method of Indian input into government policy and programs (Cardinal 1969: 104). The advisory boards were discontinued in 1967, although Manuel felt that, in spite of their problems and unpopularity, they had provided Indians with the opportunity of getting together to discuss common concerns (Manuel and Posluns 1974: 163-7).

Later in 1967 senior officials in Indian Affairs, feeling that the consensus demonstrated at the advisory board meetings was inadequate, decided to take the question of revising the Act to the Indians through a series of consultation meetings. The *advisory stage* of Indian-government relations was ostensibly to be replaced by a more systematic *consultative stage*.

RELOCATION

While the Hawthorn Report was still in preparation, the branch made other efforts to lay bare the Indian problem and seek solutions. The subarctic area contained many reserves in which the people were unskilled, and employment opportunities were extremely limited if existent at all. In 1966 the branch experimented with a pilot relocation project in which it moved twenty families from several reserves in northern Ontario to Elliot Lake for vocational up-grading and eventual resettlement in larger centres with employment opportunities. From the initial selection of the families to the lack of coordination among the government agencies, the program failed. Instead of completing their training and moving to employment centres, the Indian families returned to their reserves. Although some of the adults did improve their educational skills, the program failed to help them make the difficult adjustments to off-reserve life. The branch commissioned evaluations of the project which discouraged repeat performances without a major reshaping of the program.[27] Subsequent relocation programs in northern Manitoba (Koolage 1972) and in the Arctic (Stevenson 1968), developed in response to particular local conditions, proved equally unsuccessful. Thus the problem of economically unviable communities in the subarctic remained.

ADMINISTRATION OF JUSTICE

Yet another aspect of the Indian problem surfaced in 1964: the suspected increase in encounters between Indians and the law. Since the administration of justice to Indians was an uncharted area, in 1964 the branch asked the Canadian Corrections Association to determine the scope of the problem. Its report, *Indians and the Law* (1967), verified the large number of Indians in jails in the western provinces, but its basic criticism was the inadequacy of police, legal, and after-care services for Indians. The report recommended that the branch establish appropriate and sufficient services if it could not convince the provinces to do so. Further, it stressed that Indians could have little respect for white society if its system of justice unfairly or inadequately dealt with their problems. Although the report documented yet another dimension of the Indian problem, it did not become the basis for immediate program revisions within the branch; the training of special Indian constables began later, after the White Paper was released.

The branch's final major effort of the 1960s to cope with the Indian problem centred on the issue of land claims. In making their report the Canadian Corrections Association had reminded the government that its disregard for Indian treaty agreements had left a bitter legacy among Indians, fostering general disrespect for white society. The question of settling claims and honouring treaty agreements had been a sore point in Indian-white relations for generations and in the early part of the 1960s the government was moved to redress these grievances.

INDIAN TREATIES AND INDIAN FRUSTRATION

Indian treaties proved problematic for several reasons. Initially they were designed, among other things, to end unscrupulous land dealings with Indians and guarantee a land base for Indian settlement.[28] The British and, later, the Canadian governments signed treaties with certain tribes in which the latter surrendered specified areas of their traditional territory in return for reserves and certain payments, gifts, and services. The French regime, however, did not recognize Indian title to land, and consequently no treaties were made with Indians in Quebec and the Maritimes under its early jurisdiction. But the British colonial policy explicitly recognized Indian title (also called aboriginal title) to land. As a result, from Ontario west to Alberta many treaties were made beginning in the late 1700s and ending with the 'numbered' or post-Confederation treaties (see Table 5). Thus, land was surrendered throughout the southern-central core of

TABLE 5 'Numbered' treaties in Canada

Treaty no.	Year	Area	Square miles ceded	Major tribes involved
1	1871	Southern Manitoba centring on Winnipeg	16,700	Ojibwa, Swampy Cree
2	1871	Central Manitoba, southeastern Saskatchewan, southwestern Manitoba	35,700	Ojibwa
3	1873	Extreme southwestern Ontario and southeastern Manitoba	55,000	Salteaux tribe of Ojibwa
4	1874	Southern Saskatchewan	74,600	Plains Cree, Salteaux
5	1875	Northern Manitoba and extreme west of Ontario	100,000	Salteaux, Swampy Cree
6	1876	Central Alberta and central Saskatchewan	121,000	Plains Cree, Woodland Cree
7	1877	Southern Alberta	42,900	Blackfoot, Piegan, Blood, Sarcee, Stoney
8	1899	Northern Alberta, and NWT south of Great Slave Lake, and northeastern corner of BC	324,900	Cree, Beaver, Chipewyan
9	1905	Northern Ontario	90,000	Ojibwa, Cree
10	1906	Northern Ontario	85,800	Chipewyan, Cree
11	1921	NWT north of Great Slave Lake	372,000	Slave, Dogrib, Loucheaux, Hare

Source: *The Canadian Indian: A Reference Paper* (Ottawa: DIAND, 1966).

Canada until 1923 (see Map 3). These treaties viewed as 'legally enforceable obligations' within Canadian jurisprudence (Cumming and Mickenberg 1972: 54-8), brought their own problems.

The problems began with the conditions under which treaties were signed. At the time of signing Indians depended on certain white advisers, the RCMP officers and missionaries, for example, to interpret the proceedings, but misunderstandings arose from the outset about the actual nature of the transactions. Indian concepts of land use, ownership, and transferability were not the same as those of the European powers, and Indians should not have been expected to comprehend the British legal system. Furthermore, Indians were sometimes verbally promised certain things that did not appear in the written treaties (e.g. Fumoleau 1975). In short, because translation and cross-cultural understandings were often inadequate, treaties became contentious from the outset.

Compounding these initial difficulties was the failure of the Canadian government to live up to its treaty promises. This failure became especially obvious when, in 1917, it passed the Migratory Birds Convention

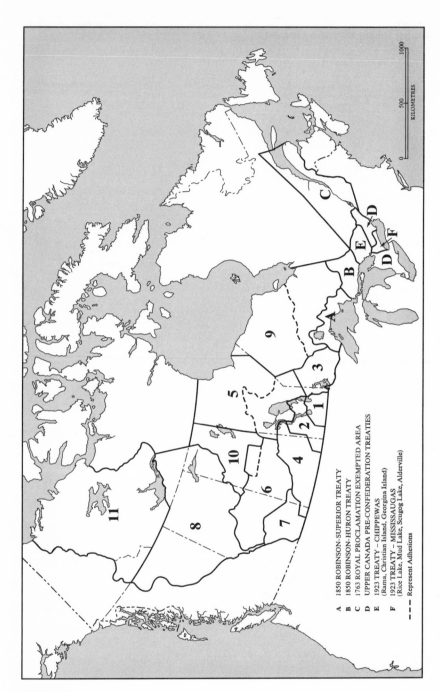

A 1850 ROBINSON-SUPERIOR TREATY
B 1850 ROBINSON-HURON TREATY
C 1763 ROYAL PROCLAMATION EXEMPTED AREA
D UPPER CANADA PRE-CONFEDERATION TREATIES
E 1923 TREATY – CHIPPEWAS
   (Rama, Christian Island, Georgina Island)
F 1923 TREATY – MISSISSAUGAS
   (Rice Lake, Mud Lake, Scugog Lake, Alderville)
– – – Represent Adhesions

MAP 3 Treaty and non-treaty areas in Canada, 1972 (*source*: Cumming and Mickenberg 1972: 2).
The numbers on the map refer to the numbered treaties listed in Table 5.

Act, a joint international agreement with the United States designed to protect migratory fowl. Although it is argued that the government simply overlooked the existence of Indian treaties, the agreement contravened the hunting and fishing rights stipulated in the treaties. Many treaties had granted Indians the right to hunt, trap, and fish on the lands they had surrendered as long as the lands remained unoccupied by white settlers. Whatever the reason for the contravention of the treaties, the government failed to correct the situation and Indians, especially those dependent on wild foods, see this failure as a symbol of white society's general disregard for their welfare and their special rights. This bitterness was further aggravated by provincial legislation promoting conservation and game control. Indian resentment over the treatment of their treaties provided them with a ready focus for political consensus.

The second issue with treaties focused on what the government called 'unfulfilled treaty promises,' which related to treaties that had been signed but which had not been granted even initially by the government. This problem occurred with Treaties 8 and 11 in the Northwest Territories, signed in 1899 and 1921, respectively. The treaties contained certain provisions for the establishment of reserves, as well as financial compensation; but in the absence of land pressures from whites, and because Indians feared that reserves would restrict their hunting, fishing, and trapping activities, the actual reserve lands were never set aside for their use. Nor were the treaty payments and annuities made. Indians lived in settlements and continued to live off the land. In 1959, when the government decided to conclude the treaty agreements, it appointed the Nelson Commission to visit the settlements in the area to discuss land provisions with the chiefs and their people. But the commission's deliberations again revealed the complex and confusing nature of treaty agreements. Indians were poorly prepared and therefore failed to understand the purpose of the meetings. Furthermore, they disagreed with the government that the treaties had surrendered their lands. The Nelson Commission Report commented explicitly on the Indian position (Canada 1959: 4):

At a number of meetings Indians who claimed to have been present at the time when the Treaties were signed stated that they definitely did not recall hearing about the land entitlement in the Treaties. They explained that poor interpreters were used and these interpreters urged the Indians to sign, saying 'It will be good for you.' It was emphasized that their chiefs and head men signed even though they did not know what the Treaties contained because the treaty parties included high government and religious officials whom the Indians trusted to look after their interests. When the Chairman pointed out that the Chiefs of each band, among others, had received copies of the Treaties the Indians replied that they were published in complicated English and they could not understand them.

René Fumoleau's study (1975) of the making of Treaties 8 and 11 reaffirms the presence of verbal promises and the absence of these promises in the written treaty documents. The Nelson Commission recommended that the government settle the land provisions by commuting the land entitlement to a cash payment. Yet, despite the commission's stressing the urgency of settlement in the face of northern development, the government did not act; neither Indian nor white interests in the area provided the needed pressure to conclude the agreement, so that when the White Paper was being formulated, the question of Treaties 8 and 11 remained unresolved. Indians maintained that they had not surrendered their lands, whereas the government held that they had when the treaties were signed.

The third and final problem with treaties lay with the *absence* of treaties. Here the question was how the government could explain to Indians the making of treaties in some areas of Canada and its refusal to make them in other areas.[29] Since the question was not of treaty rights but of aboriginal land rights, the point of Indian pressure was to convince the government to recognize their land title as a basis for making treaties, as it had done elsewhere in Canada. These non-treaty areas covered a wide arc of land beginning in Newfoundland and Labrador on the east, through Quebec, the Inuit portion of the Northwest Territories, all of the Yukon, ending in most of British Columbia. The Maritimes had treaties, but Indians and legal scholars maintain that these treaties were pacts of peace and friendship, rather than land surrenders.

Pressure from Indians to resolve the problems of aboriginal land rights came most forcefully from British Columbia where, since 1913, the Nishga tribe, who lived along the Nass River in the northern part of the province, had organized and attempted to press, though unsuccessfully, the government for land agreements.[30] In all non-treaty areas in British Columbia, Indian lands had long been occupied by whites, without compensation to Indians, and the natural resources had been controlled and developed by whites for generations. In 1927 a special parliamentary committee had been established to investigate the 'BC land question,' but the resulting annual payment of $100,000 to the Indian administration in that province (Canada 1927) had been firmly rejected by Indians from the outset as settlement of the land question.[31] In the early 1960s the BC land question became the pressure point behind the government's attempts to settle land claims. Ironically, however, these attempts by government, in and of themselves, served only to fuel Indian discontent.

AN INDIAN CLAIMS COMMISSION

After the Second World War, when revisions to the Indian Act focused greater public attention on Indians, MPs in the Special Joint Committee of 1946–48 became concerned that certain wrongs of the past should be righted and that Indian grievances over treaties, or over the lack of them, should be settled. The United States had established a claims commission in 1946,[32] providing a model which the Canadian government considered worth exploring. but the subsequent twenty years witnessed a confusing series of starts and stops as the government attempted to present legislation to establish a commission. Indeed the brief history of these attempts left a general impression that the government was not firmly committed to meeting the issues squarely and to resolving them.

Initial support for establishing a claims commission in Canada came in 1947 when the Special Joint Committee of the Senate and the House of Commons recommended that the government proceed with a commission to settle Indian land claims grievances (Canada 1947: 2004). The recommendation, however, was unacceptable to the government because Minister of Indian Affairs Walter Harris believed that the regular courts should handle such matters.[33] In his opinion, recent revisions to the Indian Act opened the way for Indians to pursue claims if they had the initiative to do so.

The question of a claims commission remained dormant until fourteen years later, when its formation was again recommended by the Joint Committee of the Senate and the House of Commons appointed to examine Indian Affairs (Canada 1961: 14). This recommendation was picked up by the Diefenbaker government, which drafted and printed a bill for introduction to parliament in early 1963.[34] But the bill never saw public light because the government fell shortly and the spring election of 1963 brought the Liberal government of Lester Pearson to power.

In its campaign the Liberal party made explicit promises to establish a rather ambitious claims commission if it were to receive a majority in that April's election. In the *Native Voice*, an Indian newspaper in British Columbia, the party pledged to develop a commission, possibly with international personnel, to settle all outstanding Indian land claims. The party's platform included full equality for Indians 'without loss of aboriginal, hereditary and usufructory rights' (*Native Voice*, February 1963: 5).

Under the new Liberal minority government, the minister of Indian Affairs was briefed on the previous claims commission bill prepared under the Diefenbaker government. The old bill would have produced a claims commission with only advisory powers, not the adjudicatory powers to settle claims with finality as the United States' commission had. After a visit to Washington to discuss the experience of the American commission, senior officials received ministerial support for a claims commission with adjudicatory powers for final settlement.[35]

The new bill laid out the form and functions of a claims commission,[36] and after its first reading in the House of Commons in December 1963, it was sent out for comment to every Indian community in Canada and to interested organizations, such as the Canadian Civil Liberties Association and the Canadian Bar Association. The disappointment of Indians and their advisers with the types of admissible claims was immediate. During the next two years the department received over 300 briefs, 70 per cent of them criticizing the bill in some respect.[37]

The most pointed criticism came from British Columbia, where Indians argued that their land claims originated in aboriginal title which was not explicitly acknowledged in the bill. Because of this omission, it was possible that the bill would not allow them to submit their case to the commission. Thomas Berger, the lawyer for the Native Brotherhood in British Columbia, went further by arguing that the bill allowed Indians to bring claims against only the federal government, not the provinces.[38] He maintained that because more Indians in British Columbia lost land after Confederation than before it, Indians would be required to bring suit against the province for their claims, and the stipulations of the bill did not permit this. Although Berger acknowledged that action by the federal government to allow the provinces to be sued was a complicated jurisdictional and constitutional problem, he stressed that it was the federal government's responsibility, under the BNA Act, to ensure fair land dealings with Indians. In his view the bill should be changed to accommodate this fact.

The claims bill rested for two years while these and other comments came forward from Indian groups. In early summer of 1965 the government reintroduced the bill, which was essentially the same with some minor concessions to Indian criticisms. This manoeuvre immediately fanned the flames of anger among Indians and their supporters in Parliament.[39] As with the first bill, this one did not explicitly acknowledge aboriginal title as the basis for land claims and it prevented suit to be brought against the provinces. The suggestions from Indians in British Columbia had been rejected, although the minister believed, as did his senior officials, that the bill would in fact allow the BC land question to go before the commission.[40] The bill was to go to committee for further review and out again to bands; however, yet another election followed so that the bill again became dormant.

Within the Indian Affairs Branch, however, Berger's comments on the bill had raised sufficient doubts among senior officials about the BC question that they commissioned an outside legal specialist to provide them with an opinion on whether the bill would allow the question to be submitted to the commission. The confidential report left the issue unresolved, for it apparently said that settlement of the BC issue would depend upon the way the commission interpreted its own mandate.

Even though this external opinion had not resolved the issue for senior officials, their position on land claims settlement was firm and they wanted the matter resolved. Their rationale for promoting the claims commission was to remove Indian distrust of the government and place Indian-government relations on a more positive footing. In 1963, when they recommended the bill to their minister, they were straightforward about their goal:[41]

The conviction in the mind of any Indian group that justice is being denied makes it extremely difficult to obtain the necessary co-operation between them and government that is so necessary in every field of endeavour that may be undertaken to improve their lot. It creates a barrier of distrust and resentment against government and the work of its officials, and seriously impedes the progress and development of the Indian people concerned.

It was theerefore deemed essential to provide a means whereby the Indians could state their claims fully and have them considered without undue formality. It was recognized that some of the claims have considerable merit, others might be doubtful, and still others might be without foundation. If a claim is good, then it should be settled. Equally important, if a claim is bad the Indians should know about it so that they can put it aside.

Significantly, their promotion of the land claims bill in the 1960s did not rest on the government's acknowledgment of aboriginal land title as the basis for settling claims but on their understanding of what was frequently called a 'psychological problem'; that is, that the negative attitude Indians held toward the government had to be removed.[42] Not one of the bills (1962, 1963 and 1965) contained the phrase 'aboriginal title,' or an equivalent. Indeed, the term had been avoided, for, as one official claimed, 'to define it would have been to limit it.' The government's failure to recognize explicitly this concept in its bills led to continued criticism from both Indians and parliamentary critics that the government was hedging on the issue and not serious in its intent. The delays in presenting the legislation, moreover, proved costly, for the senior officials rightly predicted that the longer they delayed in settling claims, the higher the payments would become.

One of the difficulties with claims settlement was determining the monetary cost of compensation.[43] In 1963 the basis for cost was set by determining what monies would have been paid to the bands if treaties had been made when whites occupied their lands. This cost was calculated by looking to adjacent areas where treaties had been made and by deriving a comparable estimate. The 1963 estimates produced by the senior branch officials showed a possible overall cost of $17.4 million for settling Indian claims. This figure did not include 'unknown claims' that might be submitted, for the department could not predict how Indian bands would respond to the legislation. At that time, the most costly claim anticipated was the settlement in British Columbia, even after the annual $100,000 grant was subtracted. The estimate was broken down as follows:[44]

1	*Aboriginal land claims*	
	British Columbia	$13,046,000
	Yukon	581,000
	Quebec	560,000
		$14,187,000
	Minus the total amount of the annual $100,000 payments to BC since 1928	3,000,000
		$11,187,000
2	*Other claims*	
	For flooding of land, improper use of funds, etc.	6,213,000
	Total	$17,400,000

The escalation in cost feared by the senior officials was borne out, for during the development of the White Paper, estimates reached as high as $1.5 billion. In 1975 the James Bay settlement in Quebec alone totalled $225 million.[45]

The final step in the saga of the claims commission occurred in 1967 when the minister, Arthur Laing, attempted to press forward with the claims bill and the BC question in particular. Laing made a firm offer to the bands in British Columbia that he would urge the government to negotiate with them if they could demonstrate that their leadership represented at least 75 per cent of the Indians in the province.[46] For reasons that are unclear, BC Indians did not respond to Laing's offer, so that when deliberations began on the White Paper, the BC land question remained unresolved. The fate of the Indian claims commission bill was also unsettled, although Laing had clearly wanted to proceed with the commission.

Thus, for twenty years preceding the White Paper, the matter of settling Indian land claims and treaty grievances had been approached in a start-and-stop fashion by the government. When, in 1963, the effort picked up momentum, the overall effect satisfied neither the government nor the Indians. In an important way these attempts had already failed: for they had enhanced Indian distrust instead of reducing it as the government had intended.

INDIANS – THE UNORGANIZED MINORITY

At the time the White Paper was formulated Indians were esssentially a politically unorganized minority. There had been a few regional associations in the past (Lueger 1977), but none became firmly established or clearly representative of their constituencies. The perceived need to organize at the regional or provincial levels had not been pressing enough, nor had the funds been available. In 1968 the question of whether a more coherent Indian movement would develop on an organizational basis was being asked by both native spokesmen and government officials. The Indian Act consultation meetings provided the first stimulus in the late 1960s to organize, yet the real thrust would not come until the White Paper was released (Cardinal 1977: 182; Manuel and Posluns 1974: 210; Whiteside 1973: 38).

Prior to the consultation meetings in summer 1968, Indian spokesmen began discussing the need for associations more powerful and inclusive than band councils to mobilize Indian people above the reserve level. But not all Indian communities agreed with this need. In Southern Ontario, for example, the Iroquois did not join forces with the emerging Union of Ontario Indians; the union was not seen to represent their interests and they did not identify with its predominantly Ojibwa leadership.

Indian spokesmen from the Prairies, however, such as Harold Cardinal in Alberta, Dave Courchene in Manitoba, and Walter Deiter in Saskatchewan, argued that provincially based organizations were vital for pressing both the provincial and federal governments to address Indian needs.[47] Given the jurisdiction of provincial governments in the field of social services, a provincial basis for Indian political organization made considerable sense. Yet, at the same time, it meant Indian organizers faced the challenge of mobilizing large constituencies. There is no doubt that the lack of congruence between traditional tribal boundaries, treaty areas, and the modern provincial boundaries imposed considerable strain on the organizing efforts of Indian leaders. There were other problems to overcome: 1/the cost and time involved in contacting the widely dispersed Indian communities; 2/the extensive cultural heterogeneity among Indians; 3/the historic inter-tribal distrust among certain groups; 4/language diversity; 5/various degrees of acculturation within and between communities; 6/poverty; 7/limited education; and 8/the lack of funding to organize or to maintain the organizations. Although some Indian spokesmen had organizational experience within their own provinces, as well as with the Indian-Eskimo Association and the National Indian Council, they still lacked expertise in organizational and communication skills. The obstacles facing Indian organizers were extensive, yet they were usually underestimated by the public and government officials, as well as by the Indian people themselves.

At the time of the consultation meetings, an overview of the provincial organizations in existence reveals an uneven picture. The most active and articulate leadership was coming from the Prairie provinces, with Ontario, Quebec, and the Maritimes being less organized. No provincially based organizations existed in British Columbia, the Yukon, the Northwest Territories, or Newfoundland. Although Indian spokesmen in all these areas were working toward, or hoping to establish, associations, they had to operate on shoe-string budgets (if any at all), out of loaned offices, or through the support of other groups such as the Indian-Eskimo Association. The difficulties Cardinal (1977) experienced in establishing the Alberta Association, and in getting government and Indian support, will probably be recounted by other Indian leaders if they document the histories of their efforts. Of these leaders, Cardinal, then 23 years old, was the most nationally known figure linked with the Indian movement, and the strongest critic of government bureaucracy.

Given the undeveloped state of provincial organizations, it is not surprising that a national organization was even less advanced in 1968. The formation of the National Indian Council in 1961 was the first attempt in Canada to build a national network of communication among native people (Cardinal 1969: 109-11; Wuttunee 1971: 19-21). The objectives of the National Indian Council were to promote Indian culture and unity, and to assist the development of regional and provincial organizations

(Wuttunee 1971). Its leadership and membership came largely from urban areas and included both status and non-status Indians, two conditions which eventually contributed to its demise. The strains between status and non-status interests had been a major problem from the beginning (Cardinal 1977), and the council's representativeness was soon questioned because it lacked rural or reserve support. As a result, native leaders disbanded the council in February 1968 and decided to start two new organizations: the National Indian Brotherhood for status Indians, and the Native Council of Canada for Metis and non-status Indians (Cardinal 1969: 111). Despite the problems with the National Indian Council, native spokesmen agree that the experience helped to develop Indian political leadership (Cardinal 1969: 110; Manuel and Posluns 1974: 163-7).

Thus, during the preparation of the White Paper (1968–69), the National Indian Brotherhood (henceforth NIB) was more a hope than a reality. It was to be a federation of the provincial organizations, but these associations, although more advanced than the NIB, were still in the developing stage and struggling for funding.

The determination of Indian spokesmen to develop their own organizations and to define their own problems and goals led predictably to their rejection of white advocate groups such as the Indian-Eskimo Association (IEA). The IEA had supported the beginnings of the National Indian Brotherhood and played an important role in assisting the growth of provincial associations. It had the expertise, the organization, and funding to draw public attention to the Indian cause, but its interests were not necessarily those of the native spokesmen or of status Indians. Cardinal (1969: 104-5) and other Indian spokesmen saw the IEA in competition with provincial Indian organizations for scarce funds, and so they urged the IEA to play a supportive role rather than a spokesman-role for Indian people. But in the fall of 1968, while the formation of the National Indian Brotherhood was being discussed, the IEA executive divided on the issue, with some favouring the new support role while others insisted on the old advocacy until Indian organizations were on a firm footing.[48] The lack of clear direction within the IEA lasted until 1972 when the association changed its name to the Canadian Association in Support of the Native Peoples to reflect the new role it had come to accept.

TAKING STOCK, 1968

By 1968, research by the Hawthorn team, the Canadian Corrections Association, and the Indian-Eskimo Association had substantiated many aspects of 'the Indian problem.' But before the results of these studies were available, the Indian Affairs Branch had set in motion a series of programs and proposals designed to relieve the vast array of problems facing both the administration and the Indians. But a stock-taking shows that most programs fell far short of their mark. The branch had responded with half-way measures which, in the end, failed to satisfy even the senior officials. In the end, there were: 1/intended proposals that were not implemented, such as the Indian Claims Commission legislation, and federal-provincial agreements; 2/programs which were mounted, only to be discontinued because they proved too disruptive to the bureaucratic order, such as the community development program; or 3/programs that proved unsatisfactory to both Indians and branch officials, such as the Indian advisory boards and the relocation projects. Taken together, these efforts made the branch appear indecisive and unable to mobilize its resources to mount the changes required to reduce the poverty and patronage of Indians. Indeed, there was a sliding scale in which the demands outstripped the branch's attempts to cope with them. In particular, the branch appeared unwilling to give Indians more than advisory roles in policy and program decisions. Consequently, the net effect of the period left the Indian problem unchanged and even more visible. More significantly, public opinion, led by journalists, academics, students, and white support groups, viewed the Indian problem largely as an 'Indian administration problem,' and doubted that the Indian Affairs Branch had the *capacity* to cope with the challenges of its mandate. For many critics, the branch suffered from a major displacement of goals by promoting its own interests at the expense of encouraging Indians to decrease their dependency on its services.

Complex factors were behind the branch's ineffectiveness, a major one being the political instability of the period. Changes in government, from the Conservative leadership of Diefenbaker (1957–63) to the Liberal leadership of Pearson (1963–68), were compounded by the uncertainties of minority government for most of the mid-1960s (1962–68). Of the eight ministers who passed through the Indian portfolio in the decade preceding the White Paper, six held terms of office of a year or less, effectively leaving the civil servants without political direction (see Table 2). The leadership vacuum brought in its wake certain bureaucratic conditions that often accompany leaderless portfolios, such as increasing complacency and resistance to change, growing indifference to public wants, and reduced accountability of the bureaucracy for its actions (Balls 1976). Such conditions also can thwart efforts by civil servants to mount new programs because they are often unable to get the necessary ministerial guidance and support for their ideas. Under minority government these conditions become aggravated, forcing civil servants to develop greater reliance on the old boy network with its informal communication and traditions (Hodgson 1976).

Branch officials experienced all these difficulties. Much of their time was spent in briefing new ministers who rarely had the time to become knowledgeable about the portfolio before being moved to another department or before an election interrupted momentum for change. With the exceptions of Ellen Fairclough (1958–62) and possibly Arthur Laing (1966–68), none of the ministers was in office long enough to become apprised of the problems facing Indians or their own portfolios.

During these years, and for that matter historically, Indian affairs had not been an item of priority on the government's agenda, nor had the Indian administration experienced high prestige within government service. Under pressure from outside government, Arthur Laing had been more involved in northern development than in the Indian affairs component of his portfolio. Indians, who had been granted the federal franchise for the first time in 1960, were not pressing for changes through their local MPs. At the provincial level, Indians in Quebec still were without provincial franchise, and although Indians in British Columbia had actively fought for many years to gain the franchise both federally and provincially,[49] many Indians refused to vote because they equated voting with a loss of their Indian rights (Hawthorn 1966: 260). This was the legacy of the enfranchisement regulations which, until 1960, had required Indians to abandon their legal status for the right to vote. Even if they had voted regularly, the fact that they were dispersed through many electoral ridings, in small numbers, rendered their influence marginal. As a result there was no persistent vigilance from MPs, although a few determined opposition members, such as Frank Howard (NDP) from British Columbia and Gerald Baldwin (PC) from Alberta, persevered as able critics of the administration. Even the governing Liberal party had not discussed Indian issues at its national biennial conventions in 1966 or 1968.[50] Consequently, without effective party pressures, organized Indian protest, ministerial leadership, and collective expression of dissatisfaction from MPs, civil servants in the branch were left to their own resources, without much political direction or support in their attempts to introduce change.

In contrast to the changing ministers and their deputy ministers, the continuity of senior officials in the branch was exceptionally strong, probably unrivalled in the civil service at that time. This stability took the form of 'the old guard,' a departmental term used to describe a small group of senior men who had been in Indian Affairs for over two decades.

These officials, long accustomed to managing the affairs of Indians, had shaped most of the branch's policies over the years, with the exception of the community development program. They clearly illustrated the powerful role civil servants had in policy-making, especially in portfolios with short-term ministers.

Of the seven senior men at the assistant deputy minister and director levels in the branch in 1968, five were of the old guard: two men had joined Indian Affairs in the late 1930s and three in the post-war 1940s.[51] Those who had come into the program in the late 1930s had themselves witnessed change in the branch, despite public opinion that Indian administration remained unaltered since the Victorian era.

After the war, the branch's military tradition was most conspicuous in the person of Colonel H.M. Jones, the director of Indian Affairs from 1953 to 1963. The analogy of the branch as a 'command post' during Colonel Jones' years was apt; senior officials addressed him as 'Colonel' and stood up when he entered the room. Researchers in the Hawthorn team still recall his sounding forth at meetings about the sanctity of the Indian Act and the branch's constant duty to protect Indian lands from land-hungry speculators and politicians. His style of leadership was foreign to civil servants outside Indian Affairs, and those who felt the branch was an anachronism sometimes referred to it as 'Colonel Jones' lost battalion.' Directives flowed from the top down to the superintendents on the reserves, line authority being highly respected. This centralist tendency resulted in an insensitivity to local needs, and the strong protectionist ethic toward Indians almost garrisoned the branch even within the federal service.

Although the military formalities diminished in 1963 after Colonel Jones' retirement, the rigidity of the administration was still apparent in 1967, when the branch began to gear up for further policy changes. With the exception of the deputy minster, the old guard filled the senior positions, each buttressed with twenty-five to thirty years' experience in one single department, Indian Affairs. In their early careers two of them had been school teachers on reserves and another had begun his career as an Indian agent, but their years in the bureaucracy had erased their first-hand experience in Indian communities. Their progression from the bottom to the top of the administration had conditioned them to an administrative perspective of Indians so that each new problem was met by developing a new set of bureaucratic procedures. Disruptions in these procedures, such as those caused by Rudnicki's community development program, met with a low level of tolerance. A strong authoritative sense of directing a specific clientele had evolved among the old guard, making them an administrative island unto themselves.

Other factors contributed equally to the rigidity in the branch. There were few professionals in the senior ranks, making its policy-research capacity very weak. Branch traditions of secrecy and of distancing Indians from its affairs were strong. Despite efforts by Colonel Jones' successor to open up the administration through inter-departmental committees, the branch remained largely isolated from other developments within the federal service. This parochialism, as the Hawthorn Report called it, was reinforced by the general conservatism of bureaucracies. For these and other reasons Indian Affairs was not an attractive place for top-ranking civil servants, and those who worked for the branch tended to be unsympathetic with its traditions and did not remain for long. As one civil servant no longer with the department said, 'Indian affairs can be a scarifying kind of experience.'

Whatever else Indian Affairs might be, it was at times a frustrating experience even for the old guard. The momentum for change, so evident in 1963, had diminished by 1967, leaving some senior officials discouraged with the results of their programs but convinced that further change was required.[52] The reluctance of the branch to relinquish or lessen its control of decision-making had been obvious, but this conservatism was not simply the result of entrenched attitudes among civil servants. Under increasing public criticism, senior officials were more frequently confronted with the dilemma that had plagued Indian policy since Confederation (Tobias 1976): how to protect Indian interests while at the same time integrating Indians into the mainstream of Canadian society on an equal basis with other citizens; if protection – and the special rights historically developed to ensure this protection – were too overpowering, integration was jeopardized; if the legal and administrative protections were minimized, integration could be enhanced but possibly at the cost of special rights and security of Indian lands. The dilemma was phrased as special rights versus equality and although often discussed by senior officials, they found the problem intractable. When representing Indian interests to other federal departments they felt the dilemma particularly acute, as one branch report revealed:[53]

There is no quarrel with the view that the Branch has a right to represent the Indians. The trouble is that this representation so often takes the form of suggesting that exceptions must be made in favour of Indians when policies or programs are being designed for non-Indians. At the same time, the Branch is advocating equality of treatment and opportunity for Indians and, therefore, finds itself too often in the paradoxical position of having to make representations in particular cases that are really in direct opposition to its announced general policy. The position of the Branch is not an enviable one when it appears at policy-making level discussions. It is certainly endeavouring to advocate the needs of the Indians at these levels, but it is most frequently in a minority position where it is difficult to obtain support.

In early 1967, amid strengthening public criticism of the branch, the government arrived at what it considered a partial solution to this dilemma when it decided to revise the Indian Act. Both Laing and his officials wanted to liberalize the relationship between Indians and the government by making the Act less restrictive.[54] The decision to revise the Act, however, was taken *within* the traditional policy framework of the branch. As a result, officials attempted a compromise between retaining the special rights of Indians and encouraging their increased participation in the wider society.

This compromise reflected the fact that during the 1960s Indians and government had begun to accent different values in their long-standing patron-client relationship. Indians, on the one hand, continued to value their special rights and protected lands, but sought an end to the policies of assimilation. The government, on the other hand, sought ways to reduce the dependency aspect of the relationship, but did not propose to terminate its trusteeship function or relinquish its goal of assimilation. Indeed, four years earlier, when Laing as minister of Northern Affairs and National Resources was involved in the federal-provincial conference on Indian Affairs, he stressed the need to retain special status for Indians and opposed suggestions from the Privy Council Office to promote the transfer of Indian programs to the provinces. Laing argued that the government would be charged with abandoning Indians and that the provinces would side-step their responsibilities, but his basic point was that it was premature to remove government protection, in short, to end the patron-client relationship, because Indians had not yet accepted the values the government wanted them to accept. He wrote: 'The prime condition in the progress of the Indian people must be the development by themselves of a desire for the goals which we think they should want.'[55] In his discussion of revisions to the Act, Laing stressed the need to keep Indian lands secure and to honour the treaties, and he had consistently pushed for the establishment of an Indian claims commission as a way to clear up the claims grievances. The ultimate purpose of government was 'to make both the Act and the Department unnecessary,' but this was not Laing's immediate goal, nor was it a hidden agenda when he proposed revisions to the Indian Act.[56]

After the decision to revise the Act was made, indeed after the draft revision of the Act was almost completed,[57] the branch decided to seek organized representations from Indians on the revisions, instead of pursuing its original plan of getting feedback from mailed copies of draft legislation. But before the consultation meetings could begin, the Liberal leadership race in April brought Trudeau in as prime minister, and the consultations were deferred until after the June election.

The decision to revise the Indian Act was the government's response to the Indian problem. By 1968, however, the sense of problem had grown to considerable proportions. The Trudeau government inherited a public perception of the Indian problem that combined the unsatisfactory living conditions of Indians with the unsatisfactory government responses to these conditions. Despite the community development programs, relocation schemes, and increased welfare budget, Indians were still poor, as the poverty reports by the Economic Council of Canada (1968) and the Senate (Canada 1971) demonstrated. Despite the government's attempt to interest the provinces in their responsibilities, Indians were still deprived of social services that other Canadians received. Indians were dying of diseases that were preventable, and their poor housing conditions only made the link between poverty and disease more visible. Instead of lessening the bureaucratic network around Indians, the government had expanded its administration, which was increasingly seen by Indians and their supporters as arbitrary, rigid, and excessively authoritarian. Even government attempts to redress the historical injustices to Indians in the field of land claims and treaties failed as the claims commission bills sidestepped the basic issue of aboriginal title, leaving the impression that government intent was less than serious. The advisory boards merely increased Indian resentment of their powerlessness in shaping the policies and programs that affected their future.

In all, the 1960s witnessed an increasing distrust of the government by both Indians and the public, particularly the media, to the point where the government, and not Indians, became the basic target of public concern. The limited gains of the branch's new programs left serious doubt in the public mind that the government was determined to grapple with the complex problems facing Indians and loosen its paternalistic hold on their communities. The Indian Act was viewed as racist legislation which denied fundamental civil liberties, relegating Indians to reserves where they were ignored by society in general. There was a strong sense that Indians had been neglected for too long, but there was serious doubt that the Indian administration had the capacity to reform.

With Trudeau's coming to power in April 1968, a new approach to policy-making was established in government and applied to 'the Indian problem.' The changes instituted by Trudeau provide the key in understanding how an exercise to revise the Indian Act turned into a policy review which gave birth to the White Paper.

CHAPTER TWO

Summer: the season for strategy

Even before Trudeau came to power there were pressures inside government for a policy review in Indian Affairs. Early in 1967 dissatisfaction with current Indian policy arose in the Privy Council Office (PCO), the office of the cabinet secretariat whose influential officials advise the cabinet of civil servants' views on policies. A special unit had been developed within the PCO to fight 'the war on poverty,' and its senior officials were becoming increasingly sensitive to the growing public criticism of the way government was handling Indian affairs. Although publicly, senior officials in the Department of Indian Affairs still disclaimed the seriousness of the Indian situation, internally they were struggling for solutions and often held discussions in their own homes about possible courses of action.[1] But as proposals went from their deputy minister to the PCO for review, before going to cabinet, a few of the PCO officials became increasingly impatient with the department's approach to the problem. The deputy minister had suggested that the department improve its information services for the public, implying that the problem lay in the public's misunderstanding of the department, not in the department's policies. In the winter of 1967 the department's persistent denial of the seriousness of the situation finally provoked strong comment from a senior PCO official:[2]

I would never suggest that improved information services are a substitute for effective policy ...

If [the deputy minister] believes that he can reverse or significantly change this trend by reorganizing his Information Division, I must dissent. If he believes that the government's position with respect to Indians will be cured by more effective information, I can only despair. To my mind the really essential problem is communications between the government and Indians and between the government and the public about Indians. That is why we have advocated a task force which tackles both communications and the solutions to the Indians' economic, social and political problems. To us, this straightforward solution is preferable to the advocacy of any one of dozens of measures which might well be advanced to improve government policies and programs ... I cannot help point out, however, that certain facts about Indian problems and government solutions will never be covered up by better organized information services. For example:

1/ Indians are deplorably poor; on the Prairies the cash income is $350 a head.
2/ Indians are deplorably unhealthy; their life expectancy is half the national average.
3/ Indians are badly under-educated; their attainment is less than half the national average.
4/ Indian housing is scandalously bad; present government programs will require a generation for correction.
5/ While Indians are becoming relatively poorer, the federal bureaucracy and federal expenditures are becoming greater.
6/ The *percentage* of Indians on relief is rising every year: in 1962 it was 32%; in 1965 it was 39%.
7/ The government is allocating $16 million to Indian relief and something like $4 million to Indian economic development.

Clearly frustrated with the department's response, the official concluded by saying, 'There are some indications that official defence of Indian policy is no longer on the same wave length as the government position.'[3]

Within a few weeks this growing sense of problem was reinforced by the three western provincial premiers at their Prairie Economic Council. They wrote Prime Minister Pearson, urging him to consider a total reassessment of programs for all people of native ancestry, including the Metis and non-status Indians.[4] The premiers were concerned about the fragmented federal programs and their provinces' inadequate financial arrangements with the federal government for native people. They recommended that a 'low-key' task force be mounted of federal and provincial officials to examine the problems in a 'comprehensive' way, hoping that subsequent consultations with the federal government would produce a broader understanding of the problems the provinces faced.

Using the premiers' letter as a pressure point, PCO officials continued throughout 1967 to stress the need for serious reappraisal of Indian policy through a task force approach. But in the ensuing months their efforts failed as Pearson announced his retirement and cabinet ministers became preoccupied with the Liberal leadership race. Instead, the cabinet decided to revise the Indian Act, and although PCO officials did not deny the Act was outdated, they were convinced it was an inappropriate response to the Indian problem.[5]

Pressure from the PCO to improve communications with Indians had some impact, for in late 1967, the department set about planning a series of eighteen consultation meetings with Indian spokesmen to discuss revisions to the Indian Act. The meetings were to begin in late April or early May of 1968 and end that fall.[6] Although the department was anxious to proceed with the revisions, on 1 May Laing announced a postponement of the meetings until the June 25 election was over. Laing felt the consultations were 'sacrificing some speed' in the process but he considered Indian support well worth the delay.[7]

However, the situation changed dramatically when Trudeau came to power and encouraged far-reaching reform in the policy-making process. The wholesale review of Indian policy which the PCO had promoted finally found political support. Consequently, in the summer of 1968, two political arenas developed simultaneously to cope with the Indian problem. One arena was *public*, in which Indians discussed legislative changes to the Indian Act with DIAND officials. The second was *private*, unknown to the public, in which only senior government officials and ministers began to develop a new Indian policy which questioned the very foundations of the Indian Act and the consultation process itself. From the outset, these arenas examined the Indian problem from different angles, bringing different values and assumptions to bear on the issue. Part of the reason for this divergence was Trudeau's own views on Quebec and special rights.

TRUDEAU'S VIEWS

Trudeau's personal philosophy on French culture and federalism was a potent force in the formation of Indian policy. His public statements on the White Paper often referred to the French situation, revealing similarity of thought on both issues, but especially on his rejection of 'special status' for both groups.[8] Other policy-makers were aware of his ideas, and his views on the French consequently provided a framework which affected their thinking. Officials frequently referred to 'the prime minister's position on the French and special rights' as they weighed certain proposals and tried to anticipate the possible reception these might receive in the Prime Minister's Office.

Although Trudeau did not write about Indians in his years as an academic, his philosophy on nationalism and federalism had profound implications for Indian policy. He viewed the Canadian federal system as flexible and broad enough in delegating powers to the provinces that special privileges for Quebec within Confederation were both unnecessary and unwise (1968: 182-203). His hostility to the notion of a nation state, a state based on a cultural entity, was well known. The concept was 'absurd' and 'illogical,' for the future of federalism lay in reason, not in the emotion of nationalism which would create ethnocentrism and intolerance, eventually resulting in political instability (1968: 4, 29).

In his ideas about society and culture, Trudeau took a strong Social Darwinian approach in emphasizing freedom and competition. Cultures, like economic systems, could survive and thrive only through competition with other cultural and language systems (1968: 35). Excessive cultural protection by the state would hinder this competition, producing a closed cultural system or 'a weak, hot-house culture' (1968: 23). The danger of protection lay in its encouragement of inward-looking attitudes among the people, creating what he variously referred to as 'a ghetto mentality' or 'the wigwam complex' (1968: 42, 211). Moderate political protections were acceptable only if they fostered equal competition, and for this reason he argued that Parliament should adopt policies to promote equality of the two major languages in Canada. Basically, however, he considered the legal buttressing of cultures 'too fragile' an instrument to guarantee cultural continuity (1968: 6).

In Trudeau's view, French Canadians had to face the external world and deal with it through their language and culture. Their success in doing so would validate their culture and give it vitality. If their language in some way suffered, this was the inevitable cost that had to be paid for the improved standard of living and technological advancement (1968: 15).

His opposition to singling out cultural groups for separate treatment is best captured in a statement he made during the election campaign: 'I am against any policy based on race or nationalism.'[9] Although his comments on Indians during the campaign were few, he took the same approach to their problem, believing that native people 'should be treated more and more like Canadians,' and when possible, not by a special minister or a special act.[10]

Trudeau's views on the minimal importance of history for current policies had equally significant implications for Indian policy. Basically, Trudeau did not believe that the future should be fettered to the chains of the past. Policies should begin with an appreciation of the current political realities, not outmoded historical constraints. In this regard he believed that the status of languages in the country necessarily reflected contemporary political fact, not historical events (1968: 31).

Historical origins are less important than people generally think, the proof being that neither Eskimo nor Indian dialects have any kind of privileged position. On the other hand, if there were six million people living in Canada whose mother tongue was Ukrainian, it is likely that this language would establish itself as forcefully as French. In terms of *realpolitik*, French and English are equal in Canada because each of these linguistic groups has the power to break the country. And this power cannot yet be claimed by the Iroquois, the Eskimos, or the Ukrainians.

His philosophy was ahistorical, and his emphasis on reason rather than emotion as the basis of government allowed him to dispense with the past as a significant consideration. As he wrote before becoming prime minister, 'politics cannot take into account what might have been' (1968: 9). In defending the denial of aboriginal rights in the White Paper he echoed these views, saying 'no society can be built in historical "might-have-beens."'[11]

In addition to Trudeau's personal philosophy, the liberal ideology which he and the governing Liberal party held provided a powerful framework for the development of Indian policy. With its focus on the individual, equality, and freedom, liberalism as a system of ideas ignores the social collectivity by framing political rights in terms of the individual.[12] Thus, even the Official Languages Act (1969) recognized the language rights of the individual as opposed to the collectivity.[13] Collective rights, such as those of minority groups, are of secondary interest, for the state is viewed as an aggregate of individuals, not groups, whose fundamental freedoms are to be respected. Special treatment of groups within society is viewed as discriminatory within the liberal-democratic tradition, although in practice elite groups are given privileges by the state.

Because liberalism disregards the social *system* as the basis of society, the liberal concept of individual choice is frequently a fallacy. It fails to detect that choices are possible only under certain social conditions and that societal forces, such as poverty, mitigate against the selection of different life styles in any real sense. Personal enterprise and motivation are considered key ingredients for individual success in life, and in its most extreme form, liberalism 'blames the victim' for any failure to use the opportunities which society is said to offer.

In practice, during the Pearson regime, there was a softening of the liberal position to the extent that government programs recognized the need to assist actively individuals if they were to benefit from the freedoms and opportunities society could offer.[14] But Trudeau brought to government his more pronounced view of individualism, and although this was known at the time Indian policy was being shaped, its effects on government policies in general had yet to be determined.

Trudeau's ahistorical approach to policies and his stand against special status for cultural groups provided strong constraints for the ministers and officials who created Indian policy. Like the liberal ideology, these constraints did not predetermine Indian policy at the outset, but they generated a strong climate of opinion in the Prime Minister's Office which other policy-makers knew they would have to address in a compelling fashion.

TRUDEAU'S REFORMS IN POLICY-MAKING PROCEDURES

Trudeau came to power determined to improve the government's capacity to make better policies. To achieve this goal, he and his advisers reformed the cabinet's operations so that policies would reflect political, not bureaucratic values and opinions.[15] Basically, Trudeau distrusted the bureaucracy and hoped to streamline the policy process by centralizing it around the cabinet and pulling it away from the incrementalism he felt civil servants preferred.

Consequently, one of Trudeau's first and most controversial reforms was to change the Prime Minister's Office (PMO) into a partisan Liberal party nerve centre within government, staffed by his own personal advisers who were to review policies from a political viewpoint, keeping re-election prospects in mind.[16] In the past the PMO had been staffed by civil servants, but the men Trudeau appointed, such as his key policy adviser Marc Lalonde, and Jim Davey, the most influential PMO figure in terms of Indian policy, had been his campaign strategists and shared his views on how the policy-making process could be improved. During the time Indian policy was being developed, the PMO became a more active and partisan influence in setting government priorities, and in determining the policy-making procedures that ministers and their officials were to follow.

Of all Trudeau's advisers, Jim Davey held the most precise view on the 'systems approach' to policy-making. He came to government with a background in physics, computer science, and communications, and he provided the vital link between the government's programs and the Liberal Party.[17] In his job as program secretary, he was to ensure that government programs were comprehensively planned and coordinated across departments.

To improve the ministers' abilities to set policies, Trudeau reformed the cabinet by establishing small permanent committees, such as the Cabinet Committee on Social Policy which handled Indian policy, and the most powerful one, the Cabinet Committee on Priorities and Planning which, under his chairmanship, set overall government priorities and coordinated programs throughout the government.[18] The committees had decision-making powers although the full cabinet could question and overturn their decisions. These committees were intended to inform ministers more fully about policies by giving them an opportunity to explore and discuss policy matters in a more thorough fashion than the full cabinet sessions of the past had allowed.

Another reform of the period that significantly affected Indian policy was the more powerful role given the PCO.[19] Its job was to provide the cabinet with advice from the civil service. PCO expertise was to be marshalled in a more effective way to make certain that cabinet received an overview of all policies from a broader 'governmental' perspective than could be gained from departments where 'departmental' interests were foremost. Under Trudeau's reforms, the PCO changed from a passive to a more active influence in policy-making, and it was staffed by some of the most powerful civil servants in Ottawa, including Gordon Robertson, the Secretary to Cabinet and head of the PCO. In the late 1950s Robertson had been deputy minister in the Department of Northern Affairs.

To improve the flow of information around the cabinet, the PCO provided matching secretariats for each of the cabinet committees (see Diagram 1). Consequently, the Cabinet Committee on Social Policy, which dealt with Indian policy, had a matching Social Policy Secretariat in the PCO. When Indian policy was being developed, this secretariat had four or five officials, but only two of them, Jordan (pseudonym) and Rudnicki, played a major role in shaping the course of Indian policy. Jordan, who headed the group, had come to the PCO a few years earlier with considerable experience in the social welfare field within government. Rudnicki, with formal training in social work, had joined the PCO a year and a half previously, after leaving the Department of Indian Affairs when it discontinued the community development program he had established. Jordan's and Rudnicki's job was to review proposals for social policies, including Indian policy, as they came from the departments on their way to cabinet, to ensure that the proposals complied with the cabinet's directives. As with most PCO reviews, this often involved examining the submissions to determine if they contained options for ministerial consideration. Under Trudeau's reforms, civil servants, especially deputy ministers who were often the major policy shapers at the department level,[20] were to provide ministers with options for choice; in short, they were to lay bare the rational approach to problems so that ministers could weigh the pros and cons of alternate actions when making their decisions. Ideally, policy proposals with a single recommendation, as was customary in the past, were no longer favourably received.

DIAGRAM 1 Cabinet and the Privy Council Office 1968–69 (adapted from Robertson 1971)

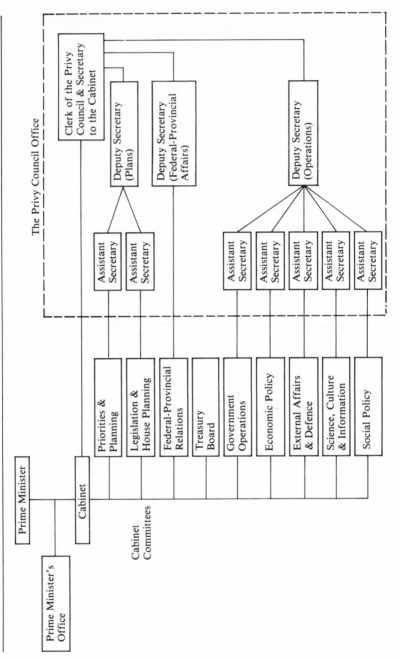

In keeping with Trudeau's own philosophy on policy-making, the reforms in the PMO, the cabinet, and the PCO, were implemented to produce policies that were more politically sensitive, carefully planned, and far-sighted in anticipating change. Ideally, cabinet ministers were to make the policy decisions, assisted by the PMO's partisan advice and the PCO's civil service expertise. By long-standing custom, 'the policy initiative' lay with the ministers who normally received the most help from the senior officials in their departments. Unlike the generalists in the PCO, department officials were specialists in their fields, and more fully informed of the details and history of their department's programs and policies.

The general procedure for making policies began at the department level where the senior officials prepared proposals for their minister. When he approved the proposals, they went to the PMO and PCO for review before going to the appropriate cabinet committee for ministerial consideration. If the cabinet committee endorsed them, they went on to the full cabinet for final consideration and approval. As an ideal procedure it was systematic, rational, and comprehensive, but when practised on Indian policy, the process became unusually complicated because of another reform Trudeau instituted.

When Trudeau selected his cabinet in June 1968, he appointed three ministers without portfolio and assigned them to departments where demands for new policies were expected to be heavy. Since Indian policy was given high priority on the government's agenda, two ministers were assigned to Indian Affairs. Jean Chrétien, then a 34-year-old lawyer from Shawinigan, Quebec, still mastering English, was appointed minister, and Robert K. Andras, a businessman from Thunder Bay, and thirteen years older than Chrétien, was appointed minister without portfolio. Although Chrétien had a brief period as minister of Revenue before the election, this was his first major cabinet positing.[21] Andras, who had been an MP for only two years, had no previous position in the cabinet.[22] As newcomers they raised some interest in the press; Chrétien because his appointment was considered proof that French MPs could be given important portfolios, and Andras because ministers without portfolio were novel, and his assignment signalled serious government intention to come to grips with the Indian problem.[23]

Although both men became personally committed to improving the conditions of Indians, they approached Indian policy from different perspectives and with very different personal styles. Compounding the difficult job that lay ahead of them, was the fact that their duties and mutual responsibilities had not been clearly established. For senior officers in the department, the prospect of having 'two masters' was initially perplexing – and rapidly became unwelcome. The Indian Act consultation meetings soon demonstrated the contrasting styles between Chrétien and Andras, and highlighted the basic differences in their approach to the policy-making process itself.

THE INDIAN ACT CONSULTATION MEETINGS BEGIN

The Trudeau government agreed to honour Laing's commitment to consult with Indians on revising the Indian Act, and the first of eighteen meetings was held on 25 July in Yellowknife, less than three weeks after Chrétien and Andras took office. Probably more than any other event, these meetings provided a major impetus to growing Indian nationalism.

With a view to focusing discussions at the consultation meetings, the department had published and distributed a booklet called *Choosing a Path* (DIAND 1968). In its foreward by Arthur Laing, the message for Indians was that they were expected to play a greater role in determining their own future. The foreword, in fact, resembled the White Paper in its emphasis on self-help, choice, and equality of opportunity, with the latter being the government's main objective.

The first item discussed in the booklet, and quickly dispensed with, was the Indian claims commission. Hoping to allay Indian fears that a commission was no longer being considered, the booklet stated that its formation had been delayed because of the British Columbia land question: the implication was that a claims commission would be set up when this issue was settled. From the government's position, the booklet set the frame of reference for the consultations; Indian Act revisions were the prime purpose of the meetings, not treaties, claims, or aboriginal rights.

The booklet then proceeded to treat various sections of the Indian Act in considerable detail, raising items for possible amendment that had initially been suggested by the department or the Indian advisory boards during the previous three years. Each item was prefaced by a statement explaining that particular section of the Act, and followed by questions to guide discussions in the Indian bands. For example,

Section 4 defines those persons to whom the Act applies. Paragraph (2) says that the government can exclude any Indian Band or Indian person from having the Act or any part of it apply to them. This has only been done on request of the Band or the Indian and it is now suggested that this consent *must* be given before anyone is excluded. Do you feel that the Indians concerned should have to agree before the government can apply this provision? (1968: 12).

At the end of the booklet there were thirty-six questions summarizing all the items as a guide to decision-making at both the band level and the consultation meetings.

The booklets had been sent out to every Indian household in the country in March 1968, just prior to the originally scheduled dates for the meetings. In addition, band councillors and band delegates at the meetings received another booklet called *Consultations with the Indian People*[24] which treated the matters raised in *Choosing a Path* in greater detail.

The department selected eighteen cities across Canada for the consultation meetings. In the southern areas they were held in hotels, and in the north in community centres. Before the meetings band councils were to discuss with community members the questions outlined in *Choosing a Path*, and then select one representative to attend the consultation meeting in their region. The organizing staff of the department had made all the arrangements and paid the total cost of the sessions.[25]

The meetings tended to be formal occasions with the delegates gathered around large conference tables and microphones (see photos). The sessions were chaired jointly by a department officer and an Indian delegate, with translators being available whenever they were needed. Verbatim tapes were made of each session so that there would be a complete record of discussions for replaying in Ottawa as the reports were being prepared and for officials to hear sessions they had been unable to attend (DIAND 1968–69).

Because the agenda was flexible, each meeting handled issues which interested the delegates. Indian delegates were told they did not have to limit their deliberations to the questions in *Choosing a Path*, with the result that discussions were far-ranging, often not touching on many items in the booklet. Some Indian delegations and organizations presented briefs, and when present, the ministers were questioned on a wide variety of issues relevant to bands in that region. The main ground rule at the consultations was that department officials and ministers were there 'to listen,' and not to discuss their own opinions.

As the meetings progressed, Indian dissatisfaction with the process was obvious, and although the department was committed to the format, certain changes were made after the consultations were underway. *In camera* sessions were added to some of the meetings so that delegates could discuss matters among themselves without government officials being present. Changes in schedule occurred in both Ontario and British Columbia where an additional meeting was added at the request of Indian delegates, and whereas two meetings had been scheduled for both Manitoba and Alberta, these were merged into one at the request of Indian spokesmen who wanted a single forum for presenting their briefs to the ministers.

At the Yellowknife meeting, which launched the series, Chrétien set the tone of the consultation process by stating it was an 'attempt at consultative democracy' which, he later said, was intended to give Indians 'a sense of participation.'[26] He considered consultation to mean 'the seeking of advice,' for throughout the meetings he stressed that the ultimate decision-making powers rested with the cabinet, not with a single minister or with the Indians. He was careful not to lead Indians to expect that his wishes, or theirs, would necessarily receive cabinet approval, or that ultimate decisions would entirely please them. In this regard his statements were straightforward and his style of dealing with Indians differed noticeably from Andras', especially on the question of encouraging Indian expectations.

With full department responsibilities and increasing activity in the Northern Affairs part of his portfolio, Chrétien had far less time to devote to the meetings than did Andras. He attended nine of the eighteen meetings, usually flying in to give the opening address but rarely staying for the day's proceedings. He had a standard delivery which began with his comments on the Act, rather than on policy; then he invariably switched to an empathic approach, stressing how his French Canadian background helped him to appreciate the problems of other minorities:[27]

Being from a minority group in this country, I understand what it is to be a member of such a group. There are many problems but there are a lot of virtues too. We have to be proud to be members of a minority group because our background becomes very important and you the Indian people of Canada have to be proud to be Indian because you were here a long time ago. You should be very proud of your culture; work to preserve that culture because it means a lot to Canada. It is part of the history of Canada and I know that you are proud of being Indians and you are proud of being Canadians and I am proud of being French-speaking and a Canadian. Canada is a great country, and all of us are a part of that country.

During the early meetings he avoided making any commitments to the delegates, being much more cautious in his statements and formal in his style than Andras. He merely repeated the need for self-help and the importance of Indians' retaining their cultural heritage. Unlike Andras, he was more concerned by the lack of consensus among the delegates on the proposed revisions to the Act.[28] Since time was of greater urgency to him than to Andras, he promised a final consultation meeting in Ottawa, probably in January, and hoped to table a new Act in Parliament by July of 1969, or possibly even in the spring.[29]

It was Andras who developed a rapport with Indian delegates early in the series of meetings. Although he attended only two more meetings than Chrétien did, his relationship with the delegates was informal and his style easy. He felt the discussions around the formal tables and microphones inhibited Indians and he preferred spending evenings with them away from the formalities and the one-sided dialogue which increasingly dissatisfied him.[30] His habit of summarizing Indian concerns at the end of each meeting contributed heavily to Indian expectations not only that Andras was sympathetic to their views, but also that Ottawa might heed his recommendations. In the early meetings, a standard part of his delivery was his emphasis on his special appointment by the prime minister to develop Indian policy. He actively fostered an image of himself as 'policy minister,' a unique and possibly misunderstood interpretation of his role, because shaping policy was the coveted right of portfolioed ministers. In his first address at the consultations he was straightforward in explaining his role:[31]

There are now as you know, two new Ministers appointed by the Prime Minister to deal with those things that are bothering you in hope that we can finally take some action to correct the situation that has developed. Just a week ago today, Mr. Trudeau, the new Prime Minister, asked me to sit down with him to discuss the role that I might take as a Minister Without Portfolio in his government and in his Cabinet. And I can assure you that I sought with enthusiasm the assignment to work with the Indian people across Canada to develop new policies for the Indian people ... and I would like to say to you what Mr. Trudeau said to me 'This matter is very close to my heart. I feel we owe a great debt to the Indian people of Canada and I want you to take a major role in finding out, identifying that debt and recommending to the government the policies that will begin to meet our obligations, those obligations we may not have met in the past' ... I am here today and tomorrow to be the eyes and ears of the Cabinet – of the Government of Canada ... I look forward to spending the next day and a half with you. Much of the finding of solutions is in your own hands and much of that depends on our ability to communicate with each other and understand each other because there are no other barriers towards solution.

At subsequent meetings he continued to promote his role as policy minister, often implying that past injustices to Indians would be rectified, possibly in the way they desired.[32] To observers who were experienced in interpreting the carefully worded rhetoric of politicians, many of these statements might not have appeared as promises, not even to Indians who had a deep-rooted scepticism about government commitments. But paradoxically, because Indians wanted to have a determining influence on their own future, they often understood his statements to be commitments, raising their expectations that government action might finally heed their wishes. Andras' sincere manner and personal commitment to the involvement of Indians in policy-making were far more compelling than the bureaucratic promises they were accustomed to and the evasive or non-committal responses they received from Chrétien.

As the early meetings progressed, the lack of consensus among Indian delegates on *specific* items for change in the Indian Act was evident, highlighting the obvious fact that the Indian political agenda differed dramatically from the one the government had laid down. Indian preoccupation centred on special rights, unsettled treaty obligations, and aboriginal claims – not on the Indian Act. Because the delegates wanted more time for exchanging ideas among themselves, they became especially anxious that further consultations occur before the government decided on new directions. Indian spokesmen wanted time to build consensus among themselves; their time-table lengthened while Chrétien's was shortening. Chrétien wanted to get on with the consultation process, assuring the delegates they would have another opportunity to offer further comment in the second round of meetings.

Although only a third of the meetings had taken place by mid-September, their significance for the public, the Indians, and the government was already evident. The six meetings, held in Yellowknife, Moncton, Toronto, Fort William (Thunder Bay), Sudbury, and Regina, had focused local Indian and white attention on the Indian Act and on Indian priorities in their own regions. As the series continued, general priorities on treaties, special rights, and land grievances emerged as repetitive themes, and the contrast between the government's plans for revising the Act, and Indian preferences, became obvious to the two ministers and department officials. Indian expectations were raised, primarily by Andras, that government might finally respond to their demands, and this anticipation fed the growing Indian nationalism, whose common refrain was special rights.

For the two new ministers, the consultations functioned to bring them into direct, face-to-face contact with Indians early in their tenure of office, to learn of Indian concerns independently of the civil servants' interpretations. The degree to which the two ministers could and did take advantage of the meetings differed considerably, but their participation created the major and most direct link of communication between the public arena and the private policy-making arena within government. In this respect their roles were unique within the policy-making arena, for unlike departmental officials and executive assistants who attended the consultations, Chrétien and Andras had ministerial authority to affect the ultimate decisions.

The consultations also demonstrated the divergent approaches taken to policy-making by Chrétien and Andras, and as the consultations progressed, the differences became more obvious to the press and to Indians. Chrétien's approach, which stressed the formal authority of cabinet, was basically the traditional one used in policy-making by the government; the cabinet held the authority to take the final decisions, not individual ministers nor the public. The decisions would be taken within the normal secrecy of the cabinet, and although Indian preferences would be considered, the ultimate decision might not please them. Once the cabinet decided, the decisions would come back to the public for a second round of consultations. In contrast, Andras' approach was decidedly an activist one, beginning with the premise that effective policies required meaningful participation by Indians. The ultimate policy should reflect their priorities and concerns, and his job as policy minister was to ensure that these priorities were made known to the prime minister. Whereas Chrétien spoke in terms of the Act and formal cabinet procedures, Andras talked in terms of policy and the need to improve the consultation process to make Indian involvement more valid.[33] In their effect, the two approaches offered Indians two options on the policy-making process itself, and it was obvious from the earliest meetings that Indians preferred Andras' activist approach. Whether these were, in fact, real options was far from clear by early September.

By mid-September, Chrétien was anxious to move ahead on claims settlement and he announced at the consultation meeting in Quebec City that an Indian claims commission would be established that fall.[34] In his urgency for action, he quickly rejected any suggestion of further studies or royal commissions, and although the public was unaware of it, his comments reflected developments in the PMO and the PCO that were then pressing heavily on the department. During the summer, while the consultations were progressing, developments on Indian policy inside government had started to take a very different direction.

POLICY-MAKING BEGINS

Under the new Trudeau regime, Indian policy ranked high among government priorities which were headed by an official languages policy and regional economic development policies. Although broad guidelines for developing Indian policy had been prescribed in the reforms Trudeau was implementing in the cabinet, and in the PMO and PCO, the summer was a time for working out a specific strategy on how 'the Indian problem' should be approached and how the policy-making process should be organized. As with most new administrations, the climate encouraged reform, but Trudeau's election promises of greater public participation in policy-making and his widespread policy reviews in most departments had heightened the expectations of far-reaching changes in policies. For some policy-makers the times offered a rare opportunity to change the status quo by instituting policies they had unsuccessfully promoted in the past. As one senior official recalled, 'That was a period of dynamism. There was much hope and expectation that significant changes could be made.'

Theoretically at least, the two ministers and the deputy minister had the advantage of being fresh on the scene and relatively free to develop their own ideas about Indian policy. John A. MacDonald became deputy minister in the spring, a few months before Chrétien and Andras were appointed, and one of the first things he did was institute an in-depth review of all department programs.[35] This review was still under way in the summer when the consultation meetings began and the government was gearing up for Indian policy. Unlike the old guard, MacDonald did not attend the consultation meetings.

The noticeable difference in approaches between Andras and Chrétien at the consultations soon gave rise to public speculation over whether the new ministers could remain free of entrenched interests among government officials long enough to develop their own views on the Indian problem. Because Andras' approach was refreshing, the press believed it was an independent effort, whereas Chrétien, it was claimed, had become 'trapped' by the old guard in his department.[36] In fact, both ministers quickly became aligned with different senior officials in government, and not with each other. Andras was soon influenced by Rudnicki, the self-styled 'maverick' in the PCO who had strong opinions on the Indian department and a deep skepticism of its stated intentions to change.

Rudnicki had initiated the community development program that the old guard found threatening, and shortly after Arthur Laing became minister in 1966, Rudnicki was transferred to the Social Policy Secretariat of the PCO. There his skills in arguing and rationalizing his own positions were more appropriately used, and his previous background in DIAND gave him a familiarity with the Indian administration which others in the PCO lacked. His maverick quality came from his activism and his adroit craftsmanship in policy review, for he was more able than most in justifying his proposals by relating them to ideas then being promoted in government, especially those on public participation.

Shortly after Chrétien was appointed, Rudnicki approached him, indicating a willingness to discuss Indian policy issues, but Rudnicki met with what he considered to be a strong rebuff. Soon after that, Rudnicki was contacted by Andras, who was then trying to familiarize himself with his new field of responsibility in Indian Affairs.[37] Rudnicki had expertise in the field, and although a loner in his style of operation, he and Andras developed a strong trust relationship which was not a normal requirement of their offices.

Thus both ministers were drawn into pre-existing conflicts among a few senior civil servants during their first months in office, creating two power alignments in the policy-making arena. One alignment followed the formal lines of authority in the department, linking Chrétien with his deputy minister and the old guard, all of whom held the traditional approach to policy-making. The second alignment, based on informal ties among the activists, connected Andras with his two special assistants and Rudnicki and Jordan in the PCO, all of whom shared the activists' approach to policy-making. Although Jordan, who headed the social policy group in the PCO, was of the activist persuasion like Rudnicki, he was not as closely allied to Andras as Rudnicki was. The activist alignment did not follow formal lines of authority, but, like the department alignment, it grouped a minister with senior officials who had previous experience and a continuing interest in Indian affairs.

The activist alignment benefited from the changing ground rules at the cabinet level of government in the summer of 1968. As traditional practices uneasily meshed with the new reforms Trudeau established, uncertainty and gray areas emerged which gave enterprising individuals, if they were so inclined, the opportunity to innovate, to define their own roles and powers. Although self-definitions were not necessarily sanctioned, there was room to try. The combination of uncertainty and self-definition particularly applied to Andras' role as policy minister, for the role of minister without portfolio had not been clearly defined from the beginning. This situation left room for misunderstanding.

Although ministers without portfolio had been used by the Pearson government, Trudeau made greater use of these appointments as a way of enhancing government efforts to develop new policies. By tradition the minister *with* portfolio was unquestionably the one to carry the policy initiative for that department as well as public accountability for its activities;[38] the question of what tasks might be allocated to the minister without portfolio remained open.

In July when Andras was made minister without portfolio, his specific tasks had yet to be defined, and like his colleagues without portfolios, he attended cabinet meetings before expressing his own preference for certain departments. Andras recalled being interested in both regional development and Indian affairs, the former being his first priority at that time.[39] In the end he was given Indian Affairs as a 'field of attachment,' and it was agreed he would handle the Indian consultation meetings, as well as assist Chrétien in policy development and parliamentary duties when Chrétien was away from Ottawa.[40] Despite this apparent agreement on his duties, it was not always clear to officials or the public whether Andras was assigned to the prime minister or to Chrétien, and for what purposes. Chrétien's responsibility for the administration of the department was not disputed. The confusion lay in the lack of understanding about the mutual responsibilities between Chrétien and Andras in the field of policy-making. Senior officials in the department felt there should have been no confusion, for they viewed Andras as a parliamentary secretary with the normal duties of assisting the minister in his portfolio and in Parliament.[41] But the press described ministers without portfolio as policy ministers, implying that they held policy-making powers beyond those of a parliamentary secretary, and Andras had capitalized on this interpretation of his role at the consultation meetings. Although it is apparent that neither minister intended that their roles should become problematic, and their spheres of responsibility and accountability blurred, this in fact happened.[42]

Publicly, the press and the consultation meeting reports described Andras as a 'policy minister' assigned to help develop Indian policy,[43] suggesting that Andras had the full initiative and responsibility for Indian policy. As the consultations progressed, Chrétien emerged as 'department minister' by defending the department's actions, and his defensiveness increased as Andras became an effective critic of the department and a persuasive advocate of Indian interests. As a result, Andras was cast by the press as a 'rebel,' a man against the traditional system of Indian administration.[44]

Even before the public relationship between Chrétien and Andras took the form of ministers in opposition, a unique version of Trudeau's concept of countervailing forces, PCO officials had begun working on a specific strategy for approaching Indian policy. The basis of their strategy was the more holistic view of Indian policy they had promoted, without success, in 1967 when the cabinet decided to revise the Indian Act instead.

THE STRATEGY

From the outset, Jordan and Rudnicki, the major figures in the social policy unit of the PCO to handle Indian policy, questioned the validity of revising the Indian Act as a means of coping with the Indian problem. Instead, as they had done in 1967, they favoured a wholescale policy review as a strategy for developing a new 'global' policy for all native people, including the Inuit and Metis. Consequently, they began a holding action against proposals from various departments, not because the proposals were in themselves ill-advised, but in an effort to prevent an *ad hoc* approach which might jeopardize the development of a new general policy. In their view, consultation with Indians had meaning only in the context of a critical reappraisal of the total Indian program and policy.

By early August, when their strategy was firmer, they proposed that a policy review group be set up within the PCO in order to avoid DIAND control which might tend to narrow the process. Specifically:

1/ it should consider a policy for all native people, not just status Indians;
2/ it should involve consultations with the provinces as well as Indian organizations;
3/ it should examine all aspects of native people's problems, jurisdictional, legal, social, and economic;
4/ it should prepare recommendations for a special cabinet committee set up exclusively to hand the Indian question.[45]

Somewhat optimisticaly, the PCO officials expected its proposals might be ready for ministerial consideration even before Parliament opened in September. Although they succeeded in keeping *ad hoc* policies from consideration, their overall persuasive powers had distinct limits which became evident in the discussions on the content of the Speech from the Throne.

In August, when the cabinet had to decide on the legislative agenda for the next session of Parliament, pressures began to build as the Throne Speech was being prepared for its September 12 reading.[46] An early draft of the speech read by the prime minister to the cabinet mentioned that revisions to the Migratory Birds Convention Act would be made during the year. Chrétien, then under pressure in the consultations to handle treaty and land claim problems, asked that the speech also include the government's past commitments to set up an Indian claims commission and revise the Indian Act.[47] But in the PCO, Jordan and Rudnicki had recommended against such specific commitments, fearing they would limit the government's flexibility in choosing a future policy direction.[48] Instead, they recommended that the government 'extend and accelerate' consultations with the provinces and the Indians. In the end, the speech made no reference to the consultations but included, albeit the last of forty-seven titles of legislation to be introduced, 'a bill to establish an Indian Claims Commission.'[49] Revisions to the Indian Act and Migratory Birds Convention Act were not mentioned, and the only other reference to Indians in the speech was brief and non-specific: 'You will also be asked to consider measures relating to Indians, to citizenship, to national symbols, to transportation ...'[50]

While the discussions over the content of the Throne Speech were going on, Andras wrote the prime minister a lengthy letter outlining his views on how the government might approach Indian policy.[51] The current consultation procedures displeased him, an opinion he had expressed publicly in one of his rare speeches by referring to 'the hypocrisy of the ritualistic consultations.'[52] He proposed to the prime minister three possible ways in which the policy issue could be handled: 1/splitting the portfolio, with Indian Affairs to be managed by himself, 2/mounting an independent task force to make recommendations to cabinet, and 3/establishing a policy review group based in the PCO to prepare recommendations for cabinet. He discarded the first suggestion because Chrétien had found it unacceptable, as well as the second one, because it would delay the process of developing a new policy.

Andras preferred, and recommended, the third alternative – a PCO-based task force under his direction; with a few policy advisers of his own, and working closely with Chrétien, he felt a Policy Advisory Group on Native Peoples could easily be established. His proposal was almost identical with the recommendations Rudnicki had made earlier that month, especially in his urging the removal of the policy review process from DIAND control.

By this time Andras' efforts to question the department from within had resulted in limited cooperation from its officials, and his public criticism of the department at the consultations simply reinforced this defensive posture. Some senior DIAND officials admitted that cooperation was indeed withheld from Andras and his assistants. Requests by Andras' staff were slowly answered, and files were often said to be unavailable. Some officials indicated that furniture was even slow in being delivered to Andras' office.

Andras' initiative to formalize his role as policy minister bothered senior officials in the PCO, particularly Gordon Robertson, who felt it went against the convention that the senior minister held the policy initiative.[53] However, in mid-September, discussions between PMO and PCO officials apparently determined that the Cabinet Committee on Social Policy should shortly consider a proposal for extending and accelerating the consultation process with Indians and the provinces. Also, further efforts toward policy review should include both the Indians and Metis, the latter being of particular concern to the western provinces, as their premiers had recently indicated to the prime minister.[54] It was felt that the policy review process should be dissociated from the department, for it was feared that departmental control could be detrimental to the consultations and 'colour the results of a review.'[55] This plan was still intended when events came to a head in late September.

On 23 September letters from the prime minister to both Chrétien and Andras asked them to undertake jointly a thorough and impartial review of government policy on Indians for submission to the Cabinet Committee on Social Policy.[56] Although it was clear from the letters that the policy initiative did not rest with Andras, their content reflected some of the recommendations he had made earlier to the prime minister. The letters emphasized the need to expand and improve discussions with the provinces and Indians in 'a low-key and sustained conversation,' and to include the Metis in the overall review. The whole range of federal programs for native people was to be examined to improve coordination at the federal level and to prepare for better cooperation with the provinces. The review was to be sensitive to federal-provincial relations and permit an Indian claims commission and other 'urgent matters' to proceed quickly. The PCO was to arrange any assistance the ministers might need in preparing the policy review for cabinet.

This formal request from the prime minister stressed the importance of policy review. But the efforts of the two ministers immediately got off to a bad start.

THE RIFT

The deterioration in relations between Chrétien and Andras occurred at the time the prime minister had asked them to cooperate in preparing a joint submission on Indian policy, and the rift was widely publicized when Andras appeared on a nationally televised program in late September.

The department was recently reorganized to bring programs for both Indians and Eskimos under the same administrative units, a move in keeping with earlier decisions to abandon the geographical basis for structuring the department. Andras claimed he had not been informed of this reorganization, and during the television interview and in discussions with the press afterwards, he was outspoken in his disapproval of the department, and by implication of Chrétien, for its recent reorganization.[57] Andras had understood that no reorganization would occur until Indians were consulted.[58] Although the reorganization left the old guard at the top, the press suggested that the changes could have serious implications for policy development, and they made much of the appointment of a biologist to head the Community Development Directorate in the Indian Affairs Branch.

Andras' constant stressing of Indian participation had obviously placed him in an embarrassing position when word of the department's reorganization was made public. This attack signalled, and contributed heavily to, his growing estrangement from the department. His stance also brought the government unwelcome charges from critics in the House of Commons of 'bureaucratic indifference' to native people, unnecessary secrecy, and inexcusable aggravation of the tension between Indians and the department.[59]

The press did not slacken its zeal in publicizing the situation. The Toronto *Globe and Mail* described the incident in considerable detail under the caption 'Indian Issue Creates Split in Cabinet'.[60] The Ottawa *Citizen* carried an article entitled 'Trouble at Indian Affairs – Can the Dinosaur Change?' in which it likened the department's reorganization to a 'dinosaur rattling its bones,' and the day's editorial comment claimed that 'there is no question that reactionary forces are in command of the department,' which suffered from an 'advanced case of sclerosis.'[61] Reporting on the strains between the two ministers, the same newspaper quoted Andras as saying that he did not 'feel responsible for or to any department, or committed to any one department ideology.'[62] Relations between Andras and the department were inflamed further when 'sources who share Mr. Andras' views', though not Rudnicki, were quoted as saying:

'As far as I'm concerned, they're [the department] are a bunch of Fascists. The deputy minister (J.A. MacDonald) wouldn't know an Indian if one walked down the street,' said one highly placed source.

This source likened the mentality of senior administrators to that of ex-RCMP officers and ex-paratroopers. The department, he said, drives out anyone with an innnovative approach to Indian problems and distrusts the view of Indians themselves.

He said there are only about 20 Indians employed in the Ottawa offices of a department with a total employment of 8,500 ...[63]

The next month the department began a program to employ native people in its administration.[64] Shortly after, however, opposition members in the House of Commons jumped at the chance of embarrassing the government as Stanfield probed the nature of Andras' role. Trudeau's firm stand on cabinet solidarity was well known, and in replying to Stanfield, his displeasure with Andras was obvious. In his reply, he clarified Chrétien's role as senior minister:

Mr. Trudeau ... The Minister of Indian Affairs and Northern Development obviously is the minister responsible for everything coming under his department. He is being assisted in one special aspect of his duties by the Minister without Portfolio. The line of responsibility, however, is clearly through the minister with portfolio. I understand the problems of hon. members with regard to this matter, and I assure them that I share them.[65]

The next day Stanfield persisted, this time focusing on the prime minister's support of Chrétien and its implications for Andras: 'The fact that the government would fail to consult even him [Andras] is bound to raise suspicions that his assignment is window dressing, his influence is nil, and that he is deliberately circumvented by the minister and officials of the department of Indian affairs.'[66]

Like Stanfield, Ed Schreyer, NDP member from Manitoba, accused the government of unnecessary secrecy, suggesting that the incident 'makes nonsense of the efforts of the Minister without Portfolio.'[67] Réal Caouette, Social Créditiste member from Quebec, phrased his criticism in terms of 'back room' decision-taking.[68]

The substance of the criticisms focused on the excessive secrecy of the department and its denial, by its actions, of the government policy to consult Indians on 'major policy objectives,' as Chrétien had reaffirmed that very morning in his defence of the reorganization.[69] In justifying the reorganization, Chrétien argued that it was required to bring programming in line with the 1966 departmental re-structuring, and that it was essentially an internal matter, properly the domain of any minister. But the implication of parliamentary criticism was clear: the department was unwilling to consult Indians on matters of importance to them.

Among a few top officials in the department, Andras' statements created annoyance and anger. They viewed Andras' attack as unwarranted and opportunistic, for they believed he had been apprised of the reorganization before it occurred.[70] Whatever the cause of the misunderstanding, the press later reported that the two ministers had 'patched up' their differences and that Andras had come to view the reorganization as a matter not requiring Indian consultation.[71]

Andras weathered the incident but the political cost could have been serious. In effect, the prime minister had reprimanded him in the House, and internally some senior officials felt he had damaged his political credibility among his cabinet colleagues.[72] From the public and the Indians, however, Andras gained considerable support and sympathy, as parliamentary comments and press reports indicated.[73]

More significantly, the rift between the two ministers drew the public's attention to the way the government was handling the Indian question. Despite statements to Indians at the consultations that the government would not move ahead on policy until the meetings were finished, the rift more firmly entrenched Indian suspicion that behind-the-scenes decisions were already being taken. Predictably, within the PMO and PCO, serious apprehensions arose that the clash between the two ministers might hinder the development of policy.[74]

Because of this incident, distrust increased between the two alignments surrounding the ministers, and officials began to tred very cautiously.

The summer had begun with Trudeau's reforms in the cabinet system and its central advisory agencies, the PMO and PCO, but the systematic and rational approach to policy-making Trudeau had hoped to implement seemed far removed from the tangles that had already developed in the field of Indian policy. The use of ministers without portfolio, a notion which at first glance had some merit, underestimated the competitiveness of politicians and their personal advisers. The consultation meetings amply illustrated this fact in addition to providing Indians with a vehicle for expressing their own priorities. The climate of reform had raised new hopes in the PCO that a task-force approach to Indian policy could be implemented, possibly under Andras' leadership. But Andras' confrontation with the department had raised doubts about the future of a task force, as it did about the chances of cooperation between the two ministers on a joint policy submission to cabinet. All this occurred, moreover, before the substance of Indian policy had even been discussed.

CHAPTER THREE **Fall: the season for review**

The notion of a task force to develop Indian policy, an idea which Andras and Rudnicki had promoted actively in the summer, was set aside in late September by Trudeau's letter asking the two ministers to prepare jointly a cabinet submission. The policy initiative clearly lay with Chrétien; thus during the fall of 1968, the department was to prepare a policy review for discussion in the PMO and PCO. As Trudeau had outlined, the review was to be a critical evaluation of the government's current policies on Indians, and it was to be broad in scope and include the Metis. The review was the first step in the ideal policy-making process which the PMO so assiduously promoted, and it was hoped the department would proceed quickly through this stage.

THE DEPARTMENT'S FIVE-YEAR PLAN

The department's first response to a policy review occurred in mid-October, although the old guard had not intended that their work be used as a policy review. Deputy Minister John MacDonald informed the PCO that a lengthy submission would shortly come from the department, giving Gordon Robertson to understand that a major policy statement was almost finished.[1] The PCO was to review the submission before it went to the Cabinet Committee on Social Policy in order to determine if the department had approached the review in the serious and probing way the prime minister had requested.

For several months the department had been evaluating its programs for the purpose of preparing a five-year forecast for budgeting and planning.[2] This exercise, begun by MacDonald in the spring when he became deputy minister, was not intended as a response to the prime minister's request for a policy review. However, MacDonald felt the plan was worth submitting in order to gain some feedback and guidelines from the PCO and PMO. Neither the director of Policy and Planning nor the assistant deputy minister of Indian Affairs felt at the time that the submission was what the prime minister and PCO officials wanted. As one official in the department described the brief: 'It wasn't a policy document, mainly a budget exercise. We wanted to get commitments from the government on long range planning. There would have been considerable increase in expenditures. It came about through a departmental review that had gone on for several months. All sectors had made a contribution.'

The brief, forwarded by MacDonald to the PCO on 30 October for an informal sounding, was basically a five-year plan for DIAND programs, consisting of a short draft cabinet memorandum and a lengthy background paper which provided the rationale for the proposals.[3] Prepared primarily by the old guard, it had been kept under tight security, as was customary with all department briefs, the copies being numbered and restricted to senior personnel. When forwarding the brief to the PCO, MacDonald indicated that Chrétien had approved in principle 'the general line' of the proposal and that his final approval was expected the following week when it would be discussed by both Chrétien and Andras.[4]

The brief's objective was to define the Indian and Eskimo problems and set down recommendations for programs 'to achieve solutions to these problems within a reasonable time.'[5] Although the prime minister's letter had requested the inclusion of the Metis, they were not considered. The plan was comprehensive in its coverage, ending with an assessment of the financial needs of Indian administration for the next five years. Essentially, it was an elaboration of the department's current programs and philosophy. The traditional thinking of the department's senior officers, at the outset of policy-making, was clearly reflected in the plan. Unlike many statements the department produced later, it was conspicuously devoid of compromises required by the PMO and PCO. For this reason, the brief provides a valuable base-line for judging the changes made by the department as the policy-making exercise progressed.

The basic problem with both Indians and Eskimos (Inuit), according to the brief, was the real denial 'of their wholly just and proper aspirations to physical and social equality within Canadian society.'[6] Their 'isolation from the mainstream of Canadian life' was seen in the fact that 80 per cent still resided on reserves, which were often economically unviable and strained by an expanding population. The general factors contributing to the problems were stated sympathetically: Indians sought good health but lacked it; they sought education, but the dropout rates indicated basic problems; they wanted good jobs, but for lack of skills and employment opportunities many depended on welfare. Indian dependency on government was seen as a 'psychologically rooted' problem, a consequence of government paternalism. Indians' strong distrust of the government was fully acknowledged and largely credited to unfulfilled treaty obligations. Generally, Indians wanted the same material benefits as other Canadians, but lacked the skills and the opportunity to achieve them. Discrimination and 'cultural disparity' were viewed as barriers to integration, but strangely enough, 'cultural variation' was seen as 'the essence of Canadianism.' Because all of these conditions were interrelated, attacks on the overall problem must occur on several fronts at once. For example, if programs for vocational training were mounted to develop work skills, the government must also ensure that opportunities for employment would be available.

Policy proposals to remedy the problems were of two types: 1/to 'enrich' existing programs and 2/to develop new programs in specific areas. On existing programs the department urged that they not be set aside simply because they had not proved completely successful:

Because total solutions have not been reached, [the programs'] usefulness should not be overlooked. More often than not they need to be enriched or supplemented rather than discarded ...

Criticisms of existing programs is valid if it results in improvement but not if it results in destroying what is useful. It should be said here that the Federal Government must expect an increasing expression of dissatisfaction from Indians and Eskimos as programs for them become more effective, simply because such expression will be a symptom of apathy loss and of climbing aspirations. As long as this is understood by the moulders of public opinion, the results will be positive.[7]

Even though critics questioned the department's claim that Indian dissatisfaction proved the success of its programs, the department made no attempt to evaluate critically its programs in an effort to defend them.

The new program areas needing development were outlined as paraphrased below:

1/ consultation with Indians and Eskimos on both planning and implementing programs and legislation;

2/ 'amelioration' of grievances from loss of treaty and traditional rights;

3/ improving the legislative base;

4/ coordinating federal, provincial, territorial, and non-government agencies' efforts to cope with native problems (including provincial 'expertise in Metis affairs');

5/ 'injection of capital' into reserves and northern communities;

6/ voluntary relocation of Indian and Eskimos to employment centres and assistance during the adjustment period.

To achieve these goals it would be necessary for Indians to receive social services from the same sources as non-Indians. This meant the transfer of programs to the provinces, as the department had attempted in 1964, even though the federal government might have to sustain the full cost for provincial services for a lengthy period to overcome the anticipated provincial reluctance.

With these 'enriched,' already-existing programs and accelerated new ones, the department calculated that within twenty to thirty years half of the Indian and Eskimo population would be 'on a par' with the general Canadian population in terms of employment, housing, education, health, and cultural achievements. The ultimate resource that would achieve these ends was money: 'a real breakthrough can only be made if sufficient funds are available.'[8] Consequently, the budget would have to be increased from $269 million in 1969–70 to $377.4 million by 1973–74 if these programs were to be effective.

On the question of Indian land claims and treaties the brief acknowledged that Indian distrust of the government would continue if 'outstanding Treaty obligations' were not settled. An Indian claims commission, already promised in the Throne Speech, received little comment; requiring special attention, in the department's view, were Treaties 8 and 11 in the Northwest Territories, and a few treaties in the Prairies and Quebec. Although the costs of these settlements were not detailed, an estimate of hundreds of millions of dollars was thought to be realistic, an estimate that underscored the rapid escalation of costs from the 1963 projection of $17.4 million.

On the question of aboriginal land rights, the brief was silent, giving only passing reference to the Nishga case, scheduled to be heard by the British Columbia Supreme Court in January 1969.[9] The Nishga Tribal Council was seeking legal recognition of their aboriginal title to their traditional lands (approximately 7,000 square miles) along the Nass River (Sanders 1973a). The department, feeling the Nishga claim would not come before the government again until the court case was completed, offered no further comment.

On the question of the Migratory Birds Convention Act, the brief proposed liberalizing the application of this act to accommodate both Indian and Eskimo hunting and fishing practices. Fish and game legislation under federal jurisdiction was to be brought in line with 'the spirit of the Indian treaties,' and Indians and Eskimos were to have the same privileges under all these changes.

The department's brief commented in some fashion on most aspects of the Indian and Eskimo problem. In the economic and educational sections, it derived much of its data from the Hawthorn Report, these being the only sections showing any detailed analytic base. However, the brief departed from the philosophy of the Hawthorn study with its equivocation on the proposal of 'citizens plus' status for Indians:

As noted [the Hawthorn] report recommends that Indians be treated as 'citizens plus.' While the Department agrees that settlement of Indian grievances over real or perceived loss of treaty and other traditional rights must take place, the extent to which special status should be maintained in terms of immunity from various legal processes is, in the Department's view, open to debate.[10]

Regarding the report's recommendation that the department play an advocate role for Indians, the brief side-stepped the issue by saying that it was 'the representatives of the people of Canada at every level of government who must collectively "act as a national conscience".'[11]

The brief contained a lengthy summary of the main recommendations of the Hawthorn Report and pointed out where the department agreed or disagreed with the report's proposals. Though there were generally few areas of different opinion, the brief stressed that implementing the recommendations would require increased funding and, in some cases, new policies. Overall, the department saw the Hawthorn Report as 'an important point of reference in the conceptualization of policy.'[12]

The most obvious deficiency in the department's plan was the pervasive inconsistency between its stated objectives and the programs proposed to meet these objectives. The brief made repeated reference to Indian 'self-determination' and 'self-help'; yet the actual proposals reflected a reluctance by the department to relinquish its control in order to realize these goals. Departmental patronage was to continue despite assertions of the need for Indians to seek their own destiny. For example, while stating that Indians must participate in programs and legislation, the department proposed continuing the Indian advisory boards, which were already being boycotted by western Indian groups. Conservativism was equally apparent in the treatment given community development programs; it recommended an acceleration of these programs, but added the caveat 'change should be evolutionary.'[13] After recommending that more local self-government should be granted, the department failed to provide any recommendations for achieving this goal, other than to comment that the current consultation meetings would determine what directions the department should pursue. A continuing 'supervisory' and 'advisory' role for the department was expected while Indian management skills were being improved. In education the brief neither questioned the continuing policy of integration, nor considered transferring control of education to the Indian communities.

In general, the brief called for a more elaborate administrative structure, with no critical examination of the merits of the current programs or of the assumptions underlying departmental policies. The programs were defended by assertions that they should not be terminated simply because they had not been totally effective; indeed, with increased funding they would improve.

However critically one might examine the department's brief, it was patently not a plan for terminating special rights for Indians. In overall tone and intent, it did not resemble the message in the White Paper of June 1969. Generally, the brief was sympathetic to the Indian problem which, it acknowledged, was largely created by past government practices. The solution was simply an expanded and more fully funded administration. In contrast to the White Paper's recommendation, the department did not propose repealing the Indian Act or relinquishing its trusteeship of Indian lands. Obviously it did not propose the phasing out of the department, although dissolution was ultimately a moot question if the goal of Indian self-determination were to be achieved. The time frame for achieving Indian self-reliance was long-term because of the 'evolutionary change' envisioned. As senior department officials phrased it, it would be 'a slow weaning process.'

While the department was waiting for a response to its brief, other events occurred in late October to increase the pressure on the department's top management. Publicly, Chrétien and the senior officials were still being criticized for reorganizing the department a month ago, while internally, another departmental submission to the cabinet, recommending the extension of provincial child welfare services to Indians in the Prairies, was rejected.[14] Although the proposal had been prepared jointly with the Department of Health and Welfare, and was acceptable in principle to the PMO and PCO, it was seen as an incremental move. It was set aside until the broad outline of a new global Indian policy could be blocked out.

THE GLENDON COLLEGE FORUM

More publicly disturbing to MacDonald than the above events was his experience at a three-day seminar on Indian affairs sponsored by Glendon College, York University, Toronto, in late October. MacDonald agreed to deliver a talk, as had Harold Cardinal, Walter Rudnicki, and others. The mood of the audience was clearly unsympathetic to any presentation that appeared to defend department actions or to be 'the same political platitudes' considered common in departmental rhetoric. MacDonald delivered his talk amid jeers and heckling from the young audience. The anti-department feeling, then growing among Indians and sympathetic university students, culminated in a free-wheeling expression of hostility. One participant demanded that MacDonald quit his job and another shredded a copy of the Indian Act in protest against the department's handling of Indian affairs.[15] For the public, the emotion of the meeting was graphically described by the Toronto *Telegram* under the title of 'Red Power Whoops It Up.'[16]

Red Power made it at Glendon College last night in a wild, whooping wind-up to a student conference on the Indians.

John A. MacDonald, deputy minister of the Department of Indian Affairs, was called a 'liar' and 'the house Nigger' by a band of heavy hecklers ...

Mr. MacDonald said they should listen for a change. 'We've been listening for 100 years ...'

The Indians then started chanting: 'What is the problem? What is the problem?'

'Right now, you're mine,' said Mr. MacDonald.

In the rear, Tony Antoine an advocate of Red Power, shot back: 'And we're going to be yours until you give us something back.'

'My office is open,' said the deputy, who's only had the job since last March.

'Your office smells.'

In contrast to the contempt shown MacDonald, Harold Cardinal was well received by the audience, and his speech, like Rudnicki's on the problems facing Indians, was obviously in tune with the sentiments of the meeting and the times.[17] Like the activists within government, Cardinal placed much of the responsibility for the department's policies on the civil servants; his statements echoed the proposals Andras and Rudnicki had been making since mid-summer. After expressing shock at the department's reorganization, Cardinal stressed the need to circumvent the DIAND bureaucracy in the government's dialogue with Indians and in policy development. He called for a freeze on further DIAND expansion, and like Andras and Rudnicki, for a more powerful role for Andras in policy formation (Cardinal 1969a: 96): whereas Chrétien would retain charge of the department's administration, a task force under Andras, including members of the National Indian Brotherhood, would develop and implement the new policies. A precondition of success was the government's acknowledgement of Indian priorities (1969a: 95): 'Firstly, the Canadian Government will have to commit itself morally, philosophically and legislatively to honoring *fully* its agreements under Treaties signed with Indians, or where Treaties do not apply, to recognize and accept the *aboriginal* rights of these people.' (Emphasis in original.) The feelings raised at the conference were common to the youth, both Indian and white, who were involved in the Indian movement, but it was the heckling of the deputy minister that was focused upon by the press.

MacDonald later recalled the event as a sign of the emotionalism governing Indian and white youths.[18] He remembered becoming increasingly convinced that this emotional climate had to be dispelled if any productive dialogue between Indians and government were to begin. The problem, he felt, was deceivingly complex, 'a snake's nest,' and it was time Indians became more active participants in their own future. But before this could happen, he felt the major hindrance of extreme sentiments, probably reinforced for him by the Glendon College confrontation, had to be removed:

The real problem was psychological and in communication needs. This had to be cut and the issue redirected to where it could be handled. We had to convince Indians they had to do something about their own destiny and we had to make a breakthrough – we had to stop this cycle of emotional rhetoric. Indian rhetoric was more and more impassioned and not focusing on the real issues to solve the problems.

The Glendon forum emphasized the rising public sentiments against the department, but more significantly, it brought MacDonald into first-hand contact with the mood of the public. Since MacDonald had purposely not participated in the consultation meetings, the experience at Glendon College probably contributed to his growing opinion that an abrupt change, a major redirection, in Indian policy was necessary to break with the past. But the department's five-year plan, just submitted to the PMO and PCO, did not reflect any serious rethinking of past policies.

THE PCO REVIEWS THE DEPARTMENT'S PLAN

During the first week of November, Rudnicki was asked by senior PCO officials to prepare an evaluation of the department's brief. His assessment vividly illustrated the activist approach to policy-making as well as his past experience in the department. His critiques, a short one and a second more detailed treatment, were often depreciatory in tone. With reason, some overstatement, and an unmistakable lack of confidence in the department's capacity to change, Rudnicki refuted many of the statements in the department's brief. He rejected its traditional philosophy and, like the other activists (and to a large extent the public), he felt Indians no longer wanted the department's special trusteeship.[19] His most devastating comment questioned the whole rationale of the submission: '[The proposal] is based entirely on the dubious assumption that current problems in Indian and Eskimo affairs are attributable entirely to insufficient money and staff. A simple exercise in mathematics is employed to come up with solutions.'[20] Not only had the department avoided a critical self-examination, in his opinion it failed to understand the need for meaningful exchange between Indians and government in coming to a mutual understanding about future policy. This emphasis on 'process' or consultation was the hallmark of the activists' position on policy-making. In his view the department was again proposing major program improvements without considering Indian participation.

Rudnicki drove his point home with a colourful style of delivery, in striking contrast to the gray memos which were the common style of policy-making:

For reasons best known to Indians, they do not trust IA&ND [DIAND] and simply refuse to mortgage their futures any longer to the deformities of existing policies. They have been saying in public statements that they will not tolerate further any 'solutions' which are pile-driven into their midst by a paternalistic 'White Father.' They are asserting their rights as Canadians to be heard in the councils power and to have some influence on decisions which affect their lives.[21]

He cautioned that the 'politically dangerous' aspects of Indian hostility would increase if the government did not recognize the 'explosiveness' of Indian feelings and respond with more open communication. As the major architect of the activist position on Indian policy, Rudnicki was skilled in shaping issues, often overdramatizing Indian antipathy and sometimes overemphasizing the stability and power of Indian organizations at that time as a strategy to get the government to consult with Indians *before* cabinet settled on a new policy. In general, however, his criticisms were incisive, leaving little doubt that the department had not met the requirements of the policy review requested by the prime minister in September, or of the prevailing activist opinion in the PCO's social policy group. Nor did the brief meet the Indians' demands for greater participation in decision-making. The following summary of Rudnicki's criticisms demonstrates his attention to detail.

On the philosophy of the report
– that it did not question the continuing 'custodial care' role of the department, and that it was not in tune with Indian demands or the meaningful involvement of native people in planning their own future.

On the budget
– that the proposed budget for welfare exceeded that for economic development, reaffirming the custodial rather than developmental role of the department.
– that the proposed department budget for 1973–74 of $377 million would average out to an expenditure of $7,000 per Indian family, and a guaranteed annual income of this amount for each family would be an easier mathematical solution.

On Indian involvement
– that it emphasized the role of 'experts' rather than Indians in approaching solutions.
– that the department was uncomfortable with the consultation process and undecided about whether it should increase its 'own advisory machinery' or use native organizations.
– that the growing strength and political importance of the provincial Indian organizations and the new National Indian Brotherhood was ignored.
– that the department was insensitive to the growing and valid criticisms of Indians about the inadequacies of the current consultation processes and that it proposed no methods for improving the procedures.
– that the problems of the Metis which concerned the western provinces, and which the prime minister had asked to be addressed, were ignored.

On local self-government
– that generally the department had no appreciation of the fact that local government meant rule by the people at the grass-roots level, not 'supervisory' activity by the department.

On education
– that the fact of the high drop-out rates was ignored, and the fact cast severe doubt on the efficacy of the programs.

On crime
– that the report totally ignored the problem of the high percentage of Indians in jails in the western provinces and the reasons for this situation.

On community development
– that the department's termination of the original community development program had shown its inability to accept the idea of Indian self-determination and its own eventual 'demise.'
– that the department's portrayal of its current community development program was misleading since only 15 of the stated 58 community development workers were in fact working on reserves; the remaining were in regional offices or Ottawa.

On provincial involvement
– that the strategy for provincial involvement was very weak.
– that there was no explanation of why the department had not pursued provincial involvement after the 1965 cost-sharing principles in social welfare programs had been agreed to by the federal and provincial governments.
– that there was no adequate response to the provincial criticism that federal programs for Indians were themselves uncoordinated.
– that there was no effort to consult with the provinces on proposed revisions to the Indian Act, yet the provinces were to become affected by this new Act.

On the Indian Act
– that the advisability of 'patching up' the current Act might not be the best direction and that there had been no consideration of examining with Indians and the provinces whether 'such legislation is really needed in this day and age.'
– that revisions to the Act which the department had sought were not a major concern of Indians at the moment.
– that the Drybones case currently before the Supreme Court of Canada might call into question the relationship between the Indian Act and the Bill of Rights and therefore have considerable consequences for legislation.[22]

Furthermore, the department's use of the Hawthorn Report to substantiate some of its proposals left him totally unimpressed. Rudnicki had little respect for experts and even less for the report:

The device is employed by the department of lending weight and authority to their brief by relating it to the Hawthorn Report. This report was prepared by academic specialists. They covered about seventy reserves but apparently did not stay on any one long enough to do a single depth study which might have been basic to their recommendations.

The study seems to have started with the assumption that the Indian Affairs Department is the only available agency to assist Indians. This is a philosophy worthy of 1867. Although the study does express some mild reservations about the department, it stops short of analyzing its structure, its resources, its policies or the qualifications of its personnel.

Only Part I of the Hawthorn report has been issued to date. Part II has not been released by the department as yet. The main value of this report in my opinion is that it describes Indian conditions and indirectly, permits conclusions about the role of the department.

A final comment on this report, it is relevant to note that none of Hawthorn's recommendations have ever been referred to Indian leaders and spokesmen for comments or discussion. The Indians were simply bystanders in a scene where experts had a conversation among themselves and arrived at their own consensus.[23]

His criticisms of the Hawthorn Report were a mixture of reasoned assessment with overstatement and inaccuracy, as were some of his other criticisms. The Hawthorn Report was based on data from a national sampling of thirty-five reserves and from seventy in-depth studies, as well as on the considerable literature on reserve communities prepared by social scientists. To imply that the study was based on purely journalistic-style reporting was a gross inaccuracy.

His critical view of the Hawthorn philosophy was, in fact, a moderate paraphrasing of R.W. Dunning's (1967: 52) critique of the report. The 'advocate' role that Hawthorn proposed for the department was exactly what Rudnicki himself was doing, believing the department incapable of advocating anything but its own interests. His statement that Indians had not been asked by government to comment on the Hawthorn Report was accurate, but the implication in his criticism, that if asked they would reject its recommendations, could have been questioned in early 1968. In 1969 the Hawthorn Report's philosophy on special status was used by Indians in their rejection of the White Paper.

Rudnicki's critiques of the department's brief were well received by senior officials in the PCO. But his proposal of a PCO-based task force raised again in his review did not gain favour. In particular, Gordon Robertson did not share the view that the department's submission was entirely misguided or that a PCO policy review group was advantageous.[24] Instead, Robertson favoured a royal commission as a means of handling the problem. This mechanism appealed to him primarily because it removed the inquiry away from the prime minister if the Indian issue were to become more explosive.[25] In addition to political distance, a royal commission could produce a more detached and thorough assessment of the issue. Further, it might divert attention away from the growing publicity of the rift between the two ministers. A disadvantage was that a royal commission would defer any action for two to three years. For this reason Chrétien, at the Quebec City consultations in September, had already publicly rejected the notion of a royal commission in favour of proceeding with an Indian claims commission.

The discussions of what mechanisms the government might use to develop Indian policy arose because the department's brief signalled much more than its substantive thinking on program expansion. Significantly, in the context of the expected policy review, the brief had become a vehicle for judging the department's capacity to carry the policy initiative. When the brief was forwarded by MacDonald to the PCO for an informal sounding, it received a thorough analysis from Rudnicki, and a more cautious review from Robertson. Neither of these critiques favoured the department's approach, and the department's brief was rejected as an acceptable policy review.

Some of the department's old-guard officials had anticipated this rejection, and in looking back over the event, one of them saw it as 'the turning point' in the policy process, especially when MacDonald reported on the brief's unacceptability because 'it was more of the same.' Another official recalled that 'it was not what they wanted; they wanted something more drastic than we gave them.' Whether or not the brief was acceptable depended, of course, on how it met the requirements of the policy review laid down by the PMO, and how it meshed with the prevailing climate of opinion in the PCO. One thing was quite certain, the brief had not envisioned the bold new directions which the Trudeau government was seeking.

Following the rejection of the department's brief, a different type of concern arose in the PCO. Rudnicki's review of the brief had been a strong indictment of the department, and by implication of Chrétien. At the same time, Rudnicki's close association with Andras was well known in the PCO. As a result of these two factors, senior PCO officials were now anxious that its officials, especially Rudnicki, appear to remain neutral in the differences between the two ministers.[26] It was feared that some briefing documents had circulated out of the PCO, through various executive assistants, and that these might get back to the two ministers, making the PCO look 'partisan as hell.' Tight security was to be kept on all the briefs and impartiality was to be maintained, or regained. Robertson's role as broker between the department and the social policy group in the PCO soon became more pronounced, but not necessarily more successful.

A GROWING SENSE OF URGENCY

Apprehension soon mounted in the PMO and the PCO over the lack of progress on Indian policy and the department's seeming inability, or tardiness, in producing a policy review. When the department's brief was returned to MacDonald in early November, he was asked to prepare a new submission which would examine the 'basic postulates' and 'principles' underlying its programs and policies. The PMO's rational approach to policy-making persisted and the impact of Rudnicki in the PCO was now felt by the department. Its senior officials found the ongoing differences between the ministers hard to cope with when they tried to come to grips with the question of Indian policy. Although department officials clearly supported Chrétien, the activist alignment between Andras and Rudnicki meant that the department faced criticism from within, as well as from the PCO.

Pressure on the department to move ahead with its policy review increased even more when, in late October, the National Indian Brotherhood invited the prime minister to attend its forthcoming meeting in Ottawa in early December. The Human Rights Conference, attracting leading Canadian and international dignitaries, was also to be held in Ottawa on overlapping dates. Jim Davey, the major figure in the PMO dealing with Indian policy, viewed both meetings with great apprehension, fearing that the government, and particularly the prime minister, might be vulnerable to political embarrassment if it were not prepared for criticism from conference delegates.[27] Because the federal government funded the Human Rights Conference, the embarrassment could be compounded. Davey felt it was vital to prepare the prime minister for any situation, especially if Indian delegates, such as Harold Cardinal, were to use the Human Rights Conference as a forum for attacking the government, or if the prime minister were to accept the National Indian Brotherhood's invitation.[28]

The possible implications of both these conferences were discussed again in mid-November when the urgency for departmental initiative increased, particularly in light of the prime minister's decision to host the National Indian Brotherhood at a luncheon during its meeting in Ottawa.[29]

IMMEDIATE ACTION ON INDIAN CLAIMS IS PROPOSED

While the PMO and PCO were pressing the department for long-range policy planning, the department was heading, with equal urgency, in a different direction. Chrétien preferred a more incremental approach and wanted to take immediate action to settle some outstanding treaty grievances. Consequently, in early November he brought forward a proposal to settle Treaties 8 and 11 in the Northwest Territories by commuting the land entitlement to cash payments,[30] as the 1959 Nelson Commission had recommended (Canada 1959). Although the proposal received some support in principle, it was seen as another piecemeal effort and failed to get cabinet approval.

Chrétien persisted, however, and sought support for introducing the Indian Claims Commission bill. In late September he had stated in the House that he intended to table the bill 'in the weeks to come,'[31] but in late November, appearing before the Standing Committee on Indian Affairs, he was asked to account for the non-appearance of the bill.[32] He said he expected the bill to come forward early in the new year, but when questioned if it was the heavily criticized 1965 bill, he reminded the committee he was not free to reveal its contents before cabinet approval.

Both the committee and Andras had reservations about the bill's contents, unhappy with the fact that Indians had not been consulted and did not know what it contained.[33] Lysyk's concerns related to the legal precedent the bill would establish. In a public address, he urged a careful examination of the bill in terms of comparative jurisprudence and of other countries' experiences with similar legislation.[34]

Chrétien's efforts to gain approval for the claims bill had failed in the fall, as did other proposals from the department for immediate action. Although there was a high degree of consensus among the policy-makers on the specific *short-range* items that could be implemented,[35] the pressures from the PMO and PCO for *long-range* policy planning on a global policy pre-empted all short-term measures.

THE PROBLEM RECEIVES CLOSER EXAMINATION

At the end of November most policy-makers sharpened their thinking and attempted to define 'the Indian problem' in a more precise way. The flurry of memos coming from all quarters (PMO, PCO, and DIAND) was a response to the many pressures requiring some government action: the pending meeting of the prime minister with the National Indian Brotherhood, the continuing disparity between the two ministers, the lack of a policy review from the department, and the fact that the Indian Act consultation meetings were scheduled to end in January.

Although most of the policy-makers had given attention to the Indian problem since at least the previous summer, some of them now pulled their thoughts together in a far more coherent fashion. The lengthy memoranda circulated within the PMO and the PCO showed a wide scattering of opinion on the Indian problem and on possible strategies the government might adopt to alleviate it. By the end of November, the exchange of ideas through letters, informal meetings, memoranda, and phone calls provided a considerable amount of material for evaluation. Although these materials could be used in briefing the prime minister for the pending National Indian Brotherhood meeting, it was now evident that no basic policy approach would be outlined by that time.

As the fall progressed the need for a global Indian policy had been reinforced by the PMO and the PCO. Consequently, the proposals now coming forward from all quarters were general in coverage and broad in their recommendations, including: 1/suggestions that PMO officials seek out external experts, 2/a flamboyant economic development scheme for Indians, 3/a royal commission, and 4/the first suggestion for a termination policy. Although many of the elements in the White Paper first appeared in this ebb and flow of ideas, as they had for many years within the department itself, the basic pattern of the White Paper had by no means yet formed.

The suggestion for a 'brainstorming' session with experts came from one of Andras' executive assistants who feared that the government might not appreciate the complexities of the Indian problem. He felt it would be valuable for a few of the officials in the PMO to discuss policy issues with persons who were well informed about Indians and social change in order to avoid a strategy that would produce unintended and undesirable consequences.[36]

Experts were often seen by PMO and PCO officials to be too narrow in their comprehension of 'the problem' because of their specialization, too insensitive to the political realities of government, and too unrealistic in their recommendations. Sometimes experts, especially academics, were seen to be philosophically 'conservative,' as was the case with the Hawthorn research team.[37] The fact that experts often disagreed with government opinion lessened their chances of being invited to even comment on proposals. For these reasons, none of the senior researchers in the Hawthorn study was involved in the development of Indian policy (Weaver 1976).

For many DIAND and PCO officials, their own administrative skills and experience provided the necessary expertise, and when these attitudes are reinforced by the tradition of secrecy on policy-making, the likelihood of seeking external opinion diminishes even further. The secrecy surrounding Indian policy was extreme, strengthened by a fear that the government might be charged with duplicity if the public were to learn it was considering basic policy changes before the consultation meetings had ended.[38] For all these reasons, the proposal for sessions with outside experts lacked credibility; one official said its advocate was on 'the lunatic fringe' to have even suggested such an approach.

Proposals from the central figures in the policy-making exercise, namely, MacDonald, Robertson, and Davey, received more serious attention.

During the fall, MacDonald had developed strong ideas on the changes required by both government and Indians if the Indian problem were to be tackled in a serious fashion.[39] In addition to the authority of his office, his forceful personality overshadowed the more reticent old-guard officials, and because of both these factors, MacDonald's ideas set the direction of the department's proposals on policy. This direction was influenced by the strong economic perspective he brought to issues, and quite probably by his experience at the Glendon forum. In late November MacDonald contributed his own perception of the situation as one in which 'something dramatic is required to achieve a communications breakthrough' with Indians.[40] The government had to show a dedication for tackling the problem and to this end he proposed 'the Marshall Plan for Indians.' He argued that by taking the economic development aspect of his earlier five-year plan, and adding a 'quantum of resources' by increasing the proposed $25 million to $100 million, the government could 'capture Indian imagination and inspire their trust.'[41] Indian bands or regional groups would receive funds from the department to hire their own advisers and prepare plans for developing their resources. His idea for this 'dramatic' program was proposed in a quickly typed memo, and it was intended simply as an immediate measure to signal the government's willingness to act on some of the Indians' complaints.

If the department's five-year plan was seen by PCO officials as merely a 'mathematical solution' to a complex social problem, Macdonald's 'Marshall Plan' was considered even more arithmetic.[42] Gordon Robertson was skeptical of it as a strategy because it would hand Indians yet another program without their participation, but he acknowledged that it was 'eyecatching.'[43]

For some months Robertson had promoted the idea of a royal commission to the prime minister as a strategy for developing Indian policy, and

during the late November flurry of memos he again urged its consideration.[44] He argued once more that the legal definition of Indians was
'artificial' and that the royal commission should include both Metis and
Eskimos in its mandate.[45] Ignoring the social and historical realities of
native people would reduce the government's chances of ever minimizing
the problems. The royal commission would consult with the provinces
and native people, and it would have the added advantage of being
removed from the distrusted Indian department. Furthermore, it should
involve the new Department of Regional Economic Expansion which was
the more appropriate agency for development programs. Robertson saw
the problems of Indians and Eskimos as being one of exclusion from
white society because of racist attitudes, and he repeatedly stressed the
need to educate the public to remove the barriers of such discrimination.[46]
Without these educational efforts, which he called 'the basic essential,' he
believed that no success could be achieved by the government.

Although Jim Davey had discussed possible strategies with officials in
both the PCO and the department since the summer, by late November he
became more forceful and assertive in steering the policy process from his
position in the PMO.[47] Officials say he was quiet in demeanour and rarely
offered much comment at their meetings but kept stressing the need for
progress on the policy and reminding them of the likely date of the next
election. His opinions carried weight and like Robertson, he remained
personally neutral in the confrontation between the two alignments,
although his approach to the Indian problem was definitely traditional in
its emphasis on government authority.

Davey's attack on the problem rather typified the rational 'technocratic'
approach to policy-making. His first step was to pare down the trouble area
to a manageable size.[48] Hence, he did not share Robertson's or Rudnicki's
view that the Metis and the Eskimos should be included in the new policy.
His argument against their inclusion was the traditional one: how do you
identify a Metis? To define the Metis would be tantamount to creating a
new problem for government, and he wanted to avoid this. In attempting to
make the problem area neater, he excluded the Eskimos on the grounds
that they had not been treated in the same way as Indians by the government. To include both groups would 'escalate the problem still further.'

Essentially, Davey viewed the Indian problem as one of racial and cultural discrimination, and of regional economic disparity. Economic disparity faced many Canadians and he felt it had to be handled on a regional
or local basis through the new Department of Regional Economic Expansion, not on the basis of uniform national programs.

Furthermore, Davey was particularly concerned that the government might inadvertently give Indians cause to organize against it. He was sceptical that Indian organizations represented the bands, as some officials claimed, and this doubt was another reason for wanting to avoid 'negotiating' with one national Indian organization.

In addition to denying the existence of a 'national problem' regarding Indians, which a royal commission would obviously acknowledge by its existence, his opposition to the idea of a royal commission rested on several other concerns: it would escalate the issue, and give it undue publicity with the possibility that such a 'side effect could be harmful'; and it would ignore the 'time-scale' problem that everyone had been avoiding. But of greater concern was the kind of recommendations such a commission, with its external experts, might produce.[49] He had 'looked at' the Hawthorn Report, but his reaction was one of distrust and apprehension. In his opinion the recommendations for 'citizens plus' status for Indians had political consequences that were 'enormous and endless.' He said he shuddered to think about the possibility of a royal commission coming forward with similar recommendations, especially around 1972 when he expected the next election.

Davey had monitored news clippings on the Indian problem and these gave him some basis for assessing the strength of the Indian movement. Possibly this checking gave him some reason for detecting Rudnicki's strategic exaggeration of the development of Indian organizations at that time. But in arriving at the 1972 time frame, he turned to the figures on Indian education, and as he frequently did, he illustrated the information with the aid of graphs and charts. He projected that as many as 1,000 Indian students could be in universities by 1972. As the university environment was a place of 'intense social action,' he believed this milieu would heighten the growing unrest among Indian youth, especially when the cold realities of a discriminatory society confronted them in their search for jobs, even if they were properly qualified. From this exercise, he concluded that 1972 would be the time for 'the major escalation of Indian problems.' Moreover, by that time the 'department will have completed much of its accommodation program,' its five-year plan, and Indian organizations would have increased in strength. If his prediction of 1972 as a critical year proved incorrect, Davey felt it erred on the conservative side by predicting too late a climax for Indian unrest.

In his urgency to set a time frame, Davey felt that the immediate step for the government was to decide upon some course of action for guiding its policy and program developments. He listed six alternatives:

1/ continue with the *status quo*;
2/ proceed with five-year plan and wait for positive results;
3/ negotiate with 'a corporate group' he labelled 'The Indians';
4/ proceed with total termination of the department and special rights, and solve the land problems;
5/ let the Indians continue to create their own associations, which would become 'disruptive';
6/ shift the responsibility for Indians to the provinces and/or municipalities.

Aside from disliking the idea of negotiating with a corporate Indian group, he did not indicate his own preference, although it was implicit in his emphasis on the need to treat Indians in the context of regional development programs, and avoid singling them out on racial or cultural grounds. His fourth and sixth options were termination proposals, but these were little more than notions at this point.

Although all these proposals – including consultation with experts, 'the Marshall Plan,' and a royal commission – were discussed by the prime minister and the two ministers in late November, no substantive decisions were taken.[50] Davey's options were still conceptually limited, and although he had instigated an exchange of ideas, the net gain seemed minimal. MacDonald's Marshall Plan for Indians was not a substitute for the policy review, and Davey had rejected consultation with experts, as well as the establishment of a royal commission. There was little doubt by then that the prime minister would be meeting with the National Indian Brotherhood in early December without a government position.

THE DECEMBER CONFERENCES

The Human Rights Conference, which Davey felt had the greater potential for politically damaging the government, passed off quietly. Harold Cardinal's speech was similar to the one he had delivered at Glendon College, and the critical attacks that Davey had anticipated, did not materialize (*Labour Gazette* 1969: 66).

Neither were Davey's apprehensions about the meeting with the National Indian Brotherhood borne out by the events of the day. In fact the meeting passed with a controlled discussion over a gala luncheon. PCO officials concluded that the presence of the prime minister, together with the elegant ballroom setting, had overwhelmed the delegates and 'defused' the danger. The PMO considered the event a 'success.'

In describing the luncheon to Marc Lalonde,[51] Davey was clearly moved by the affair and almost waxed poetic in relating how some of the old chiefs expressed their deep pleasure in being honoured by the prime minister. For Davey the luncheon reinforced his opinion that it was the younger leaders such as Harold Cardinal who, through 'the pointedness and tone of the questions,' would be the group the government would ultimately have to deal with. Davey noted the different attitudes between the young and old Indian spokesmen, observing that the younger men appeared uncomfortable with their elders' show of enthusiasm for the cabinet members and the prime minister. Trudeau's talk, Davey reported to Lalonde, stressed the role of Indians in solving their problems, and his belief that if it were merely a question of abolishing the Indian Act, it could be done immediately.

The humility of some of the chiefs, which was to be expected given their traditional backgrounds, caused Davey to say the meeting had 'the stuff of history' about it. George Manuel, later to become the president of the National Indian Brotherhood, recognized its quality of historical 'replay,' but not with any sense of pleasure:

But most of the Indian Chiefs at the feast knew from the Prime Minister's statement that some sinister plans were taking place within Government. I believe what took place at the luncheon meeting with the Prime Minister was a 'replay' of what happened when the Queen's representative met with our forefathers in earlier history ... to persuade our forefathers to sign away our Indian territory. At the luncheon meeting the Prime Minister was trying to persuade us to surrender to them what little we had left of our heritage.[52]

Publicly, the luncheon with the prime minister had all the appearances of an open and accessible relationship with the government, a relationship in which the government would listen, and wait for, Indian opinions at the consultation meetings before making decisions on a new policy. However, Indian spokesmen suspected that decisions were being made before their opinions were heard, although they had no direct evidence to confirm their suspicions.[53]

Press coverage of the luncheon was positive, reporting that the Indian delegates, some twenty-five from the various provincial and regional organizations, were generally pleased with the meeting and the opportunity to discuss their concerns with the prime minister.[54] Trudeau was reported to have been non-committal in his replies to Indian questions, telling the delegates that 'It is up to you to give me the answers.'[55] But the younger, more militant Indian spokesmen, such as Harold Cardinal, were not inclined to believe government intentions and openly expressed their distrust. In an interview with the press Cardinal called for the gradual abolition of the department, charging that 'the department had tried to turn Indians into nice little brown white people, it had a white supremacist mentality, and it used welfare the way the Romans used bread and circuses – to keep the poor happy and tame.'[56] Despite negative comments such as these, which Davey had carefully noted, the luncheon did not prove embarrassing for the government, nor did it require any quick decisions.

At the luncheon the National Indian Brotherhood (NIB) presented the prime minister with a brief, outlining the strategy it favoured in developing new policy directions. The brief supported Cardinal's recommendations (made at the Glendon forum) and left no doubt that Indian spokesmen wanted to discuss their future with Trudeau and his cabinet, not with lesser officials in the department. It stipulated

1. That the National Indian Brotherhood be recognized as the advisory body to the Prime Minister and his Cabinet on matters pertaining to Indian people (Treaty and Registered) of Canada
2. That a Task Force consisting of Indian people be appointed by the Prime Minister through the National Indian Brotherhood and that this Task Force report to a Ministerial Committee. The Task Force would be established to develop new policies and programs which would begin to transfer the major responsibility for Indian matters to the Indian people. It would implement meaningful consultations, communications, and adult education programs through Indian organizations in preparation for the new roles and responsibilities that the Indian people are aspiring to.[57]

Trudeau's opinion of such a task force became known a few days later. In responding to a question in the House as to whether the government would accept the NIB's suggestion, he stated the matter was under advisement, but 'we are not as yet convinced that this would be the most effective way of arriving at a policy which would be to the greatest advantage of the Indians.'[58]

As a result of the meeting with the NIB, Trudeau asked both Chrétien and Andras to take the brief into consideration when they prepared the long-awaited department submission on 'policy options.'[59] There was also a reminder that it would be embarrassing to the government if the submission were not prepared shortly.

Within two weeks' time the Manitoba Indian Brotherhood, under the strong leadership of Dave Courchene, presented Chrétien with the most forceful and eloquent statement of the Indian rights philosophy yet expressed in the consultation meetings.[60] Not only were Indian rights to be honoured, they were to be incorporated in the new Indian Act and in the BNA Act Trudeau hoped to revise. There was no uncertainty on the part of the Manitoba Indian Brotherhood, or of the Alberta delegates the week previously,[61] in their insistence that the beginning of meaningful dialogue between them and the government was predicated upon a forthright, legal honouring of their special rights.

The fall season had been a stormy one with no end in sight to the pressures on the department. Department officials, like those elsewhere in government, were unfamiliar with the new policy-making procedures, and their efforts to comply with them were less than successful. Continuing differences between the ministers, and the Glendon forum episode, had an unsettling effect on the department. Even worse, none of the department's efforts to gain approval for immediate action on the social welfare agreements with the Prairie provinces, on the settling of Treaties 8 and 11, the introduction of an Indian claims commission bill, or the Marshall Plan for economic development, had succeeded. By mid-November the department's priorities on quick, piecemeal policies were obviously out of phase with the long-range planning priorities of the PMO and PCO, and its submission of the five-year plan as a policy review raised doubts, especially in the PCO, of the department's capacity to manage the policy initiative. But alternative, non-departmental methods of preparing Indian policy, such as a PCO-based task force or a royal commission, were unacceptable to the PMO. The National Indian Brotherhood's proposal for a task force had received non-committal comment from Trudeau, creating doubt the policy process would be opened up to Indians. Indian demands for entrenching their special rights, uneasily received in the PMO, were becoming more forceful.

Thus, by early December, the policy initiative seemed to lay somewhere between the PMO in practice and the department in theory. The scope of the new policy had been established in the sense that it was to be a global approach rather than a segmental one. The urgency in the PMO to proceed with the policy process had limited impact on the department, but events in the policy arena peaked in mid-December, suggesting a change in the department's approach.

CHAPTER FOUR

Winter: the season
for dramatic change

The winter season of policy-making began in an explosive fashion. Apprehension over the National Indian Brotherhood meeting had no sooner died down when tensions, which had been building between the PCO activists and the department during the fall, abruptly burst into the open. The winter season witnessed major advances in the policy-making process, demonstrating how publicly disturbing events could provoke the action that prodding from the PMO had failed to achieve.

Troubles began when Chrétien did not appear at the Edmonton consultation meetings on 12 December, as Indian delegates had expected. Andras arrived instead, but the angry Indians, led by Harold Cardinal, initially boycotted the meeting, refusing the begin the session if it was to be chaired by civil servants.[1] Cardinal considered it an insult to meet with 'junior officials,' claiming they might just as easily meet with the staff at regional office. Chrétien's absence was even less defensible, publicly, when the regional director of DIAND supported the Indians' position, telling the press the minister had received sufficient advance notice of the meetings.[2]

As a result of this confrontation, the press again speculated on the different approaches to Indian policy taken by Chrétien and Andras. The problems within the policy arena, especially those focusing on Indian participation, were graphically described for the public in the Calgary *Albertan*:[3]

INDIAN POLICY RIFT IN OTTAWA?
A strange and bitter power struggle that evidently reaches all the way up to Prime Minister Trudeau raged like a boiling undertow just beneath the surface at Indian Act review hearings here this week.

A reporter caught between the opposing forces found it hard to discern facts from factionalism. Minister without portfolio Robert Andras was unwilling to offer much enlightenment, although by implication he suggested there is some opposition in Ottawa to giving the Indians too large a say in what happens to them in future.

He told the Albertan he is determined to see at least two results from this review:

– Participation by Indians 'at the top level' in the final policy-making process leading to whatever changes are made in the Act.

– After a new Act has been approved by Parliament, participation by Indians in the administration of the revised laws.

But whether his head will survive the turbulent forces being generated in the process of this revision remains to be seen.

Andras fared much better at the meeting than the boycott might have suggested, for at the end of it he was described as 'a tremendous guy' by Cardinal, and the press coverage was definitely sympathetic to his stand on Indian participation in the policy process.[4] The department, however, was not so fortunate.

Department officials, frustrated by the innuendos made to the press by Andras' supporters, found many of the consultation meetings trying experiences. One official, overcome by the strain over the two ministers and unhappy over the boycott, finally lost control at the meeting, and his undiplomatic remarks about the situation were immediately picked up by the press for public consumption:[5]

One department official, whose sense of discretion seemed rather blunted, offered scathing corridor criticisms of Andras, claiming he was trying to further his political ambitions at the cost of the Indian Affairs Minister Jean Chretien.

He spoke of how unfortunate it was to see two ministers in the same cabinet carrying on such a tasteless power struggle between themselves.

By mid-December these feelings were running high and senior officials felt that Andras' adversary tactics were unnecessarily aggravating an already complex problem of trying to cope with the task of developing a new policy. The dual ministership of the department, from their perspective, was becoming intolerable, and the fact that the press continued to describe Andras as 'the cabinet minister responsible for coming up with a new federal policy on Indians' only increased their aggravation.[6] These sentiments were still fresh when, a week later, a second incident further provoked the department.

THE ELK INCIDENT

On 1 December, a young Indian woman by the name of Flora Elk died while returning from a correctional institution in Saskatchewan to her reserve in Manitoba. Her body was found at the side of the road, and press reports, noting a considerable alcohol content in her blood, gave the probable cause of death as over-exposure. Since she reportedly had been given $2.00 at the institution for her return fare home, it was claimed that the department had not made appropriate arrangements to assist her in travelling to her reserve.

By mid-December the press in Montreal and Toronto picked up the issue of Flora Elk's death and rapidly made it a nationally publicized symbol of the alleged inhuman treatment of Indians.[7] The department was charged with 'cold indifference' to human suffering and callous treatment of Indians. In the Commons, under questioning from the opposition, Trudeau said he would have the matter investigated.[8] Chrétien, then attending the Winnipeg consultation meetings, agreed to look into the matter, but in his view he doubted Flora Elk's death was the department's responsibility, stating to one reporter 'It's true that we are responsible for the Indian people in Canada, but at the same time they have their own freedom.'[9]

When the prime minister's letter arrived in the department asking for a report on the department's role in the Elk incident, Chrétien was in Mexico for the Christmas break. The letter also asked Chrétien to proceed quickly with 'rationalizing and expediting' the policy process, reminding him that this had been requested last September.[10] But the suggestion that the death of Flora Elk might have been avoided sent a few senior officials into even greater agitation. Some of them, feeling that the department was being unfairly maligned in the incident, resented the implied culpability in the letter.

The letter caused considerable antipathy among the few top officials who saw it, and they proceeded to draft a reply for Chrétien's consideration when he returned.[11] In recalling the episode, one senior official said the prime minister's letter was basically a catalyst to their thinking that the department's patronage of Indians, especially the implicit notion of custodial care, had to be fully examined. Like MacDonald's experience at Glendon College in late October, the Elk incident created strong public sentiments about the relationship between Indians and the government. The public reaction to Flora Elk's death had all the features of 'excessive emotionalism' which, in October, MacDonald had pinpointed as the prime target for government action, mainly because this emotionalism masked the underlying problems and prevented their being considered in any serious way by Indians and the public. He felt the situation called for dramatic measures on the part of the government to cut through the public sentiments and demonstrate to Indians the government's willingness to tackle their problems.[12]

When MacDonald's belief in the destructiveness of emotionalism, compatible with Trudeau's views on reason as the proper basis for public action, combined with the old guard's frustrations with the Elk incident, departmental thinking 'turned right around,' as one official described it. More accurately, MacDonald's thinking turned around.

THE DEPARTMENT SEEKS A NEW DIRECTION

Chrétien's reply to the prime minister on the Elk incident was, in fact, an exploratory discourse on Indian policy although it could not be considered a position paper nor a fully argued set of policy alternatives.[13] By the tone of the letter he was clearly unhappy about the charges of moral 'culpability' levelled at the department. He considered Elk's death regrettable, but at the same time argued that the government could not be expected to be responsible for the lifestyles individual Indians chose to adopt, anymore than it could be responsible for the actions of hitchhikers or drivers. After providing information on the details of the woman's death, he went on to record his views on the new direction Indian policy could take. The liberal values of equality, individualism, and freedom, so prominent in Trudeau's thinking,[14] wove their way through Chrétien's arguments in important ways as he searched for solutions.

Chrétien acknowledged the need for an overall global Indian policy, but there was no backing down from the 'enriched' programs he proposed the previous October. Education needed further expansion, and programs aimed at developing local government, now showing some progress, had to be continued. Social welfare programs were singled out for immediate attention because Indian need for these services was considerable. He urged the government to reconsider federal-provincial cost-sharing arrangements for social welfare programs, much as he had tried to do in the fall, and reminded the prime minister of the provinces' reluctance to assume these services.

As with the five-year plan Chrétien's point of departure for discussing policy was financial. Until the government firmly committed funds to Indian Affairs, he felt the department could do little to develop future plans. This approach was bound to find little sympathy from both the social policy officers in the PCO and perhaps the prime minister himself, who had just firmly stated in the House that viewing the Indian problem as a funding issue was 'a gross oversimplification'; his government took 'a much more profound view of that problem.'[15]

Chrétien went on to argue that, once the financial resources were committed to the department, it would be 'an advantage' to consult with the native people on the distribution of these funds. On the question of decision-making powers for Indians, the department's reluctance to relinquish its own power was still obvious. The National Indian Brotherhood's proposal for a task force was rejected in favour of improving the existing consultation procedure. Although Chrétien agreed that funding should be made available to the NIB, he disagreed with the Brotherhood's request to stop the expansion of the department.

On the subject of treaties Chrétien was firm in his stand that 'our policy is to honour the concluded pacts,' and he was pointedly critical of the government's past failure to come forward with an official statement 'on its interpretation of treaties.'[16] The different interpretations among Indians of what treaties meant were fully described. He urged the government to take a clear stand on the question by either making its own interpretation of the treaties or accepting those of the Indians. The other alternatives he suggested for handling treaties were apparently unacceptable to him: passing the issue to the courts was ruled out because he felt some Indians would not accept the court's rulings; renegotiating the treaties, as had been proposed by the Manitoba Indian Brotherhood, was left without comment.

The new direction in department thinking became evident when Chrétien claimed that the whole purpose of the Indian administration needed rethinking. In his letter, he posed two possible alternatives for the new Indian policy: the continuation of special 'privileges' for Indians, or the granting of full 'equality' based on the total extension of provincial services to them and the removal of all special arrangements. In both these approaches Chrétien recognized, but did not address, the larger question of whether all ethnic groups in Canada should receive the same type of treatment from the government. Although there was no full conceptual exploration of either option, or a clear indication of which one the department would ultimately choose, it was evident Chrétien preferred equality.

The policy I intend to follow must make possible the treatment of Indians on the same footing as other Canadians. This approach is in accordance with Article 7 of the Universal Declaration of Human Rights under which all men are equal before the law and must be treated in the same manner. You will certainly agree that this kind of equality cannot exist when certain services are provided specially to one group of people, or to a single group ... In short, if we take equality as our objective, this implies equal services for all individuals. If we accept this approach, it follows that not only are the Indians entitled to the same services as others, but that these services should be provided by the same organizations ... Moreover we must maintain that every Indian be free to choose his own destiny and to live as he sees fit, regardless of the consequences this choice may have.[17]

In Chrétien's opinion, Indians should be allowed to choose their own lifestyles and make their own mistakes, much as Flora Elk had done. In his traditional, liberal approach the individual, not the society, nor the government, was responsible for his own destiny, and any policy which accepted this objective would be non-paternalistic. His letter reflected the long-standing frustration felt in the department, especially by the old guard, about 'the damned if you do' and 'damned if you don't' dilemma: if government performed its protection role, it was charged with 'paternalism' and if it did not, it was seen as 'indifferent' and 'callous.' As the Elk incident had illustrated, the department was caught in a cross-fire and Chrétien felt the time was ripe for a direct assault on this basic dilemma. The issue, as he saw it, was squarely related to the question of keeping special rights or abandoning them for equality. In short, Chrétien's letter to the prime minister suggested that a redirection in the department's position might be in the offing.

This conceptual breakthrough came directly after Chrétien's response to the Elk incident and resembled Jim Davey's views. The flow of ideas between the PMO and MacDonald increased at this point, and unlike the strained relations elsewhere, Davey and MacDonald are said to have had an easy and more open relationship. Though Davey was sympathetic to the stress the department was experiencing, he kept up the pressure for getting on with the policy-making process.[18]

The turn-about in the department's thinking occurred primarily through the efforts of MacDonald. About Christmas time he approached Davey to explore informally with him the political acceptability of a 'bold' proposal to end the conventional Indian-government relationship.[19] He wanted to determine the possible receptivity of the idea in the PMO, and was told a short while later that such a proposal would not be entirely unacceptable. By that time MacDonald was convinced of the counter-productive force of emotionalism, and felt that whatever the department did, 'it had to be so dramatic that it would startle and upset people but get them on a new direction.'[20]

The redirection of departmental thinking was put forward in a draft cabinet submission in mid-January,[21] but it did not contain the policy options, as the PMO had requested. Instead, it presented one proposal for transferring federal Indian programs to the provinces. The department now doubted that its programs, including the enriched ones proposed in its five-year plan, would solve the Indian problem. This change carried the department a long way from its initial position, because implicit in the submission was the termination of the department. The Indian problem was seen as 'discrimination' against Indians in both a positive (special rights) and a negative sense (lack of provincial services), and the devolution program was proposed as the means of overcoming it.

The response to this proposal was not encouraging, as it was not considered a breakthrough in either a substantive or a procedural sense. To Rudnicki in the PCO, it was little more than a restatement of the cabinet's 1964 decision to seek federal-provincial agreements, and to the PMO it failed to provide the requested policy options.[22] As a consequence, Davey again asked the department to prepare a statement on policy options for the government to consider. Each option was to be evaluated in terms of its advantages and disadvantages, and the department was to indicate its own preference.

Although the department was attempting to move in new directions, its efforts to date were unsuccessful. Policy planning was clearly not its strong point, or its preferred approach. As in the fall, its preference was for immediate action, not planning. Thus, there now occurred yet another episode in Chrétien's up-hill battle to gain approval for a claims commission bill.

INDIAN CLAIMS COMMISSION IS AGAIN PROPOSED

Chrétien hoped to introduce the claims bill when the House reconvened in January,[23] but when the House met, the bill was dropped from the order paper. The new rules for procedure in the House required certain practices with bills requiring monetary expenditures, and ostensibly because these practices had not been followed, the claims bill was set aside. The motion to drop it brought a flurry of criticism from the opposition and renewed pressures to reintroduce it. Some of the speculation about the bill's removal came close to the mark when Robert Stanfield suggested that 'the government in power has no legislation ready.'[24] New Democratic Party leader David Lewis, agreeing with Stanfield's comments, demanded that 'the government has a duty to inform the house when the legislation will come before the house.'[25] After other MPs joined the attack Chrétien finally cleared the air by stating: 'I cannot bring it in today, but I can assure the house that the bill will be tabled in the forthcoming weeks, probably before the end of the month.'[26] Chrétien's efforts to get approval for the claims bill were hitting stormy waters within the policy arena, despite the government's commitment to introduce it in the September Speech from the Throne.

The indecisive way the claims commission issue had been handled since 1962 had not been a credit to any of the governments, and Chrétien's criticism of the way governments had avoided taking a stand on the interpretation of treaties was unquestionably warranted.[27] Because government promises had been followed by hesitant action, verbal assurances no longer held credibility with Indians or MPs. Chrétien had made many public commitments to the bill, and although he was now anxious to honour them, he was getting minimal support.

Andras, who questioned whether a claims commission should be established at all, had written the prime minister the day before the claims bill was dropped, appealing for a holding action on the bill until a new comprehensive Indian policy could be developed. He indicated that he was working on a policy paper which he would submit shortly.[28]

Andras was doubtful that any meaningful objective would be served by a claims commission. His position was based on several points, one being that since the necessary research had not been done, the government was likely to commit itself to a course of action which had unknown consequences and costs. The probable cost of the settlements ranged from estimates of 500 million dollars to over a billion dollars, but this cost, he said, was still indeterminate, as were other matters such as the number of Indians who would benefit from settlement, the amount of land involved, and the efficacy of a commission in removing basic Indian grievances. In addition to these concerns, Andras objected to the historical or 'past orientation' which he felt claims and treaty settlement would reinforce among Indians at the expense of redirecting their horizons to the future and of the need for social development. Furthermore, if such large sums were directed to Indians through claims, he thought this action would probably reduce funds available to communities without claims and limit social development programs in those areas. However, his overall objection was that no claims policy should be mounted in the absence of a new global Indian policy.

The views of the two ministers collided at a meeting of the Cabinet Committee on Social Policy on 15 January, the day after the bill was dropped in the House and Chrétien reassured his critics it would be reintroduced.[29] Chrétien had publicly committed the government to action, but since a new policy submission from the department was not available, the question before the committee was whether to proceed with the bill in the absence of a policy review.[30] Andras argued against considering the claims bill, whereas Chrétien, wanting to proceed quickly, reminded the committee of the Liberal party's promise as far back as 1963, stressing that claims held high priority among Indians. The committee, agreeing to review the bill at its next meeting, concluded that it should be introduced to the House because the government and the party were committed to that course of action.

The session on the claims bill only reaffirmed the distance between the two ministers, a matter of increasing concern to the PMO. Consequently, during January, Davey tried to maintain a sense of urgency for developing policy options by attempting to open up areas of agreement between the two ministers. He held meetings and informal discussions with Chrétien, Andras, and MacDonald, and his mediation continued as he became increasingly unhappy about 'the current atmosphere of uncertainty and the government's vulnerability' due to the lack of a policy.[31] Formally, the policy initiative still rested with Chrétien, but with the continuing stalemate between the two ministers, the 'option' paper had yet to come from the department. The arena lacked decisive ministerial leadership. Davey felt the situation was increasingly difficult for the department's personnel who were unable to channel their energies into policy considerations without some effective direction from 'the government,' from the PMO.[32]

Working against any effective prodding by the PMO were certain counterforces. The first was that the department put a limited value on a policy-making exercise. Probably even more basic to this reluctance was the similarity in decision-making styles between Chrétien and MacDonald. Both were pragmatic, impatient, and action-oriented. Intellectual exercises in reasoning through policy matters held little interest for them. As one senior official described Chrétien: 'He wants to find a solution right away – to be decisive and to be seen to be decisive.'[33] Another official's description of MacDonald's style is remarkably similar: 'He had the answer before you finished giving him the question.' But counterforces to PMO prodding lay outside the department as well.

The ideological alignments, formed during the summer, had in significant ways precast many of the arguments about the policy. The activists, Andras, Rudnicki, and Jordan, were convinced that the policy process had to involve Indians in a direct and meaningful way, while the department did not question the exclusive authority of the cabinet and the minister to develop policy and implement it. In a real sense these were options on the policy process itself, but as the alignments became more entrenched, which they now proceeded to do, rationalizing the process seemed even less likely.

CONFLICTS STOP PROGRESS

Although the department had proposed two possible policy options in mid-January, pressures from the PMO and PCO for more careful planning and rationalization persisted. Within the department less than a handful of officials had participated in this exercise since its inception in the summer, and the secrecy about the process even at the top level of DIAND was so excessive that many officials were unaware of the policy-making exercise. MacDonald was the prime mover in the department and the principal architect of its official position, whereas the old guard, who were far more reserved in style and sometimes intimidated by MacDonald's forcefulness, provided advice and comment which sometimes had limited impact. Furthermore, MacDonald's steering of the policy toward termination of the department was not particularly palatable to most of the old guard who felt Indians would reject such a proposal no matter how it was packaged. Nor was MacDonald's assertive style and his concern with secrecy palatable to the activists who felt these features typified the traditional approach to policy-making in the department.

The activists considered MacDonald the major opponent of their own approach, believing he was more suited to a business or financial position in government than to a 'people portfolio' such as Indian Affairs. MacDonald was aware of their views of him. He was as able a proponent and defender of the department's prerogatives as Rudnicki was of the activist ideology. Each was convinced of the correctness of his own ideas and used the power of their offices with skilful determination. MacDonald did this primarily through his forceful personality, whereas Rudnicki managed it by shaping issues and strategies.

Rudnicki's overriding objective in the policy-making process had been to get the government to adopt a consultative approach for developing Indian policy prior to cabinet approval. His strategy for achieving this end was to build arguments promoting the values and benefits of public participation, which Trudeau had espoused, and to avoid confrontations on substantive issues which were firmly held in the PMO. Although liberal in his outlook and dedicated to the removal of the department, he was not concerned with terminating Indian rights, nor was he adverse to arguing for termination if the end result were agreement to consult with Indians. He believed that the substance of Indian policy would take care of itself in that it would be determined jointly by Indians and the government in negotiations. If, however, his notion of policy *process* – the joint Indian-government shaping of policy – were accepted, it would preempt the power of Chrétien and MacDonald in formulating the new policy.

Because of his strong advocacy of this approach Rudnicki was vulnerable to department disapproval, and during January the policy-making process began to circumvent him. Although not totally excluded from the flow of ideas in the PCO, his formal involvement in reviewing department submissions ended as the 'freezing-out' manoeuvres set in. His informal ties with Andras and Jordan, however, allowed him to have some continuing input.

Quite obviously, Rudnicki's role as the prime strategist of the activist position, and his criticism of the department's submissions had been effective, indeed too effective, leading one old guard official to openly acknowledge that 'we were no match for those aggressive guys in the Privy Council Office.' Senior personnel in the PMO and PCO were deeply concerned about the relationship between the two ministers, and predictably, as one official recalled, 'something had to give, someone had to go and clear the air.'

In recounting the period Rudnicki described himself as 'an outcast'; he had played the 'maverick role' consciously and deliberately.

I picked up the Indian issue which wasn't a popular thing to do. I had no mandate to do it. I began to get together with Indian leaders and I was accused of subversiveness. As energies got mobilized I tried to keep up the pressure points from within the Privy Council Office by reporting on events going on [outside] and by interpreting them. It was quite successful. Then the campaign [of isolation] was launched and it was quite effective drawing room assassination. Files stopped coming to my desk and I was suspected of leaking documents. I was suspect because of my philosophical orientation. I was told that it was not a good thing to get between the bark and the tree – this was upsetting [a senior PCO official who] said 'my advice to you for your sake is to abandon it.' I never took threats seriously. I was isolated for several months but I carried on ...

Rudnicki's isolation weakened the activist alignment, placing greater weight on Andras and his assistants to carry the ideology forward. They were at a further disadvantage because they lacked the formal policy initiative. But countering this power question was their ability, especially Rudnicki's, to conceptualize policy issues in an appealing way and in accordance with the procedures Davey kept reinforcing. Although the activists were far more adept at arguing and rationalizing policy positions than departmental officials, Davey invariably attributed the department's lack of progress to the conflict between the alignments, not to the lack of aptitude or the disinclinations of department personnel.

By January, after six months of struggle, the policy process was a tangled web of ideologies and individuals, and the government was still without a new Indian policy. The confrontation between the alignments now preoccupied the policy-makers far more than the process of conceptualization. The emphasis in the government on 'new directions' and 'bold action,' together with the general devaluation of experts and Indian opinion, seemed to overwhelm them. The situation led them to seek solutions almost entirely from within their own world views and reasoning abilities. In this sense they became inward-looking and conceptually closed. The policy-making arena had become a cocoon of self-searching and soul-searching among a very small group of people. Early on in the process, academics were dispensed with as being out of tune with many realities, and with the exception of the old guard, no one read the Hawthorn Report. Indians were not fully accepted as knowing their own priorities, and their spokesmen were suspected of not being representative of their constituency. Even the activists were not above deciding what Indians really sought and wanted. Individuals in each alignment screened Indian demands through the two ideologies – the traditional and the activist – and this screening process became more selective as the opposition between the alignments hardened. The conflict made each alignment more rigid and less receptive to modifications as the months of tension wore on. By removing Rudnicki from formal participation, the department would have less interference as it tried to produce the policy submissions the PMO required. The larger question of how influential the department itself would be in shaping the new policy remained unanswered.

THE PMO FOCUSES ISSUES

By mid-January 1969 'the problem' was less how to solve the Indian problem and more how to solve the policy-making problem. Since the process was unmanaged and directionless, Jim Davey again moved in to steer the process by sharpening up the sense of the Indian problem and to spur the department into action. In refining his ideas, he described the Indian problem to the prime minister as a political one which could not be solved simply by expanding the department's programs, and like MacDonald, he considered it vital to dispel the emotional climate around the issues. But in his opinion the key factor was the government's vulnerability because it practised discrimination: '*Any government will have great difficulty in solving problems when it is open to the emotional charge of discrimination. This* colours all argument and makes near impossible, rational discussion. The first step in the development of a solution must be the elimination of specific status for Indians which is the cause of discrimination' (original emphasis).[34] Davey opposed any programs that would be either negatively or positively discriminatory; he distinguished between discriminatory practices of the government which could be eliminated with policy change, and societal discrimination over which the government had no direct control. It was necessary to examine the several bases of discrimination which, in his opinion, were primarily economic, legal, and racial, the last of which resulted from the economic and legal distinctions. He singled out the major instruments of discrimination as being the Indian Act and the Department of Indian Affairs.

Given all these conditions, Davey argued that the inevitable solution, and his own preference, required the government to remove all forms of discrimination in its treatment of Indians. His ideas had gelled since the fall, when he initially suggested termination as a possible option, and MacDonald's influence on his thinking was now more apparent. To achieve a non-discriminatory policy Davey set down a series of clear-cut steps the government should take, going far beyond what the department had proposed. In summary: 1/the Indian Act should be abolished; 2/discussions should be started with the provinces as soon as possible so they could adjust to their responsibilities for Indians as provincial citizens; 3/a program should be devised to 'phase out' the Department of Indian Affairs; 4/settlement of claims should be handled in the way that other citizens seek redress against the government; and 5/the government should stress the fact it will not condone special treatment for any of the country's citizens. Davey was proposing a wholescale termination policy. A crucial component of his solution was the settlement of treaty and land claims. If these were not properly addressed, the government would not be able to absolve itself of charges of discrimination. Consequently specific claims settlement was mandatory and the high cost of such settlement was unavoidable.

If such large sums of money are involved there will be a tendency to avoid paying them and to attempt to work up a package deal for the Indians involving some continuation of special status or treatment. I feel that this will be a very poor trade-off. Any long-term plan proposing a status for Indians that permits the charge of discrimination to be levelled is far too expensive, no matter how much it appears to save. We have to separate out the problems and apply the appropriate solution to each. If there is discrimination, remove it. If the Indians have claims against the government, give them redress.[35]

As in his fall proposals, Davey's solution totally disregarded Indian demands for direct involvement in the policy-making activities of government. The only consultation he recommended was with the provinces. Here he followed the hard line that the government should not be financially generous with the provinces, for it was their obligation to assume the responsibility for all their citizens, including Indians. Davey felt it was urgent to move forward on a new policy, for he feared delay might result in the Indian problem becoming a 'racial problem,' which the federal government could not expect the provinces to accept.

Davey's proposals contrasted sharply with Andras' on the point of Indian participation, but not in the ultimate goal. For several months Andras and his assistants had been preparing a major policy statement summarizing their position, and shortly after Davey came to his own conclusions, Andras completed his statement and circulated it among ministers and officials.

ANDRAS' PROPOSALS

Andras' style of discussion at the consultation meetings had led both departmental officials and Indians to believe he would support Indian priorities, and indeed his practice of restating their demands at the end of the meetings reinforced this notion. His proposals, however, shocked senior department officials as they would have Indians, if they had become public. Andras recommended a termination package far more extensive than the one Davey and the department had suggested. But unlike the department's or Davey's approach, Indian consultation was basic to his scheme, for it was through this process that he envisioned Indians negotiating an end to all special rights with the government.

Andras' 'Working Paper on Indian Policy' was by far the most detailed and rationalized presentation yet produced by either of the ministers, but it proposed a single direction for the new policy, not a set of options.[36] The activists' hallmark, their emphasis on the process of policy development through Indian participation, was its most prominent feature. Essentially it was a polished elaboration of the activist ideology, reflecting many of Andras' earlier proposals and his close collaboration with Rudnicki.[37]

Andras' basic recommendation was that a task force with Indian and government membership be the mechanism to develop a full policy 'package' that would be a radical departure from current policies. He believed that the special rights and legal status of Indians, as well as the paternalistic administration, lay at the basis of Indian apathy and poverty.

Only with the removal of this status, the rights, and everything that reinforced them, would the goal of Indian self-determination and 'full participation' in Canadian society be attainable. In the meantime, the government would have to commit itself to a 'sustained program of social development' to end the poverty of Indians. This was a key feature of his proposal. Without this development plan he felt Indians would regard legal equality 'as mere symbolic gesture.' Formal legal equality would not alleviate poverty, nor would the proposed settlement of claims by large sums of money. In the evolution of the social development plan, the task force would play a crucial role and Indian involvement would be mandatory.

When it came to the settlement of treaty and land claims, Andras found himself in a dilemma, at times appearing to equivocate in his proposed remedies. Although he felt these claims could not be denied, he feared their settlement would focus Indian attention on 'the past' and on special rights, at the expense of the future and equality. He considered the settlement of claims to be a part of the patron-client tradition of the department, and restated his previous doubts that a claims commission would be an effective method of removing grievances.

In contending with the complexity of the problem, he separated treaty claims from aboriginal land claims, at the same time recognizing that both were 'moral, if not legal obligations.' He felt that settling claims on treaties, such as Treaties 8 and 11, should not lead to a renegotiation of those treaties because this would have the detrimental effect of reopening the past. In his opinion, the department's proposal to commute the land provisions in Treaties 8 and 11 to cash payments would amount to a renegotiation of these agreements. Furthermore, this action might lead to pressures to renegotiate other treaties.[38]

Although he did not dwell on the topic, Andras felt that some compensation for aboriginal land rights should be considered, suggesting the task force as the proper mechanism for undertaking negotiations on these claims.[39] In his view, the ultimate goal of the task force was to terminate all special rights. Although he did not use the phrase, his proposal was for universal commutation of all claims and grievances to programs which the new policy would establish. Not only could the task force reorient Indian thinking and time horizons to the future, in the end he felt it could obtain a less costly settlement of claims for the government than the one that was likely under the proposed claims commission. In contrast to the department's current estimate of $1.5 billion for settling aboriginal claims, Andras proposed that the task force keep all its costs within 100 million dollars; however, should it be necessary, for the sake of achieving its objectives, this sum could be increased.[40]

Andras' only reservation on the possible success of the general commutation proposal was that it might not be acceptable to Indians.[41] Because of this concern, he felt potential opposition might be reduced if treaty and other claims were connected to transitional programs agreed upon by both Indians and government.

The overall tone of Andras' paper reflected a cautious optimism that if the task force were properly structured and operated, it could pilot the matter of claims settlement through to the conclusion he preferred. The success of his proposals depended entirely on the consultation process and the attitudinal change within the task force. Even though there were no simple solutions to the Indians' problems, the consultation process would maximize the chances of reaching mutually acceptable policies in specific areas. The government needed only a general policy 'direction' or 'objective' such as equality to start the process of consultation with Indians, and that this objective would become developed to the mutual satisfaction of all parties. The task force was to work essentially as a fact-finding, opinion-setting, and discussion-facilitating group under both the minister of Indian Affairs and the Cabinet Committee on Social Policy. It would be the major liaison with Indians, involving 'Indian working groups,' possibly provincial organizations if they were strong enough.

His timetable required the task force to recommend a comprehensive policy that was acceptable to all parties in two years' time, by 1971. Meanwhile, all specific moves by the government to handle Indian claims should be stopped. A further ten years was needed for special funding of social and economic development programs, ending in 1981. At that point special rights for Indians would have terminated and Indians would no longer have 'a perpetual claim' to special status in Canada. Any continuation of development programs beyond 1981 were to be negotiated with the provinces.

Andras' 'Working paper' had been several months in preparation by his advisers, and when it was completed, copies were circulated to all the major actors in the arena. Its formal discussion in cabinet committee, however, required Chrétien's approval. Since this approval was not granted, it never appeared on the agenda of the Cabinet Committee on Social Policy.[42]

Even though Andras' position paper lacked official status, its informal circulation within the department meant there were three policy approaches for consideration in early February: 1/Davey had produced the most extreme plan for terminating all special privileges for Indians, but he supported the department's position on settling specific claims; 2/Chrétien and MacDonald had proposed transferring the department's programs to the provinces, although they had not yet developed the full implications of this approach for either the government or Indians in any systematic way; but they had 'decided to go the route that would end the department,' according to one official; 3/Andras was still proposing a task force, but in sharp contrast to the traditional approaches of Davey and the department, his conditions for a successful termination plan were social development programs and Indian participation. The common theme of all these approaches was now obvious: equality was a goal they could all accept for the new policy.

Although there were still deep-rooted differences between the activist and traditional alignments on how the government could implement this goal, Davey's efforts to advance the policy's development had succeeded to the point when, in mid-February, he felt it was necessary to get cabinet's reaction to the objective of equality.

CABINET DECIDES THE POLICY OBJECTIVE

Interpersonal relations were very tender between members of the two alignments, and so instead of taking the proposal to the Social Policy Cabinet Committee, as would have been normal, the ministers in that committee discussed them privately in the office of Jean Marchand, the chairman of the committee.[43] Tension between civil servants had reached the point where it was feared that their presence would inhibit frank and open discussion among the ministers, and for this reason officials were not invited to the meeting. Despite the delicate atmosphere, the ministers agreed on equality, now called 'non-discrimination,' as the policy objective, and to bring forward only the policy *objective* to the full cabinet the next day.

In his briefing on the meeting in Marchand's office, the prime minister was advised that the cabinet discussion be restricted solely to the policy objective because it was the only area of agreement between the ministers.[44] No memoranda were circulated before the full cabinet meeting because Chrétien feared that the implications of dismantling the department might cause anxiety within government or the department.

The next day, 13 February, cabinet approved the policy objective of 'full non-discriminatory participation' for Indian people in Canadian society.[45] Chrétien was asked to prepare a statement setting forth both a policy and a plan by which the objective could be most effectively implemented; these were to be presented to the Cabinet Committee on Priorities and Planning the following month on 14 March.

This decision set the basic value of equality for the new policy and 'non-discrimination' became the conceptual anchor, the benchmark around which a policy statement and a strategy for implementation was to be determined.

THE DEPARTMENT'S RESPONSE

Given the personal styles of Chrétien and MacDonald, it is not surprising that the department responded quickly to the cabinet's directives. Within a week they completed a cabinet memorandum proposing certain measures intended to achieve the non-discriminatory objective. The steps outlined were:

1/ repeal the Indian Act and substitute legislation which would secure Indian land title for the bands and protect it from reversionary interests of the provinces;

2/ dismantle the department leaving only those programs that provinces were unlikely to offer (e.g. lands and treaties);

3/ negotiate with the provinces to extend a full range of services to Indians;

4/ settle all outstanding Indian land claims (including the BC land question and Treaties 8 and 11) by establishing an Indian Claims Commission;

5/ amend the Migratory Birds Convention Act to liberalize its provisions.[46]

The memorandum was a mixture of the department's preferences and the proposals Davey had made in January. Its tone, and its inclusion of specific treaty settlement, bore no resemblance to Andras' position paper.

The department anticipated that the general Indian reaction to its proposals would be negative but that most of the public would support it, especially 'the silent majority.' Indians were expected to respond by asserting their special rights and demanding that the programs on housing, health, education, and local government continue. It was thought they might also insist that their traditional exemption from income and property taxes on reserves remain unchanged. The basic hedge against total rejection on the part of Indians would be the policy's provisions to secure Indian lands and to guarantee their not being sold without the consent of the bands.

In general, the proposal was noteworthy in its lack of certain features. There was no mention of Indian participation: the policy was to be developed by cabinet and delivered *post facto* to Indians. Nor were the provinces to participate except through a federal-provincial conference which would determine the financial arrangements of the transfer after cabinet approved the policy. The provinces would also receive the policy after the fact. There was no reference to the timing of these measures, nor was there any rationalization for the establishment of an Indian claims commission, which Andras and others saw as incompatible with the policy objective of non-discrimination.

After being reviewed in the PMO and PCO, the proposal was returned to the department for revision.[47] The questions of implementation and time-tabling, as well as the inclusion of special rights elements such as the Indian claims commission, all needed to be worked out. Dismantling the department, repealing the Indian Act, and transferring services to the provinces[48] were fully acceptable.

Within a week, on 25 February, a revised version of the proposal was completed, but the changes Chrétien and MacDonald made were minimal.[49] The revision consisted of the first draft, identically worded, together with a short section on tactics and a draft speech for the immediate introduction of the policy in the House of Commons. The department wanted the policy released immediately, justifying this wish by arguing that a quick release would have the greatest public impact and allow the government to retain the initiative to interpret the policy to the public. The section on tactics read as follows:

TACTICS

(a) All other things being equal, it would be desirable to announce the new policy immediately in the House of Commons. This would have the greatest impact and would enable the Government to set the tone and dimension of the public debate and editorial comment that would follow, based on a clear statement of its policies and objectives. The initiative would lie with the Government. There is risk in delay and the possibility of the policy becoming public in stages with the Government being put on the defensive and being forced into the awkward position of having to reveal its plan bit by bit, not on its own terms but on others' interpretation of what the policy might be, and thus allow those who might be opposed to consolidate and further their opposition.[50]

The desire to capture and maintain the initiative in delivering the policy led Chrétien and MacDonald to focus on the announcement rather than on a comprehensive plan for implementation. Because of this urgency, the question next posed by the department was whether the government should 'inform' both the Indians and the provinces of the general outlines of the policy *before* it was announced in the House of Commons. The decision was to notify the provinces lest they oppose the policy on the grounds of non-consultation. But Indians fared differently:

[TACTICS ... cont'd]

(b) The question of prior consultation with Indians must also be considered. After six months of consultation on revisions to the Indian Act, it is clear that Indians are frustrated by the present trust relationship and want to run their own affairs. However, no consensus has emerged as to what should be done and moreover, given the problems inherent in this, it is not likely to develop. For this reason, prior discussion on the policy would not lead to a constructive result and, instead of support of the policy, might even generate a strong negative response even though the policy now being proposed flows in large measure from the position taken and views expressed by the Indian community in the consultations. Once the policy is announced, however, the Indian leaders would be consulted as to the legislation required to deal with lands and the implementation of the policy.

The power of the provinces to thwart the policy was judged to be greater and more damaging to the policy's ultimate and immediate success than Indian power. But the government's limited success, since 1965, in persuading the provinces to assume more services for Indians, even when it was willing to cover 97 per cent of the total cost, made the department's proposal of gaining provincial support seem unduly optimistic.[51]

Although land claims were considered by Chrétien to be a crucial aspect of the policy,[52] the department did not present any further defense of the claims question other than to state in a perfunctory fashion that the federal government would handle 'the past,' and the provinces 'the future.'

The department, especially the old guard, were highly sceptical of the activists' proposal for a general commutation of all treaty and land grievances to the new policy and programs, and there was good reason for this scepticism. The activists failed to understand the strength of Indians' attachment to their treaties and land, and the particularistic nature of specific grievances at the local level. Because the activists viewed the Indian movement through their own liberal ideology, they lacked an appreciation of the trustee relationship and collective rights that were so important to Indians. Being more informed about the Indian administration than about Indians, they assumed that Indians would trade their special rights for participation in the policy process and the transitional programs it would produce. It could have been argued quite readily, of course, that Indians had a right to these programs without any trade-offs. The activists' proposals rested on certain questionable assumptions, particularly the belief that native people valued 'Indianness' only because they had been excluded from normal social relations and economic benefits in white society. Indian ethnicity was seen as a negative concept, the result of Indian reaction to exclusion, not a positive feature in its own right. Class, not ethnicity, was the basic framework for their analysis.

By the end of February the fact remained that the department had so far failed to argue its own case convincingly. It persisted in advocating certain

Indian demands, but it had not been as incisive and rational as the PMO and the new policy-making procedures demanded.

The most obvious feature of the department's proposal was that it was in a hurry. In the urgency to end its own administration it set itself a three-year deadline. But in the more immediate sense, it was in a hurry to announce the policy and stop the futile submission and revision of proposals.[53] The department's position was that the policy was finished, but, more to the point, that the PCO had become little more than an obstruction. According to one senior official: 'Indian opinion was forming and getting more and more negative. It was important to get it out quickly, and the Privy Council Office did nothing but delay it. The thing was getting no where with the Privy Council Office and the Social Policy Committee. They were killing the proposal.' However, despite the department's impatience, its revised proposal was reviewed by the PMO and the PCO and, much to the department's frustration, it was again returned for further reworking.[54] Its faults were still the retention of some special rights features, such as the claims commission, and the lack of 'strategy and implementation' which the cabinet had specifically requested.

By then, the end of February, both alignments were rigid with all but one or two of the major figures being firmly committed to one of the camps. Opposition had become so entrenched that a proposal by one side was bound to draw rejection from the other, not on its merits but on the basis, as one official phrased it, 'of being agin everything.' Time was running out and the final national consultation meeting with Indians was scheduled in a few weeks' time. Once again progress in the policy-making arena reached a stalemate.

Although the department's proposals had not yet been sent to cabinet, speculation of what the new policy might entail curiously began to appear in the press. The Toronto *Star* reported that a new course for Indian Affairs was being discussed within government, and in an editorial on 22 February, the writer directed attention to 'the revolutionary program that Mr Chretien has recommended to the cabinet.'[55] Two days earlier, Anthony Westell had gone even further by providing an outline of the new program on Indian affairs, which he said 'the cabinet will approve within the next 10 days.'[56] His outline resembled the department's proposals, not those of the activists. But the expectation of cabinet approval turned out to be premature.

Internal delays in decision-making were publicly evident a few days later when Chrétien announced the postponement of the final consultation meeting scheduled for 6–14 March without specifying a future date. But the press interpreted the postponement optimistically as a gesture of respect to Indians' wishes to read the recently published reports on the regional consultation meetings.[57] Inside government, however, there was little reason for this optimism.

The winter season of policy-making had had a stormy start in December with the Elk incident and the confrontation with Indians over Chrétien's absence from the Edmonton consultation meeting. The department's efforts immediately after to produce an acceptable policy proposal had shown some progress, but its further attempts in late February were rejected as incomplete and premature. Chrétien was not allowed to release the policy he and MacDonald had shaped, and he was denied approval to introduce the claims commission bill, whose future, as the weeks passed, became dimmer and more endangered. Andras' proposals, which shocked department officials by the scale of termination envisioned, nevertheless influenced the thinking of the major policy-making figures, although his 'Working Paper' still lacked official status. A dramatic breakthrough occurred when MacDonald focused on emotionalism as the impediment to communication, an idea which Davey then incorporated in locating the basic problem in the government's vulnerability to charges of discrimination. Davey then proposed a full-scale plan for the termination of all special rights for Indians. His steering of the tangled process resulted in the cabinet's mid-February approval of the policy objective of non-discrimination, breaking significant new ground in Indian policy. However, although the proposals from MacDonald and Davey for dismantling Indian Affairs and repealing the Indian Act were accepted, the cabinet's requirements for careful rationalization of the policy and systematic planning for its implementation had not been done. More accurately, the department felt it was unnecessary, for in MacDonald's and Chrétien's views the policy was complete and ready for public announcement.

The winter season had been a strain for everyone concerned with Indian policy and relations among the ministers and officials were frayed by the end of February. No agreement had been reached on how to implement the new policy objective and compromise seemed remote. Department officials were irritated by the continual review and rejection of their proposals, especially by 'those boys in the PCO looking over our shoulder.' By early March, as one official described the situation, 'things were getting no where.'

CHAPTER FIVE

Spring: the season
for rationalization

In the first few days of March 1969 several questions about the future of
Indian policy hung in the air. What kind of action was possible to ensure
that a plan of implementation was prepared? Who was to remove the
inconsistencies in the department's proposals and rationalize the policy?
On 4 March Indian policy was to be discussed in the Cabinet Committee
on Priorities and Planning, the senior cabinet committee chaired by the
prime minister; it was obvious that a new approach had to be found. The
department had blocked Andras' 'Working Paper' from the agenda of the
Social Policy Cabinet Committee, and even after Rudnicki was ostracized,
department officials had been unable to produce an implementation plan
acceptable to the PMO and the cabinet committee. Since the two ministers
still had different approaches to implementation, the basic process of
rationalizing the policy remained to be done.

Senior officials in the PMO and PCO searched for ways to break the
stalemate[1] and at the 4 March meeting one was finally decided upon.

The policy process was removed from the department's jurisdiction and
assigned to a task force to be set up in the PCO. The PMO's insistence on
rational and systematic planning was obvious in the specific mandate
given the task force:

1/ to examine all the implications of a non-discriminatory status for Indians;
2/ to set down the time table and procedures by which the government was most
likely to achieve full participation of Indians in Canadian society;
3/ to resolve the 'apparent contradiction' between the objective of equality and
the special rights proposals the department promoted;

4/ to use both Chretien's and Andras' submissions in undertaking their work;

5/ to refer to Brophy and Aberle's 1966 study which evaluated the results of the United States termination policy and;

6/ to prepare a draft White Paper for cabinet's consideration in 3 to 4 week's time.[2]

Given the direction of events in the winter months, the inclusion of the Brophy and Aberle study was rather startling. The report showed how the United States' termination policy (1953–61) had been hastily conceived and poorly planned, the effects of which subverted the intent of the policy. Brophy and Aberle provided detailed recommendations on how a termination policy should be developed, stressing two fundamental principles: Indians must be fully involved right from the initial stages of policy development and be fully aware of the consequences of termination; and termination should be applied only after careful and extensive planning among Indians, the local and state governments, and the federal government (1966: 211-14).

It was the activists, more accurately Rudnicki, who suggested that the Brophy and Aberle study be examined, for they feared that if the department's proposals were accepted, Indians would be bypassed in the policy-making process and socio-economic development programs would not be mounted to tackle the real problems of poverty. Although Andras' 'Working Paper' had most closely approximated the Brophy and Aberle recommendations, the cabinet's acknowledgment of the Brophy report now reflected a wider concern over the implications of termination for both the government and Indians.

The question of the policy's incorporating Indian values, a condition which Brophy and Aberle considered mandatory for achieving a successful policy (1966: 179), in major part had already been answered by the cabinet's decision on a non-discriminatory policy objective. The value of equality, not special rights, was to guide the formation of the new policy. The other main Indian priority, participation in the policy process, would depend on how the White Paper was to be used by the government.

The department had not proposed a White Paper previously as a means of delivering the policy, although the mechanism had been discussed within DIAND as far back as spring 1968.[3] The notion had been set aside at that time as other administrative matters took precedence. It now emerged from the cabinet committee.

The idea of putting Indian policy forward in a White Paper was adopted, but how firmly the government would commit itself to the policy was not decided. As Doerr (1973) has shown, White Papers had been used for purely informational purposes in announcing completed policies, or as mechanisms for enhancing consultation with the provinces, the public, and opposition members in Parliament during minority governments. The only use of a White Paper by the Trudeau government before the Indian policy debate was the White Paper on Price Stability, released in 1968 (Doerr 1973: 111-15). As with the paper on Indian policy, the public was unaware of its preparation, but following its release, it received low-key publicity because the subject was considered a politically sensitive topic. Only minor changes were made before it was implemented in spring 1969.

The decision to use a White Paper for Indian policy reflected a new trend in the Trudeau government toward greater use of these documents to enhance discussion on policies before the legislative stage was reached. Theoretically, White Papers could open the policy process up to debate, focus consultation, provide a means for educating the public, and hopefully gain support for the legislation. But there was no set pattern regarding the degree to which the government would acquiesce to the changes that the public might demand. Consequently, the decision to issue Indian policy as White Paper could mean many things.

The decision to release Indian policy as a White Paper was described by personnel in both alignments as a 'natural' or 'obvious' decision, given the increasing use of White Papers within government and the commitments to Indians to have another series of consultations. Given the developments on Indian policy to date, however, the choice of a White Paper strongly suggested the policy process had become so tangled that few people were convinced that the final product would fare well with the public. It left an escape route if the policy hit bad weather, relieving the government of defending a policy not well received, or perhaps not well conceived. Consequently, the mechanism of a White Paper had many aspects to commend its use in Indian policy. In the end, though, it probably reflected an uncertainty concerning unresolved internal differences and probable Indian response.

Task forces, like White Papers, were increasingly used by the Trudeau administration (Wilson 1971) largely because they facilitated policy development by providing a broader perspective on issues than was likely to come from a single department; among the advantages of these interdepartmental committees were the greater use of expertise in many departments, the increased chance that most aspects of a problem would be detected and examined, and the benefit of previous experience with similar policy issues.

Although most of the policy-makers felt the decision to use a task force for Indian policy at this point was a rather normal procedure, there were mixed reactions to it in the department. MacDonald considered a task force to be a negative reflection on the department, a lack of confidence in its judgment, and some senior officials resented its intrusion into their jurisdiction.[4] Those who were convinced that the recent policy proposed by the department was timely thought the delay was unwise and unnecessary. Predictably, the activists welcomed the task force; with the department in 'receivership,' as one of them phrased it, the activists now had a greater opportunity to influence the policy process, a hope they had entertained since the previous summer when they originally proposed a task force.

THE TASK FORCE

The task force was assembled after the cabinet meeting, and although Rudnicki was initially expected to participate in it, he was removed at the last minute at the department's insistence; nevertheless, he remained 'backstage,' as he phrased it. The old activist alignment, consisting of Andras, his two executive assistants and Rudnicki, was not directly involved, but many of their ideas were carried into the task force by Andras' 'Working Paper,' which now had official status, and by Jordan, who organized the task force and headed its operations. Jordan, the head of the social policy group in the PCO, had played an important but low-key role in the policy process since the summer, and his views were decidedly of the activist persuasion.

Jordan's initial concern, that the task force would lack credibility if it did not include officials of deputy ministerial rank, or its equivalent, was respected by senior officials, and the group consequently included them. But Jordan was equally concerned about the philosophies of the committee members, fearing that 'the White Paper is a dead duck if the process surrounding its production is weighted in any way to political commitments on *de facto* special status.'[5] Even though he was in a position to shape the task force's product by recommending specific members whose philosophies were in keeping with his own and the cabinet's directives, his recommendations could be disregarded because departments sometimes sent officials of their own choice. By the very nature of the task force's structure, however, DIAND control was unlikely because the task force was firmly based in the PCO.

Jordan, then in his early forties, had considerable experience in the social policy field within government before joining the PCO during the

Pearson regime. Like Rudnicki he had come from Manitoba, but he was of French background, fluently bilingual, and lacked Rudnicki's background in Indian affairs and substantive knowledge of the field. He read both the recommendations of the Hawthorn Report, but not the full report as it was 'too voluminous,' and the Brophy and Aberle study after he became involved in the task force. Although he and Rudnicki were of kindred spirits in their general approach to policy-making, their personal styles of operation were quite different. Whereas Rudnicki was largely a loner who related to Andras at the ministerial level and tended to promote confrontation as a mechanism of instituting change, Jordan operated in an easy and more indirect fashion in the system and related to Jean Marchand at the ministerial level.

The task force was simply structured (see Diagram 2). At its head was 'the deputy minister's group,' a dozen senior officials from several departments, many of whom Jordan recommended because he had worked with them before and knew their expertise, styles of operation, and personal philosophies.[6] The group's job was to review the proposals coming from the two smaller working groups to ensure they were realistic in terms of the various department's perspectives. Department interests played a significant role at this level, more than they did in the informal working groups, for the members had to keep in mind their department's eventual participation in the implementation of the new policy. The group was chaired by a senior PCO official who played a very minor role in the process, whereas Jordan, its secretary, was the prime mover and organizer. The PMO representative was Davey, and DIAND's was MacDonald.

The real work of the task force was done by the drafting group, or more accurately, the core working group, the smaller group of officials who constituted its actual membership. The finance group was a smaller, less active unit with a narrower mandate to examine the problems of transferring funds for DIAND programs to the provinces.

In general, the task force opened up the policy process within government. A wider expertise and outlook were brought to bear on Indian policy, rapidly shifting the frame of reference from the department to the government. Unlike the pre-task force phase, deliberations now pivoted on the policy objective of non-discriminatory participation of Indians in society. Although the major value of equality underlying the new policy had been set, some flexibility remained, depending on the ability of the officials and ministers to develop compelling arguments. Consistency and rationality, key concepts in Trudeau's own philosophy on policy-making, were to guide the process.

DIAGRAM 2 Task Force on Indian Policy

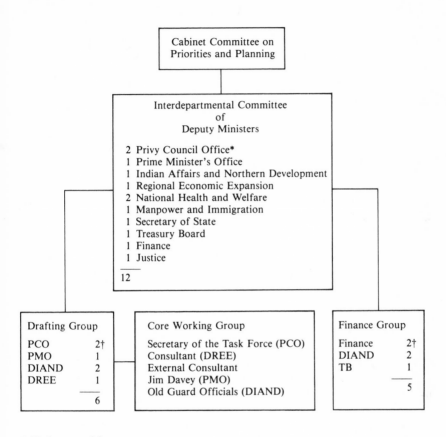

* Chairman and Secretary

† Chairman overlap with DMs' group

TABLE 6 Task Force timetable

1.	Initial period of establishing the committee and outlining the procedures	1 week	4–11 March
2.	Information collection and preparation of recommendations by core working group	5 weeks	12 March to 16 April
3.	Discussions of recommendations with the full committee, and revision of the recommendations	3 weeks	17 April to 7 May
4.	Presentation of the recommendations to the Cabinet Committee on Priorities and Planning		8 May

THE CORE WORKING GROUP

Conscious of the short time available, Jordan launched the core working group within a week of the cabinet meeting. Its pace was hectic and intense during the end of March and early April, and work often extended into the evenings and weekends. Jordan organized the work schedule and pulled out issues needing close examination through small group discussions. As new questions arose, different officials were called in, and background papers were prepared by the relevant departments.[7] The task of organizing the flow of ideas into coherent proposals was done largely by Jordan himself who set the pace of events to ensure the deadline was met (see Table 6). Secrecy prevailed, but it was most intensive within DIAND where civil servants sometimes prepared position papers without knowing how their work would be used.[8] Although the task force was given the power to co-opt other officials, none of its members, including the consultants, was Indian.

The core group was a microcosm of the two policy-making alignments: the traditional ideology was represented by two old guard DIAND officials and Jim Davey, and the activist ideology was carried by Jordan and the two consultants he brought into the group. One of the consultants was a senior official from the Department of Regional Economic Expansion and the second was a specialist in public participation from outside government. Jordan and the two consultants formed the nucleus of the *new* activists in the task force, supported by an official from the Department of Justice who was not a mainline activist in his approach or training.

The core group's basic tasks were to rationalize the inconsistencies in Chrétien's and Andras' proposals in keeping with the non-discriminatory objective for the new Indian policy, and to develop a plan for implementation. The process of rationalization took the form of open debate among the core group officials as they thrashed out and argued over detailed issues.[9] The sessions were free-wheeling exchanges involving 'some good heated discussion' and strenuous efforts 'to convince' others of their own line of thinking. Both the old guard and the activist members tried 'to educate' Davey, whose 'hard line' and lack of familiarity with both Indian affairs and social development processes distressed them. In turn, the activists and old guard attempted to persuade each other of the correctness of their own perspectives, and although there was little agreement on many issues, there was a general respect among them and a ready flow of ideas and arguments.

The new activists

From his experience in government Jordan knew other civil servants of activist persuasion and he drew upon this network in constructing the deputy ministers' group and the core working group. The network linked civil servants who had worked together on past programs or interdepartmental committees related to ARDA, FRED, CYC, and the Challenge for Change Program. The two consultants in the core working group both had a PhD in sociology and had recently left academic institutions to pursue government careers or independent consulting; the two also shared a background in community development programs of the 1960s. At the ministerial level they related to Maurice Sauvé, former Minister of Forestry and Rural Development who, they speculated, might have promoted their notion of Indian participation in the policy process had he been in cabinet. These new activists typified Kernaghan's notion of civil servants as agents for social change (1976: 439), being very much in tune with the citizen-participation movement of the 1960s. Collectively they wanted to move Indian affairs programs under the auspices of the newly emerging Department of Regional Economic Expansion where they felt officials would view Indian development in the holistic manner it deserved and accommodate Indian participation.

None of the new activists, including a like-minded official from the Secretary of State on the deputy ministers' group, were newcomers to the field of social development policy. Even though they came to the task force with different career paths and different styles of operation, they shared an ideology of policy-making that was firmly based in public participation. They viewed social development, as one of them phrased it, as 'an holistic process that couldn't be chopped up into separate programs.' They also believed that a more flexible government structure was required to accommodate this process. Though, as one of them said, they 'believed it was proper for civil servants to fight for certain principles,' they made a careful distinction between their style of activism and that practised by the CYC workers: 'We believed that the organizational framework of government had to be flexible, it had to have dedicated civil servants who wouldn't run to the press as the CYC had done, it needed to relate directly to politicians who could support it and cause departments to cooperate when cooperation wasn't coming.' Their idea of government organization envisioned 'freer' civil servants who could operate responsibly within a more tolerant and elastic bureaucratic structure. At the one end of this structure civil servants could be more receptive to the needs of the public, and at the other end, because of this responsiveness, they could better advise ministers who made the policy decisions. This perspective contrasted sharply with the rigid chain-of-command characterizing much of government organization, and the new activists found it particularly inconceivable that a department like DIAND could function in this way.

In addition to their common approach to policy-making, the new activists shared a similar view of both the Department of Indian Affairs and the Hawthorn Report. They thought the Hawthorn Report was a conservative document which reinforced the traditions of the department – although only one of them had read much of the report. They thought it was 'too dated' and philosophically inappropriate to be of any current relevance. One official viewed the report as promoting 'acculturation through administration' rather than 'acculturation through Indian action.' Its emphasis on special rights was in direct conflict with their own liberal belief that equality was a proper value to guide the new Indian policy. These activists were firm, if not doctrinal at times, in their belief that the policy objective was an inherently 'good' one. As one of them stated, 'We were all of the small-L liberal philosophy. It [equality] was the only way to go ...' None of them had attended the Indian consultation meetings or read the ensuing DIAND reports.

Although their view of the individual officers in the department was tempered by contact with them in the working group, their collective perspective of DIAND was uncompromisingly negative; they found its approach to policy unnecessarily rigid, closed, and secretive. Seriously doubting the department would actually support the principles of the new policy, they believed it was both ideologically and structurally incapable of meeting the needs of Indians. They viewed the old guard officers as too ingrained with the departmental ethic of paternalism to change at this point in their careers, even though as individuals they might be altering their approach to the policy process and to Indian demands.

The new activists' view of the department derived partly from their past experiences in working with its officials, although none of them had been in the Indian Branch as Rudnicki had. One activist, for example, had worked with DIAND officials on an inter-departmental committee that reviewed the Indian Act and prepared recommendations for revisions; for him the department's reluctance to consider even minor changes to the Indian Act and grant more power to the bands emphasized its conservatism and rigidity. Another official, who had been in Northern Affairs earlier, had a similar experience with DIAND officials over an Indian treaty matter; believing the department had beaboured a simple issue, making it far more complex than was necessary, he failed to understand why the department 'didn't give them the binder twine and be done with it. The treaty *said* the Indians were to receive the binder twine.'

Finally, the activists viewed the department as having 'a detailed administrative mentality' which tended to produce 'an administrative solution' to every problem that arose: 'You just add more rules and regulations and that will cure the problem.' Another activist believed the department 'was simply not able to perceive social issues, and to understand what was happening.' This comment applied equally to Davey who, in their opinion, held the simplistic notion that Indians would assimilate if the legal and administrative barriers were only removed.

Like the old activists, the new activists advocated Indian participation in the policy process, but they differed from their predecessors in their stronger commitment to the substance of the newly emerging policy – the notion of equality (although not in a legal sense) and the notion of termination of special rights. Also unlike their predecessors, they had close and direct contact with senior officials in DIAND.

The department's participation

Although two old guard officials represented DIAND in the drafting group, only one of them was a regular member of the core working group. The other, who had a legal background, became impatient with the group's deliberations and less committed to the exercise. In demeanour they were less assertive and aggressive than the activists, but they persisted in advocating Indian demands for claims settlement and land security. They thought the activists had a blind spot when it came to special rights and land claims. Both were then in their fifties and had had full careers in the Indian administration. The official who stayed with the core group had been a major organizer of the Indian Act consultation meetings, and his regular exposure to Indian demands and opinions made him the only direct link between the consultations and the task force. He prepared some of the background papers for the task force, which accurately described Indian priorities and demands.

Like other old guard officials, the two in the core group believed that even though the goal of equality was ultimately both desirable and necessary, they were convinced that under the equality rhetoric of Indians and their white supporters, there was a basic Indian dependency on, and a desire for, special rights; these rights, as they saw them, included treaty and aboriginal rights, hunting and fishing rights, and the various tax benefits attending Indian land-holding and residence. They believed it was mandatory to settle Indian grievances before Indians could look to the future and self-determination. Since the two officials considered land claims as moral and psychological issues, not simply legal ones, they were sceptical of Andras' ideas that claims could be totally commuted to money payments through negotiations, although they felt some Indian groups might be so inclined.

These two officials acknowledged that the department had inhibited Indian self-determination, but that ending paternalism or 'cutting the cord,' as it was commonly phrased, was a complex process because they firmly believed Indians would resist the end of trusteeship. For these reasons and their belief that Indians would defend their historic privileges, the two supported a much slower 'weaning period.' On the basis of their previous efforts to develop educational and social-welfare agreements with the provinces, they doubted the provinces would readily extend their services to Indians.

But a crucial factor was their belief that they 'knew' Indians in a way that the activists did not. Thus many of the activists' proposals seemed untenable and unrealistic. Activists were often described as 'theoretical,' as 'social philosophers' or 'academics,' and as 'lacking in practical sense' when it came to realizing the implications of their proposals. One old-guard offical described the drafting group sessions and the activists as follows:

Jordan was a good chairman. He brought up all sides of issues, played devil's advocate, and you couldn't tell where he stood on issues. I couldn't see that it [the group] accomplished much of use. Much of it was nonsense – academic theories. They were full of ideas they'd read about and they didn't know the first thing about Indians or administration. We provided the practical side. We had to bring the discussion down to earth, not these theories up in the air. I lost interest in the committee but I attended all the meetings. It was an academic exercise – we got off the practical end and got into the social science end, and in the end I hope it brought Jordan and [one of the consultants] down to earth. Indians aren't lamp posts to be handled. Anyone who has never worked with Indians has great ideas about what to do with Indians. We had to convince them that hunting and fishing rights were important to Indians, they couldn't understand why these would be important.

Opinions among the department's old guard were mixed on the value of the task force and on the PCO in general. At one pole were those officials who saw the PCO as 'interfering' in departmental matters without 'the proper authority' to do so. At the other pole there were fewer officials, including the assistant deputy minister of the Indian-Eskimo Program, who generally felt that interdepartmental committees were useful because the department could no longer be expected to handle all the programs for Indians; these few men, although not entirely supportive of the task force, were not entirely negative either.

The task force was important because it brought old guard officials into direct contact with the policy-making process and with the new activist officials outside the department. The old guard officials now argued their positions with the activists who, through the process, saw the differences between the old guard and MacDonald. However, because of the secrecy within DIAND about the task force, few other senior officials in the department even knew of its existence.

THE PROCESS OF RATIONALIZATION

Rationalizing the policy was a systematic and thorough process, as Jordan led the discussion of each topic through to its logical conclusions and implications. As task force members mulled over ideas and sought a logical consistency in their arguments, they invariably ran headlong into certain political realities that threatened to undermine the practicality and firmness of the logic. Indeed, the politics of the issues seemed to get in the way of the logic. Discussions seesawed between the rational conclusions of certain ideas and the realities of acceptance by Indians and the provinces. As they examined incongruities and disparities in reasoning, they experimented with various arguments and interpretations, trying to explore all considerations and to reconcile differences of opinion. In particular, they tried to ensure that all the proper questions were being posed. DIAND members, however, tended to be more concerned about what they felt Indians would accept or reject rather than the logical neatness of the arguments.

The process of rationalization can best be illustrated by the core group's first meeting when it debated whether Indians were being given a choice in the policy option of non-discrimination. The conclusion was that neither the policy nor the pressures of society at large allowed Indians a real choice.

THE OPTION

Main points:

1. The policy objective is to help the Indian achieve non-discriminatory participation in Canadian society. Question: are Indians being given any real choice in respect of this objective?

Not if the choice is between the above option and a return to traditional Indian life in some pure form. There are too many pressures the Indians would have to be protected against if this were to be a real option for them. A basic choice in any real sense, because of the pressures of modern industrial society upon everyone, is not available to Indians nor to any other Canadian. Everyone is free, of course, to make the hermit's choice, but that is a matter of individual decision which cannot be binding on future generations and which cannot allow individuals to exact services from governments. The policy should make no room for choice in the sense of providing Indians a permanent possibility of opting for some permanent maintenance of the reserve system, or some special relationship with the federal government. This is not to say that many reserves won't transform themselves into prosperous corporations or co-operatives; this is a real choice for them, and anyone.[10]

As the above discussion illustrates, the prevailing liberal ideology was strikingly obvious. All manner of issues were raised and as one official commented, 'you name it and we discussed it.' But deliberations tended to focus on four recurring questions: 1/Should Indian land and treaty claims be recognized, and if so how? 2/What mechanisms should be used to implement the new policy? 3/How firmly should the government commit itself to the new policy? 4/How soon should DIAND programs be transferred to the provinces and to the other federal departments? Because certain issues were more important to some officials than others, different alignments occurred depending on the topic, although the activist/traditional split was still generally apparent.

The issue of Indian claims settlement

Settling Indian claims, or disregarding them, raised numerous questions in the core group. Would claims settlements really reinforce the past time-orientation of Indians? Could the government afford to disregard claims and expect Indians to accept the new policy? If claims were to be recognized, was an Indian Claims Commission an effective method of settling grievances? What form should a commission take and what criteria could be used to determine a claim? What would be the cost of a claims commission in economic, legal, political, and ideological terms?

The issue of settling claims was couched in terms of 'the past and the future,' calling to mind Trudeau's strong ahistorical approach to policy and his belief that governments could not solve the problems of the future if they were constrained by irrelevant events of the past. Discussion focused on how important the past was for Indians and how readily they would, or must, relinquish certain rights for the future. Whereas the activists emphasized the need to dispense with the past, stressing Indians' desire for future self-determination, DIAND officers stressed the need to satisfy Indian grievances, 'to clear up the past,' before Indians would look to the future. One department officer recounted that the claims issue was 'the most argumentative' one they dealt with. The other DIAND official in the core group found that the importance of claims to Indians was the most difficult point to convey to the activists:

Our job was to educate those who didn't know anything about Indians, to educate the others how they could expect their ideas to be met by the front lines, down at the level of the Indians. We had to tell them that although treaties don't have any status in law, they were very important to Indians and that was the department's position. We said it was important that things like treaties be settled before they go on to other things. The problem was that government and Indian priorities were different. The [drafting] group spent time trying to manage two worlds – the desirable and the possible. We [in the department] had had much experience trying to sell ideas to Indians and failed badly. We knew it wasn't going to be accepted.

The same officer repeatedly tried to convince the activists of the importance of claims settlement to the policy's receptivity by Indians. For him, claims was 'a moral issue, not a straight legal one – you simply couldn't look at it that way.' He found it particularly difficult to persuade the lawyers on the task force of this fact. Because of their conventional training in property law, they had problems grasping the concept, but more significantly, they had difficulty understanding the consequences of denying claims settlement to Indians. This difficulty applied particularly to the notion of aboriginal title.

Although the economic and political consequences of recognizing aboriginal title were not irrelevant to the argument, officials in both alignments agreed that 'the idea' of aboriginal title was the major stumbling block. The problem was one of simply understanding what the term meant. For example, a few officials outside DIAND felt that recognizing aboriginal rights for Indians would require the same recognition for the French in Canada. The concept was confused sufficiently without the added complication of those who opposed it in principle. The standard reluctance to consider the concept was often phrased as 'What are we supposed to do? Give all of BC back to the Indians?'

In the core group sessions, the activist position on claims clearly prevailed as the record of the discussion indicates:

Doing something special to settle claims and grievances has these problems:
(i) it involves a continuing identification of Indians
(ii) it opens up a series of unanswerable questions regarding – original rights allegedly violated; dependent's rights for which settlement cannot be binding; it turns attention to the past; it has enormous financial implications e.g. a move to settle B.C. claims entails action on Quebec claims, and in either case what would constitute a reasonable settlement?

Claims and grievances cannot be processed through the courts unless there is a legislative or legal embodiment of the recognition of the right, and to this extent the broadest range of claims of Indians for compensation cannot be taken to the courts.

There have been special vehicles created for the assessment and settlement of quasi-legal claims based upon race, and other unique characteristics e.g. expropriation of Japanese lands in B.C.; Halifax Claims Tribunal. It can be said these usually 'put money into the right pockets' but they must be recognized for what they are – *political settlements* where (a) only limited public funds should be engaged, (b) a settled claim cannot be appealed to court, and (c) a time-limit must be placed upon the claim time.

As to the argument that a national commission or tribunal creates a false generality in claims and an artificial nationality among all Indians, perhaps it would be possible to break up the process of responding to claims by establishing either different commissions for different types of claims, or regional commissions for all claims.[11]

It was obvious that if these arguments were accepted by the deputy ministers' group, and later by cabinet, the new policy would not recognize specific claims in any form.

The issue of the mechanism of implementation

The second major issue for debate in the core group was the mechanism the government should use to implement the policy. Discussions focused on who should do the implementation and how it should be managed and scheduled. One question predominated: were the conditions surrounding the Indian problem, and Indian policy, unique enough to require 'unorthodox procedures' in implementation? Rephrased, was the conventional means of implementations through the department best suited for the policy or did Indians so distrust DIAND that a new mechanism should be created to do the job? These questions raised many others. How critical was the implementation process to the ultimate receptivity of the policy by Indians and the provinces? How and when should the provinces be brought into the process? How 'firm' should the government's commitment be to the new policy? What were the advantages of 'firmness' versus 'flexibility' in the delivery? All of these questions focused on the desire to bring about the greatest degree of public compliance with the policy.

Discussions in the core group soon moved to the activists' preference for an innovative implementation procedure. Basically the activists' proposition called for a public task force, anchored in government at the PCO level and reporting to a special group of ministers in the Cabinet Committee on Social Policy. Instead of labelling it a task force, however, they referred to it as 'a coordinating secretariat,' or more commonly as 'a special piloting group.' Its job was to take simply the new policy objective of equality to the public, and with feedback on public response return to cabinet with specific recommendations on a full policy that would be mutually acceptable to Indians and the federal and provincial governments. According to this approach the White Paper was to be used as a skeleton mechanism for proposing a policy direction, not affirming a policy statement, since the final policy would grow out of agreement and compromise between government and Indians. In principle, the piloting group was almost identical to the one Rudnicki had suggested in the summer and developed further in January when he argued that the government should decide upon an initial bargaining position which would be 'firm, yet tentative' before consultation began.[12]

In further developing the idea of a piloting group mechanism, Jordan claimed that independence from DIAND was necessary because the department was occupied with on-going programs, and if DIAND were to become involved, it would inevitably defend past department policies.[13] He further argued that a new 'framework' for delivering the policy would redirect Indian thinking toward new agencies in government, thus launching the implementation process in the right direction. For this same reason he recommended the immediate transfer of DIAND's federal programs, such as cultural affairs, manpower, and economic development out of Indian Affairs to the appropriate federal departments.[14]

The piloting group, composed of well-respected figures in the federal government and the Indian population, would report to the minister of Indian Affairs through its own director at the deputy ministerial level.[15] With the concurrence of the minister, the group's recommendations would ultimately go to the cabinet for consideration. The timetable, longer than the one Andras had envisioned, reflected Jordan's scepticism about the efficacy of social change programs, and the rate of social change expected of Indians and the public. The first year would see the policy announced and the piloting group established to interpret the policy to the public. During the next three to five years the consultations and negotiations between the two levels of government and the Indians would be completed and the transitional policies determined. The final stage would cover the next twenty to thirty years, during which federal financial support to the provinces for transitional programs for Indians would decrease and eventually end. In short, policy development and negotiation would require a five-year period and the full implementation would take a generation. Jordan was far more critical than the old activists of the assumptions that programs could be mounted to facilitate Indian adaptations. He drew attention to the limited track record of governments in alleviating problems of marginality and underprivilege, concluding that there was little to inspire Indians to believe such change was possible and to encourage them to abandon their traditional privileges:

What has been done in comprehensive (FRED-type) socio-economic planning is not readily visible to the majority of Indian communities. Indians are not likely to take very enthusiastically to the eventual repeal of the Indian Act and dismantlement of the Department of Indian Affairs. (Better a devil you know than one you don't). Being treated like other Canadians is not a very positive concept for them: a good many 'registered' Indians live next door to Metis ('other Canadians') whose fate is often worse than theirs. Early visibility of the new policy at regional level, through demonstration projects, is therefore highly desirable. Concurrent research capacity of an applied nature is essential to allow the groups interacting to learn as they go along.[16]

Equally important to him was the involvement of Indians themselves, for in his opinion there was a need to build on Indian cultural features which whites could also respect:

An approach to integration which is not imbedded in the Indian cultural stream which is foreign to Indian ethics or which purports to do for them rather than with them is bound to flounder. The strategy for implementation should therefore systematically build upon Indian socio-cultural traits which majority society sees positively and refrain from doing anything about those which may, prima facie, appear to be negative. This requires that responsible Indian leadership be given status and power and implies that the federal authority is prepared to further define its policy of cultural diversity as a positive force.[17]

Theoretically, by the end of a generation, Indians would have achieved equality of opportunity, but this expectation bothered Jordan because it rested on certain unrealistic assumptions about the practical rate of socio-cultural change among Indians. Even if Indians could change that rapidly, he doubted there was any method for determining if a state of equal opportunity had been achieved by Indians, or by anyone else for that matter.

In his general approach, Jordan was much more sensitive to the aspect of social change among both the general public and the Indians than the previous activists had been. More significantly, he was worried about the post-termination monitoring process, and wanted to ensure that Indians were not left in an administrative vacuum. One of the major functions of the piloting group would be a sustained monitoring activity, involving the assessment and improvement of social development programs. The old guard members of the core group had influenced his thinking to the extent that he was less convinced than the old activists that Indians would trade off their rights for transitional programs; hence his heavier emphasis on social development programs and Indian participation. Jordan believed that Indians must be involved at the outset in shaping the policy and interpreting it in ways that were acceptable to them; that the ultimate success of the policy depended on changing the attitudes of both Indians and the general public, and for this reason the communications component of the piloting group was more important than the substantive issues of treaties and claims.

Jordan's overall approach resembled the recommendations in the Brophy and Aberle study, which he had summarized for members of the task force. His analysis of the Indian problem was invariably cast in terms of Indian communities and the wider society, not in terms of individuals and the government, as Chrétien, Davey, and MacDonald had argued. Their analysis, more firmly in the liberal mould, saw development in terms of economic capital, whereas Jordan's approach was that of a social analyst, viewing development in a holistic socio-economic framework.

Jordan's relations with the old guard were easy, and even though there were many areas of disagreement between them, there was also mutual respect. In one important aspect of their discussions there was also mutual agreement: that the notion of a piloting group was reasonable, given the Indians' strong distrust of the department. As one of the old guard commented: 'We didn't have any objections at the time. It had some merit because of the very nature of the proposal. At that particular time there was quite a bit of hostility to the department. Hostility in the sense of Indians seeing the department as overbearing and paternalistic – but mainly overbearing I guess.'

In all, the idea of a piloting group had many features to commend it. It would bypass the distrusted department and reduce any chance of prejudice from this source in delivering the policy. It was compatible with Trudeau's notion of participatory democracy, and it was flexible in terms of the promised second round of consultations with Indians. Furthermore, it lent itself easily to the White Paper procedure, and by focusing on participation, it avoided issues such as special rights which might arouse Indian opposition to the policy. The core group, including the old guard members, were quite optimistic that the deputy ministers' group would accept this proposal.

The issue of the timing of termination

The final issue for debate in the core group centred on the timing of the termination of special federal services to Indians. Discussions focused on whether there should be an abrupt severing of Indians from the department or whether there should be a slow withdrawal. This question was closely related to the matter of making the policy a credible statement by linking the department's demise to a specific date in the new policy. A credible statement would convince Indians and the public that the department would, in fact, be dismantled. MacDonald feared that if a time were not specified in the policy statement, the public and the Indians would not believe it would be done. As a result, the department's position was to be precise about the time, and, like its February proposals for three years, make the phasing out process of short duration. However, the new activists did not believe the department would 'self-destruct,' and they felt that a specific date would become a negative point of fixation for Indians, causing them to dwell on what they were losing instead of directing them to the future.

In his recommendations to the deputy ministers' group, Jordan stressed the advantages of leaving a termination date out of the policy statement, and encouraged the more open-ended, flexible approach to developing the policy that the piloting group could offer. He further urged them to avoid any negative aspects of the policy in its public statements, such as termination of special rights, but instead to emphasize the process of policy formulation.

The basic recommendations of the core group were finished by mid-April, and their overall tone was clearly activist. The key mechanism for implementation was the piloting group through which government-Indian negotiations would take place, resulting in a mutually acceptable policy. The informality of the core group had resulted in some softening of positions among its members, and although they felt the deputy ministers' group would find their proposals acceptable, they doubted that MacDonald would accept them.

TASK FORCE DECISIONS

Six weeks after the task force was established, the core group sought comment and guidance on its proposals from the deputy ministers' committee. The full task force convened on 17 April, and after weighing the pros and cons of the core group's proposals, the deputy ministers were able to agree on the following issues:

1/ claims should be finally settled;
2/ enabling legislation will be needed for the immediate transfer of land title to Indians;
3/ the Indian Act and the section in the BNA Act dealing with Indians should be gradually repealed;
4/ consultations and negotiations should occur between Indians, the federal and the provincial governments on transferring programs;
5/ Indian communities should receive socio-economic and cultural development programs;
6/ a greater financial commitment by the federal government for Indians will be needed for the next 30 years;
7/ both the white community and Indians should be the target of a 'sustained communication effort';
8/ that vested interests of both Indians and whites will be affected by the policy and that for everyone involved it will be 'a painful exercise.'[18]

Beyond these points, however, the deputy ministers' group was unable to agree.[19] MacDonald's opposition to the notion of a piloting group which would by-pass DIAND jurisdiction had been known for some time, and at the session he forcefully defended the formal interests of the department. MacDonald maintained first that DIAND must implement the new policy which, secondly, must recognize Indian claims if Indians were to receive the policy positively. Despite his opposition, there was considerable support among other deputy ministers for the notion of a piloting group. Jordan's White Paper, a rough draft that emphasized the *process* of policy-building by a piloting group, was apparently found acceptable enough to the group that he was asked to polish it before submitting it to the cabinet committee. He was also asked to refine his arguments so the ministers were left with options in each of the three areas that the core group had wrestled with for several weeks; namely; Indian claims, the mechanism for implementing the policy, and the timing of transferring DIAND programs to other federal departments.[20]

The activists and the old guard in DIAND had expected MacDonald to oppose the notion of a piloting group. Even some of the old guard who were not members of the task force supported the idea of a piloting group, although they still held firm on specific claims settlement. However, the activists were reasonably encouraged with the outcome of the meeting and were optimistic that the piloting group approach would be sanctioned by the ministers at the cabinet committee meeting in two weeks time. At that point the finance group's recommendations would be completed, and the whole task force report would be delivered.

THE FINANCE GROUP

The finance group's job was to propose a formula for federal-provincial cost-sharing agreements which would encourage provincial compliance with the new policy. Federal-provincial relations were in a particularly precarious state as the provinces, led by Quebec in the 1960s, were demanding more financial autonomy from the federal government, especially in areas constitutionally mandated to them (Simeon 1972). The larger question of federal-provincial relations applied directly to Indian policy because the majority of services provided Indians by DIAND were constitutionally mandated to the provinces and the new policy required the provinces to pick up these services in the future.

When the finance group made its final report to the task force, there remained certain inconsistencies which bothered its members. One was particularly troublesome: what assurance was there that Indians would receive similar treatment to that of other citizens unless the funds going to the provinces were earmarked as Indian funds?[21] If Indians were identified in the transfer payments to the provinces, this identification in itself would be discriminatory and inconsistent with the new policy objective; other provincial citizens were not identified by their ethnic affiliation in administrative arrangements. This problem was left unresolved by the finance group which turned to the more pragmatic and politically sensitive job of developing proposals for the federal government's use in negotiating with the provinces.

Because the overriding concern of the finance group was how to encourage the provinces to extend their services to Indians, they began their work by listing reasons why the provinces might reject the new policy:

1/ provincial belief that Indians fall exclusively within the jurisdiction of the federal government;

2/ provincial fear that their treasuries will have to carry a substantial cost if Indians do not become educated and integrated into the mainstream of Canadian society;

3/ general provincial concern that, as in any joint federal-provincial program, the federal government might withdraw its support when expenditures were still at a high level;

4/ provincial reluctance to assume programs for Indians which they do not provide their other citizens;

5/ provincial difficulty and perhaps 'embarrassment' when their services do not favourably compare to some of those granted Indians under special DIAND programs (e.g. housing subsidies, grants for physical facilities in communities such as sewers and water systems, and two year kindergartens);

6/ provincial concern as 'a matter of principle' that Indians do not pay either land tax or income tax when resident on reserves;

7/ provincial difficulty in persuading local municipalities to provide services to Indians if Indians are not required to pay local taxes.[22]

Against these specific concerns was the more general one that the BNA Act provision for Indians meant that the federal government, as one official phrased it, could not simply 'schuck off Indians onto the provinces.' Negotiations would be required, occurring in the increasingly uneasy climate of federal-provincial relations. It was also recognized that even though the poorer provinces would be hardpressed to provide these services to Indians, Indians should not be shortchanged because of this fact.

These considerations, together with the anticipated provincial reluctance to accept the policy, produced what one member called a 'political' decision: that the federal government should make a 'generous offer' to the provinces so they would not reject the policy on purely financial grounds. This proposal, running counter to the federal government's general desire to reduce its expenditures, was also designed to ensure that provinces had sufficient funds to provide Indians with the same level of services granted other citizens in the provinces.

Recognizing that many of the services currently provided Indians were substandard, the finance group argued that a transitional period of enriched programs, administered by the provinces, was required to bring Indian communities in line with provincial standards.[23] If Indians were not granted the same services as other citizens in the areas of health, education, and welfare, this deprivation would become 'readily apparent,' presumably providing evidence of provincial non-compliance. If these discrepancies became too great, it was expected that Indians would organize to put pressure on the proper provincial authorities to improve the services.[24]

On the basis of their assessment of likely provincial resistance, the finance group provided specific recommendations for the government's preparation for provincial negotiations. Since the provinces would be worried about the financial burden, the federal government must be prepared to make long-term fixed agreements, probably in the range of twenty to thirty years. These agreements should indicate what costs could be expected by the provinces up to the 'normalization' period when the federal government would end its contributions on the basis of 'Indianness.' From that point on Indians should be included in the regular provincial programs, or in any future federal-provincial agreements as normal provincial citizens.[25] For the western provinces whose proportion of Indians was higher in relation to the total population and which were likely to insist on 100 per cent federal contributions, the need for clarity on the long-range implications of the transfer was considered particularly important. Here the negotiations might have to include the Metis.

The finance group believed the federal government should be prepared to fund the programs to the full amount (100 per cent) for at least the early part, possibly ten years, of the transitional thirty-year period, even though this funding departed from the normal 50 per cent federal contribution. This open-handed interpretation of cost-sharing was viewed as particularly necessary to cover the higher costs of the crucial transitional programs for Indians. Consequently, in recommending a timetable for the transfers, the finance group suggested that 'a neat package might be ten years of escalating federal compensation, ten years of stablized amounts, and ten years for phasing-out.'[26]

Although many other problems remained to be worked out by the group, two were particularly difficult. One was determining the current standard of programs in the many provinces, and the second was the problem of monitoring the transfer to guarantee that Indians would in fact receive comparable services. The range of standards and structures of programs among, and even within, provinces was extensive. When the full range of services theoretically requiring such evaluation was considered (e.g. housing, education, health, social welfare, sewer and water systems, road construction, and local government), the task became monumental. To overcome the pre-termination evaluation and post-termination monitoring problems, the finance group recommended against a uniform or blanket federal-provincial agreement on the transfer of funds. Instead it advised that bilateral agreements be made between the federal government and each province to allow for flexibility. Services would be monitored by requiring each province to 'pledge' provision of services to Indians in the same manner it provided its other citizens. Auditing of the financial statements would provide further control on the expenditures made by the provinces.[27]

In keeping with its general recommendations, the finance group worked out a rough formula for the transfer of funds to the provinces.[28] A financial base line, or 'lump sum amount,' derived by obtaining the actual cost of federal services (DIAND and the Department of Health and Welfare) to Indians in each province in 1969/70, would be supplemented by a 'growth factor' of possibly 9 to 10 per cent a year. The growth factor, designed to cover population increase, and price and cost changes, was to be bilaterally negotiated with the provinces.

After the first ten year's expenditures were calculated and compared with the estimates in the department's five-year forecast (October 1968), it became evident that it would be to the federal government's advantage financially to phase out its Indian administration. The department had forecast a more costly program with its 'enriched services' than the finance group had for its 'escalating' period of financing, even when health and welfare costs were included (see Table 7).

In addition to other more technical aspects of the transfer, the finance group recommended against the development of provincial departments of Indian Affairs. Instead, it suggested that the point of contact between the federal government and the provinces, whose various departments would be advancing claims on the federal treasury, should be the provincial treasuries.

In general, the finance group's recommendations were designed to provide guidelines for federal-provincial negotiations which would maximize the chances of provincial compliance with the new policy. Its generous formula was in sharp contrast to the recommendations Davey had made in mid-January when he favoured a harder line with the provinces, arguing that 'we should be most careful about appearing to be over-

TABLE 7 Cost forecasts for Indian programs

Year	DIAND five-year forecast (millions)	Finance group's ten-year forecast[†] (millions)
1969/70	269.9	189.9
1970/71	329.4	208.9
1971/72	350.8	229.8
1972/73	364.6	252.8
1973/74	377.3	278.1
1974/75	–	305.9
1975/76	–	336.5
1976/77	–	370.2
1977/78	–	407.2
1978/79	–	447.9
1979/80	–	492.7
Five-year total	1.6 billion	1.1 billion
Ten-year total	–	3.5 billion

* From DIAND's five-year program forecast, 30 October 1968.
† From finance group's report, 5 May 1969. These figures include the cost of both DIAND and DNH&W programs.

generous in this instance,' because the provinces must accept the fact that Indians are provincial citizens.[29] However, MacDonald agreed with the finance group's generous recommendations because he hoped to avoid provincial rejection of the policy on purely financial grounds.

The Brophy and Aberle study, which the task force was to consult, emphasized the need to guarantee that Indians received adequate services after termination. It recommended detailed pre-termination planning and post-termination monitoring of programs to achieve this end, but the finance group found this difficult to cope with. In the end, implementation of its recommendations could not guarantee that Indians would receive services similar to those granted other provincial citizens. The conclusion reached by the finance group was that if the provinces disregarded their pledges and if audits indicated that funds were not going to Indians, Indians would have to pressure the proper provincial authorities to ensure provision of comparable services.

The finance group did not directly address the question of what the federal government could or would do if the provinces would not comply with their pledges. This problem was part of the much larger one of provincial compliance with federal-provincial agreements, but recognition of this fact would not benefit Indians, nor would it provide any assurance that the policy objective of non-discrimination could in fact be implemented.

One, more general, observation on the economic considerations of the policy is worth making. The policy-making exercise was not burdened by a concern about the financial costs of the policy. Although the open-endedness of land claims settlements concerned officials, the basic opposition to a claims commission was not funds. The policy-makers were ready to accept high economic costs in implementing the general policy if they felt this would result in enhancing compliance with the policy.

In summary, the task force, through weeks of intensive work, rationalized the new policy and prepared a plan for its implementation. Despite the department's opposition to the task force, DIAND's old guard officials generally accepted the basic proposal for a piloting group, although they still strongly supported a special claims settlement. In its general approach, the task force report derived squarely from the activist ideology: in fact a more elaborate statement of this ideology evolved through Jordan's management of the rationalization process. The piloting group proposal, predictably opposed by MacDonald because it bypassed DIAND's jurisdiction, had many features to commend it, including its flexibility, given the promised second round of consultations with Indians, and its compatibility with Trudeau's notion of participatory democracy. For these and other reasons, Jordan and many other officials in the task force were quite optimistic that the cabinet ministers would accept the basic notion of a piloting group and greater Indian participation in the policy process.

The spring had been a season for rationalizing the policy. It began with the department's determination to announce its own version of the policy in late February, but quickly changed direction at the cabinet's insistence that the policy be rationalized and systematically planned by a PCO-based task force. March and April saw the task force examine the issues and inconsistencies in considerable detail, with a view to determining the policy's implications for both Indians and the government. By late April the task force's proposals were completed, and were to be polished by Jordan for presentation to the cabinet in early May. For the activists the spring had been an encouraging and productive season, but for the department it had been a time for mixed feelings.

CHAPTER SIX

Early summer:
a time for
final decisions

In early May the momentum on Indian policy quickened as the government tried to complete its task before Parliament recessed in June. While Jordan was refining the task force proposals, over fifty Indian delegates came to Ottawa for the final Indian Act consultation meeting. The anachronism of the meeting was sensed only by the policy-makers, for the public and the Indian delegates were not aware of how far the government had already gone in formulating the new policy. Whether the consultations would change the direction of government thinking at this late date was a moot point.

THE LAST CONSULTATION MEETING

The National Conference on the Indian Act, the last meeting in the first round of consultations, convened on 28 April in Ottawa. This meeting was the culmination of the regional consultations begun in July 1968, but more significantly it was the first national conference in Canadian history to bring together Indian representatives from every region of Canada. Many of the representatives were the founders of the National Indian Brotherhood. Walter Deiter, the first president of the NIB, was absent because of a family death and so George Manuel, who took over the leadership in 1970, presided over the sessions.[1] At this time the brotherhood was largely a hope; its organization had yet to take shape and its Ottawa office would not be established until the summer. Although some conference delegates were critical of the NIB as a representative body, most looked to the future, seeing the potential in the NIB as a vehicle for achieving consensus and for lobbying in Ottawa.[2]

Senior officials from DIAND did not attend the meetings; instead the department provided rapporteurs who taped the proceedings and later published a verbatim report and a shorter summary of the deliberations.[3] Several Indian delegations had brought their own lawyers, at least one of whom played an important role in formulating the conference's resolutions; the content of the resolutions came from the delegates.

Chrétien opened the conference with a brief speech on the 'bold new initiatives' he intended to take in the new policy, and although this was a preview of the White Paper, his statements were so diffuse the delegates could not have discerned this.[4] Andras was also present at the opening session, after which they both withdrew from the next four days of meetings, leaving the delegates to discuss matters among themselves. Chrétien said he would return if asked. Andras, whose role in Indian policy was nearing completion, did not address the session. Discussions about his reassignment had been going on for a few months, and in the week following the conference he was given a new portfolio in housing, filling the vacancy created by Paul Hellyer's resignation from cabinet.[5]

After solving several procedural issues, the delegates rapidly focused on the long-standing discrepancies between the government and themselves on the meaning of their special rights, and they wanted the necessary resources from government to undertake research on this matter. In short, they wanted to define their own rights, free of government interpretations and any 'mechanisms' which Chrétien might propose.[6] Many delegates saw the exercise as the 'next stage' in the consultation process in which they would present their own material to the government for the second round of consultations. One delegate described the next stage as the preparation of their own version of *Choosing a Path*, 'only the shoe is on our foot so that we could present it to them [government] with our questionnaire.'[7]

Indian delegates were impatient with the government's stalling on claims and unhappy about the current consultation process which failed to respond to their own priorities. As they had done in December at the Manitoba and Alberta meetings,[8] they again presented Chrétien with a brief stating their own priorities:

It has been made abundantly clear, both by the consultations to date and through Indian meetings throughout the land, that the principal concerns of Indian people center around:

A) recognition of the treaties and the obligations imposed by same

B) recognition of aboriginal rights

C) reconciliation of injustices done by the imposition of restrictions on Indian hunting through the ratification of the Migratory Birds convention and subsequent federal and provincial legislation
D) Claims Commission

It is our opinion that before meaningful consultation on amendments to the Indian Act can take place, these four items must be dealt with and a position of mutual understanding and commitment reached.[9]

Though claims always took precedence over the Indian Act in any Indian agenda, the delegates now moved one step further when they asked the government for funds to establish a National Committee on Indian Rights and Treaties to research an exhaustive list of rights. This research would provide the basis for further negotiations with the government. The conference decision read as follows:

Resolution: To enable the Indian people of Canada to establish its own destiny and priorities.

1. Be it resolved that a National Committee, composed of the representatives of province or region at this meeting be established to effect the following purposes:
   −a) investigate the rights, including treaty, aboriginal, acquired, residual, and human rights of the Indian people of Canada;
   −b) formulate a draft an [sic] Indian Act for presentation to this delegation, reassembled as a whole, at a date to be specified; and
   −c) research, the rights of Indian people generally with special reference to treaty rights, hunting rights, fishing rights and rights to medical, educational and local government services, foreshore and riparian rights, forest and timber rights, land, mineral and petroleum rights.[10]

The resolution, after later attempts to refine it, was not clear on the relationship between the new National Committee and the NIB.[11] Even though Chrétien was concerned with this omission when he was asked to support the request, in the end he agreed to meet with the new executive at a later date to discuss the financial requirements for 'future consultations.'[12] The delegates were delighted with Chrétien's reply, and Cardinal welcomed the response as an indication of a new relationship between government and Indians: 'We are happy with the recognition of yourself that we in this meeting have entered into what you call a new era. Because for the first time our people as a whole are proposing to work with you on a basis of partnership rather than on a basis of directives from your officials. Our delegation is extremely pleased that this has occurred.'[13]

This was the high point of the meeting, but as Colin Tatz noted in his analysis of the event, Indian spokesmen were highly gratified by the conference because unity had been achieved among the Indian delegates, creating a strong sense of common purpose.[14] The conference ended on an even more optimistic note when the press described the meeting as a significant breakthrough in Indian-government relations and a 'triumph' for Indians.[15] One account viewed Chrétien's remarks as evidence that Indian, not government, priorities would shape the new policy.[16]

Thus, despite criticism of the regional consultations by Indians, the final national conference concluded on an encouraging note. In a very real sense the conference was the Indian equivalent of the Priorities and Planning Committee, and it had unmistakably reaffirmed Indian priorities for special rights and participation. The meeting had demonstrated Indians' hope that the authoritarian, paternalistic approach to policy-making had been abandoned in favour of a constructive partnership between them and the government.

Indeed, as the cabinet committee meeting approached, there was a good deal of optimism, publicly among Indians and the press, and privately among the activists in the task force.

THE TASK FORCE REPORT

By the time the conference ended, Jordan had completed the task force report. In keeping with the deputy ministers' request, he examined the three sensitive areas which had caused problems in the core group – Indian claims, the method of policy implementation, and the timetable for transferring DIAND programs to other federal departments – and each was presented as a set of options for the ministers to consider.

On the question of handling Indian claims, three options were put forward: 1/to establish an Indian Claims Commission which recognized special claims as Chrétien had proposed; 2/to commute all claims in a generalized way to socio-economic development programs under the new policy as Andras had proposed; 3/to announce special negotiations between Indians and the government which would determine ways to approach claims settlement.[17]

Option one was clearly the department's preference. Option two, the activists' choice, was described by Jordan as 'renegotiating the past' in a global sense; instead of the government's negotiating with specific bands or treaty groups to settle their individual claims, a general commutation would take place without the recognition of specific grievances, compensation taking the form of development programs. In this sense 'all the past is renegotiable,' but in global, not specific, terms. Specific 'wrongs' would be addressed by generalized 'rights.' Department officers disagreed with this proposition, for as one of them argued, 'You couldn't deal with claims on a basis of economic need when you were righting a wrong.' They also felt Indians would reject such generalized compensation because it failed to recognize the historical depth and regional nature of the grievances.

Option three, calling for special negotiations, was a compromise option favoured by the activists if their first choice were not accepted. As one official remarked, 'It left the door on claims,' giving the ministers the opportunity to keep the issue of settlement alive but not prominent in the new policy.

On the central issue of how the policy was to be implemented, two options were put forward: the conventional departmental implementation, and the unorthodox method involving the piloting group or special secretariat, which was generally favoured by the task force. In Jordan's draft of the White Paper, the piloting group's functions were clearly outlined:

The Government will establish a Coordinating Secretariat reporting to the chairman of a special Cabinet committee. It will have the following responsibilities:
(a) It will assist the Government in the further development of policy, particularly with regard to settling historical claims.
(b) During transitional periods it must function as an ombudsman to protect the rights of the Indian people against intentional or inadvertent harm.
(c) It will evaluate the effect of change.
(d) It will be a communications centre through which all interested parties may channel their enquiries and receive information about changes.
(e) It will be a body for consultation and negotiation with Indians, with the provinces and with interested citizens' organizations.
(f) The Secretariat will provide for liaison with other federal departments. It will guide agencies in extending their activities to include Indian interests. It will also lead a decentralization of Indian Affairs activities to appropriate federal departments and ensure that such change occur with no loss of services.[18]

Even though some of the old guard had accepted the notion of a piloting group, but not its role in settling Indian claims, the department's official opposition remained firm. The divergent approaches to policy were most striking in the drafts of the White Paper prepared separately by the department and by the task force. The basic principles underlying each

TABLE 8 A comparison of the drafts of the White Paper principles underlying the new policy

Activists' Draft [late March 1969]	Department's Draft [late April 1969]	White Paper [25 June 1969]
What should be the principles of the new policy? Though the consultation meetings have only begun, principles which should govern the direction of new policy have become apparent. These include:	The Government believes that new policies must be based on the following principles:	The Government believes that the framework within which individual Indians and bands could achieve full participation requires:
(a) Full participation of the Indian people in the resolution of these problems.	(1) The Indian people have the right to full and equal participation in the social, economic and political life of Canada	(1) that the legislative and constitutional bases of discrimination be removed;
(b) Recognition of the cultural importance and the diversity of Indian peoples as a major building block in the Canadian mosaic.	(2) Legislative and constitutional bases for discriminatory treatment must be removed.	(2) that there be positive recognition by everyone of the unique contribution of Indian culture to Canadian life;
(c) A policy of non-discrimination which will have the result ultimately of extinguishing all special arrangements for the Indian people.	(3) There must be recognition of the importance of the Indian heritage and its cultural diversity in the Canadian mosaic.	(3) that services come through the same channels and from the same government agencies for all Canadians;
(d) Consultation must grow between the bodies which are concerned – provincial, Indian, and other federal organizations.	(4) Full participation will only follow redress of legitimate grievance.	(4) that those who are furthest behind be helped most;
	(5) Agreements must be honoured until they have been fulfilled.	(5) that lawful obligations be recognized;
	(6) Indian people should be free, as are all others, to control their own property.	(6) that control of Indian lands be transferred to the Indian people.
	(7) Services should be available to all Canadians on an equitable basis and ought not to flow from separate agencies established to serve separate ethnic groups.	
	(8) Those who are furthest behind in material things must have enriched services to help them catch up.	

approach differed significantly, revealing the disagreements over the firm or flexible approach and over the past or future time orientation (see Table 8). Worried that Indians would oppose the loss of their historic rights, the department's drafts were long explanations of how past policies had been counterproductive and why they should be abandoned for a new future.[19] The policy was emphatically presented, leaving no doubt that its implementation was all that remained. Since the department was to implement the policy, there was no mention of the piloting group. A late-April draft of the White Paper was submitted by the department to the cabinet committee, along with the task force's report favouring the policy objective of equality but a flexible implementation.

On the third issue, the timing of the transfer of DIAND programs to other federal departments, the task force report offered two options: an immediate transfer, which the activists preferred because it would reinforce the intent of the policy, and a deferred transfer, which the department favoured. This issue, not as contentious as the others, tended to be overridden by the question of whether the White Paper should specify a particular date for the department's dissolution, as MacDonald preferred, or whether a date should not be specified with emphasis instead on the process of consultation, as Jordan and the other activists wanted.

In its final form, the task force report was a low-key rationalization of the policy that favoured the activist approach and supported the generous formula for federal-provincial agreements which the finance group had proposed. Specific dates and deadlines were to be avoided, with the thrust of the White Paper on the process of policy-making through the piloting group.

The day before the task force report went before the Cabinet Committee on Priorities and Planning (7 May 1969), the PMO called for a briefing of the implications on the policy of the final Indian Act consultation meeting. The conference resolutions had clearly supported the department's advocacy for claims settlement; furthermore, a few days earlier, Chrétien indicated in the Commons that a claims commission would probably be a part of the new policy.[20] But the activists in the PCO downplayed this aspect of the conference, and stressed instead the new partnership that Cardinal and other delegates expressed a hope for at the end of the session. This interpretation lent support to the piloting group recommendation on which the PCO had pinned all their hopes for the new policy. Consequently in briefing the prime minister, the PCO predicted no difficulties with the policy if it met the expectations of a new government-Indian relationship and if the policy were announced in June, as promised. The briefing memo read:

In considering the implications of the meeting held last week on the policy statement which the Government is preparing, it would appear that:

(a) the general thrust of the government position is receivable by the Indian
leadership;

(b) the policy statement will have to be carefully worked out on rights, lands and
claims – but need not embody a definitive statement on a Claims Commission;

(c) an ongoing national committee undertaking research into the field of rights
will quickly become obnoxious unless the discourse which has begun between
Indian groups and the government last week can be carried on, in action
terms, at regional and sub-regional levels;

(d) there could be serious difficulty if the oft-repeated commitment to a policy
statement in June is not met and if the combination of ingredients in the
pronouncement belies the partnership expectations which have been aroused;

(e) the creation of an effective Indian lobby such as recommended by the Conference last week – if it can be financed jointly by government and private
sources – might reduce the need for a Coordinating Secretariat to implement
the new policy. A combination of the two measures would be the ideal ...[21]

The PCO brief showed that the activists had made a rather remarkable
interpretation of the last consultation meeting and, as we shall see, seriously underestimated the strength of Indian determination to maintain
their special rights. The closest approximation of the Indian option in the
task force report sent to the cabinet committee would have been a claims
commission combined with a special piloting group. Indeed, scope for
recognizing any part of the Indian option was becoming narrower and
narrower.

DECISIONS ON THE TASK FORCE

The meeting of the Cabinet Committee on Priorities and Planning on 8
May was a major turning point in Indian policy. In normal fashion it was
chaired by the prime minister, but it was far more explosive than usual.
Task force officials, including Jordan, were present to discuss their report,
and Chrétien and MacDonald represented the department. Other officials
and ministers attended, including Andras, although much to the regret of
western Indian spokesmen, Andras had just been assigned to housing.[22]

The meeting, described by officials as 'a real showdown,' was a major
confrontation between the two alignments, and predictably the most
heated debate centred on the task force proposal for a piloting group.[23]
According to officials, Chrétien and MacDonald adamantly refused to

accept the proposal, considering it an affront to the department. They emphatically defended the department's right to implement policy, and persevered in an effort to keep some semblance of a claims commission in the new policy. In contrast, the task force proposal, lacking ministerial support, or advocacy as forceful as MacDonald's, fared poorly. As the session progressed, all hopes of accepting the piloting group proposal vanished.

On the question of Indian claims, the cabinet committee decided in favour of a compromise position put forward by MacDonald: to retain a claims settlement component in the new policy by establishing a mini-royal commission on Indian grievances.

Indian grievances related to legal or quasi-legal claims or breaches of Indian Treaties should be considered by a commissioner for Indian grievances, appointed under Part II of the Inquiries Act. The commissioner would not make awards or adjudicate claims, but he would hear Indian grievances and engage in discussions with Indian groups on possible solutions in order to make recommendations to the government on what action would be appropriate.

The terms of reference of the commissioner would be prepared by the Department of Indian Affairs and Northern Administration for consideration by the Interdepartmental Committee on Indian policy; and by the Cabinet Committee on Priorities and Planning.[24]

This alternative was MacDonald's 'fall-back' position. As one department officer described the decision, it 'was, in essence, to defer, to have a study, and to have a commissioner do it.'

This proposal would produce an advisory commission that lacked adjudicatory and award-making powers, since the commissioner was merely empowered to discuss grievances with Indians and recommend suitable action to the government. As a compromise it avoided giving a claims commission a focal position in the new policy, but, at the same time, it indicated that the government was not dispensing with the idea entirely. As a step in the evolution of a claims commission, it was regressive in that it took the decision back to 1962 when the government first proposed an advisory commission for settling claims. The decision was clearly not intended to meet the issue squarely and definitively, but to the extent that claims would even be acknowledged by a weak-mandated commissioner, it satisfied the department and predictably disappointed the activists. MacDonald had succeeded in keeping the notion alive.

When it came to the most contentious issue on the agenda, whether the department or the piloting group should implement the policy, the cabinet committee took the conventional approach, deciding that the department should implement the White Paper.[25] Although the notion of a piloting group had many features to commend its use, it did not embody the traditional principle that a minister is responsible for implementing policies in his portfolio.

On closer examination, the piloting group had many of the characteristics of Andras' role as 'policy minister' which had been so troublesome to the department. Direct and continuous contact with the public in shaping the policy would have been made by the piloting group, not by the minister nor the deputy minister. The opportunity would have existed for the piloting group to foster certain expectations among the public, intentionally or not, about what action the government should or might take in the future. A minister then might have been confronted with certain proposals, not of his own making or choice, and been pressured into agreeing to these positions or forced to defend his rejection. In addition, the piloting group would have had the power only to recommend policy directions to the minister and the cabinet, not the power to implement these recommendations. It would have been the minister, in the end, who would have been responsible for the actions of the piloting group. The effect, and the intent, of the piloting group would have been the removal of policy interpretation from the minister and the department, but not the responsibility for the results of that interpretation.

The approval of the piloting group approach could have resulted in a replay of Andras' role, which embodied the negative aspects of free-lance opinion-setting and lack of accountability.[26] Chrétien and MacDonald were aware of these aspects and argued against the piloting group.[27] In the end the traditional principle of departmental implementation proved stronger than the desire of the Trudeau government to mount innovative procedures. Consequently, the task force recommendation was rejected and the department was asked to prepare a plan for implementing the policy.

The rejection of the piloting group proposal ended the activists' hopes that the policy process would involve Indians through the White Paper. They also failed to get cabinet approval for their proposal that federal-level programs currently operated by DIAND should be transferred within one year to other federal departments. The cabinet committee decided to support the department's preference of delayed transferral because the delay avoided assuming the policy's acceptance by Indians and the provinces.[28]

The policy's reception by the public was a major concern at the meeting, but as the policy now stood, it contained neither of the conditions each alignment considered imperative if the policy were to be accepted by Indians. The cabinet committee decided that the 'tone' and the 'thrust' of final policy statement should not prejudge its acceptance by either the Indians or the provinces,[29] and so the department was asked to revise its draft of the White Paper, changing its assertive and directive tone to one more in keeping with 'a proposal' than a firm and final statement. This decision, reflecting uncertainty about the policy's reception, suited the activists, but it was based more on winning public acceptance rather than on a desire to undertake a policy process which the activists had promoted.

The cabinet committee's final decision was to forward the recommendations of the finance group for transferring funds to the provinces to the Cabinet Committee on Economic Policy and Programmes, where the department's recommendation for a $50 million dollar development fund could also be assessed.[30]

The activists' struggle to establish Indian participation in the policy process ended with their failure to get ministerial compliance for the piloting group. They saw the meeting as a repudiation of the task force and the open-policy approach. Some of them recall a strong sense of defeat after witnessing or learning of the decisions, and a few were extremely bitter over the outcome. One claimed that the White Paper was a department statement that 'could have been written eight months ago by IAB [Indian Affairs Branch].' Another felt the merits of their approach had not been seriously considered by the cabinet committee:

It would have worked too, if the piloting group had been allowed to take the policy to the public. There was no hope for it if the department got ahold of it – which it did. It got shot down without a hearing. Our group wanted to bridge the gap between Indians and whites and cut down the distrust and misinformation. But it proved that the department was very skilled at survival.

Rudnicki summed up his feelings when he said, 'The countervailing influences [are] now almost eliminated ... a sense of battle lost.' In his view the PCO had been 'battered and bruised' after its encounter with the department, and more particularly with MacDonald.

The activists were now certain that the policy would not get Indian compliance because of the limited participation for Indians in any implementation scheme the department might devise. For them, the cabinet's decision ended any realistic hope of Indian involvement. In hindsight, many activists felt their approach was idealistic because the government was 'far more closed and formal' than was evident to them at that time.

One claimed that 'the open policy process was anathema to Trudeau.' They believed their chances of enhancing public participation were seriously weakened because there had been no effective ministerial support for their ideas. Despite the government rhetoric of the day, they tended to agree that the policy-making process had changed very little and that the department's retention of policy control unduly compartmentalized policies and their implementation. But the climate of the times had been conducive – perhaps illusive – to the expectation that this rigidity could be changed.

Andras, also displeased with the outcome of the meeting, wrote the prime minister a few weeks later expressing serious reservations about the direction Indian policy had taken.[31] He hoped the decisions could be reconsidered before final cabinet approval. Andras believed the proposal to appoint an Indian claims commissioner was inconsistent with the objective of a non-discriminatory policy and a further move to treat Indians as a separate ethnic group. Given that the idea of a commissioner was a delay tactic, he expected the public would react negatively, and if it were intended as a measure to open the door for large claims settlements, he felt it was misguided because it assumed that claims could be separately treated from the broader issues of Indian policy. Whatever the intention for a commissioner, Andras thought the terms of reference were far too narrow and would preclude meaningful dialogue with Indians.

Furthermore, he considered the retention of federal-level services by DIAND to be ill-advised because it appeared to reaffirm the need for a special department for Indians. Since the policy was not conducive to Indian participation, he thought it should not be approved by cabinet simply because it was the sole policy available. He recommended that the Indian claims commissioner be replaced by a different commission, tentatively titled 'Indians in Canadian Society,' which could begin intensive consultations with the Indians and the provinces about the total range of needs and roles of the three parties.

Like other activists, Andras saw the new policy as a minor variation of the department's January proposals, and his assessment of it left little doubt that he felt it was an inappropriate and conservative approach to the Indian problem.

Despite Andras' parting comments, cabinet proceeded with the decisions. The preparation of the White Paper and the plan for implementation returned to the department. As a result of this and other decisions, the policy arena again changed its composition in mid-May. Andras' move to a housing portfolio ended the activists' representation at the ministerial level, which, in the end, had not proved compelling enough to defend the activists' proposals. Rudnicki, by then well removed from the policy process, left the PCO during the first week of June, joining Andras in the housing portfolio. The core group in the task force disbanded as the department set up its own drafting group to define the policy statement and devise an implementation plan. The task force's committee of deputy ministers was to continue its review function by commenting on the department's proposals before they went back to the cabinet committee for decisions-making.

As the department began to prepare its implementation plan, a new approach developed that appeared to contradict the activists' views that DIAND would remove Indians from the policy process altogether.

ANOTHER OPEN APPROACH FAILS TO INFLUENCE THE POLICY

While the department was preparing its implementation plan in mid-May, differences among senior DIAND officials on the prospective shape of the new policy became more pronounced.[32] Although there had been a full gamut of opinion, from MacDonald's firm approach to the more compromising one of a few old guard officials, a more radical view now came from Christie (pseudonym), a new 'young blood' official who had joined the Indian-Eskimo program during the department's highly criticized reorganization the previous October. So far he had not participated in the department's deliberations on the new policy. At this point, however, being liked and respected by the old guard, Christie was drawn into the inner circle to assist senior officials in preparing the department's implementation plan.

Although his formal training lay in the natural sciences, he viewed Indian policy from a community development perspective, and his proposals on how Indian policy should be shaped were a thinly veiled critique of the current state of the policy.[33] In his opinion, formal (administrative and legal) equality was not the ultimate goal of the policy. He believed the focus on government paternalism was a red herring, and though deep-rooted dependence of Indians on government existed, it did not have to continue into the future. For Christie the basic issue of the Indian problem was 'the conditions and not the dependence' of Indians, and the appropriate government response should be to improve its social development programs.[34] Consequently, like the activists, he advocated a wide range of social development approaches as a basic component of the new policy.

Of even greater concern to Christie were the probable implications of the policy for Indians. He argued that further research was needed before any services be transferred to the provinces because the consequences of this transfer were at that time poorly understood. He was highly sceptical of the finance group's assumptions that Indians could compete successfully with non-Indians in provincial political systems, particularly because of their minority position in the electorate and their lack of ties to political parties. He was even more concerned than Jordan had been that Indians might find themselves in an administrative vacuum, a federal-provincial no man's land, in which neither government accepted responsibility for their well-being. If the provinces were to default in the transfer of services, he felt the federal government must be prepared to supply the needed assistance.

Given the current shape of the policy, he was convinced Indians would find it unacceptable because it ignored the importance of their 'charter rights.' Citing the Hawthorn study in British Columbia (Hawthorn et al. 1958), he argued that although these rights might seem vague and undefined, the 'related claims are strong and vigorous.'[35] He felt Indians would accept the policy only if 'their charter rights remain unabridged,' and if they could participate in the policy-making process as they had been led to expect. To deny this involvement invited rejection of the policy. Like the activists, he felt the policy should go forward as 'a statement of ultimate objectives' with a flexible implementation, especially in its timing. The policy must be discussed in a direct and meaningful way with Indians prior to any public release. He was unimpressed with the department's official position that Indians were to be consulted after the policy was released; rather, the process should be reversed and the government should be listening to what Indians were saying:

It is a widely accepted view that this Department has made a commitment to consult with Indian people in the process of policy-making. It has just completed a country-wide exercise in this respect, the stated objective of which was to amend the Indian Act. To be told now that the Act is to be repealed, without prior consultation, would seem to be inviting bitter reproach from all sides. This would merely reinforce the view of those who hold that the Departmental consultation is *ex post facto*.

The proposal to make a significant change in policy with a limited choice of action available to the people concerned negates the community development principle that people must be involved in decisions which affect them. To violate that principle, in dealing with Indians in 1969, is inevitably to reduce credibility and to run the serious risk of creating real barriers to acceptance of the policy.

It is essential that implementation of the proposal take these very real and vital human factors into account by extending the period of meaningful consultation and by paying some attention to what is said. To do otherwise will lead the Indian people to conclude that their views and feelings are of no consequence. They would see themselves again relegated to the bottom of the heap, and there would be severe social and psychological consequences to both Indians and non-Indians. The advances of the past few years can very well be undone overnight unless attention is paid to these factors.[36]

Christie's pointed criticisms made in May reflected a refreshing concern that seemed to have evaporated months ago as the policy process became tortured and preoccupied with power struggles. Of all the policy makers, he had come closest to promoting the Indian option, the combination of special rights and participation. Although a few of the old guard felt they had some merit, Christie's proposals did not become the basis for the department's implementation plan.[37] His emphasis on charter rights was incompatible with the policy objective and the climate of opinion in the PMO, and his stress on opening the policy to Indians before its release contradicted the secrecy practices in the department. Furthermore, his ideas did not go beyond the department, so that officials in the task force were unaware of his efforts to open up the policy approach. The department drafts of the White Paper reflected none of his concerns.

POLISHING THE WHITE PAPER

With a few exceptions, the *content* of the draft White Paper by mid-May was similar to the final version, but cabinet required changes to make its *tone* less assertive and confident of a positive reception.[38] However, MacDonald and a few senior officers wanted the statement to be 'firm' in two ways: firm in the sense of being credible, of convincing Indians that the department would in fact phase itself out of existence; and firm in the sense of government commitment to the policy, of conveying the belief that the goal of equality was worthwhile, and that the government was correct in its proposed actions.[39]

Throughout the remainder of May and into early June the department's drafting group worked and reworked the White Paper – as one officer described the process, 'changing the "musts" to "shoulds."' Revising the drafts resulted in the final one in which Indians, not the government, were said to want the changes being proposed. The stylistic changes simply softened the delivery by substituting 'the government proposes ...' for 'the government will ...' A comparison of the drafts in Table 9 illustrates these points.

TABLE 9 Comparison of mid-May and final White Papers

Mid-May draft*	Final White Paper†
The Government has been engaged in a thorough review of its programs for Indians and of the effects of those programs on the present situation of the Indian people. The review has drawn on the knowledge and experience of officers of many departments of government and of consultants in a variety of professional fields. Most significantly, it has drawn on the experience and opinion of Indian leaders who have attended consultation meetings in every part of Canada during the past year.	The Government has reviewed its programs for Indians and has considered the effects of them on the present situation of the Indian people. The review has drawn on extensive consultations with the Indian people, and on the knowledge and experience of many people both in and out of government.
The Government believes that the time is ripe for a change, indeed, the times *demand* a dramatic change. Indians must be freed *now* from the stultifying paternalistic relationship that is kept alive by the Indian Act and by policies of differentiation.	This review was a response to things said by the Indian people at the consultation meetings which began a year ago and culminated in a meeting in Ottawa in April. This review has shown that this is the right time to change long-standing policies. The Indian people have shown their determination that present conditions shall not persist.

* Draft 'Statement of the Government of Canada on Indian Policy, 1969,' prepared by DIAND officials, dated mid-May 1969, pp. 1, 4.
† DIAND (1969: 6).

To convince the public of the department's dissolution, the White Paper proposed a five-year limit, a change from its February proposal of a three-year phase-out period. Some of the activists, sceptical that the department would self-destruct, and anxious to avoid specific dates in the policy, thought the focus of a five-year limit was a calculated move by the department to destroy the policy by eliciting a negative reaction from Indians. One activist referred to it as 'an attempt to subvert the policy, to scuttle the whole idea of it.'

It is interesting to note that the mid-May drafts of the White Paper made no explicit mention of aboriginal rights in the proposal for a claims commissioner. Rights became the topic for the last confrontation.

THE QUESTION OF ABORIGINAL RIGHTS

While the department was refining the policy statement and drafting the terms of reference for a claims commissioner, the question of aboriginal land rights surfaced more pointedly as a specific issue.[40] Throughout the policy-making exercise settling claims had been a focal issue, with aboriginal rights being discussed in this context. The department had supported aboriginal rights in its efforts to reintroduce the claims commission bill, still holding to its 1965 position that aboriginal claims would be admissible under the bill. As one senior official described their position: 'One clause [5a] in the claims legislation made it possible for Indians to bring forward aboriginal claims, at least that was the intent. We held firm to that view throughout. If one proceeded with the bill, one would cover aboriginal rights and all other claims.'

The approach to aboriginal title introduced during the task force denied the existence of aboriginal land rights. This approach was new only in the context of the task force since it had been the government position for the past decades. This approach, advanced by a senior official in the Justice Department, was a straightforward legal interpretation of the issues, resembling neither the department's nor the activists' arguments. The lawyer in the task force who raised and advocated this approach, argued against any recognition of aboriginal rights and the inclusion of aboriginal land claims in the terms of reference of the claims commissioner. His basic argument was that the concept of aboriginal rights itself lacked any basis in law. The legal consequences of recognizing Indian title, in his opinion, would be extremely disruptive to the land title system. Even beyond the law, the concept lacked clear definition in public usage. The department's proposal of a claims commission, he thought, lacked careful planning and clear conceptualization: 'They had no criteria in mind as a basis for claims, no guiding principles, and no notion of the conse-quences.' In his view, department officials had failed to prepare their case with any conviction, and their assessment of American claims commis-sion procedures, on the basis of their 1963 visit to Washington, was uncritical and indicative of their inability to approach the question in a discerning and discriminating way. For him, the settling of treaties and land claims required distinguishing between 'justiciable issues,' which were amenable to the judicial forum, and political issues, which were more properly handled in the political arena or were matters of 'social contract.' He personally believed that the Indians' relationship to land should not be the focus of both Indians and government regarding the complex problems facing native people. Nor was he convinced that Indians would actually receive any funds if they were granted settlement, fearing that 'paper transactions' by government would substitute for actual payments.

In general his position on aboriginal rights was a legal one which held that 'legally enforceable' claims should be honoured, but that aboriginal land title did not exist, nor should it exist. Basically, the notion of aborigi-nal title was inconceivable. This was the view on aboriginal rights that the prime minister supported and defended in his public statements following the release of the White Paper.[41]

The department, however, had not conceptualized the idea of aboriginal rights in legal terms, and had avoided doing so in drafting the claims commission bills during the 1960s. Its officials wanted the mandate of the claims commissioner to include aboriginal rights; in fact, as one official said, 'We assumed aboriginal rights was included all along.' In discussing the focal attention aboriginal rights received at this time he commented: 'The problem came out primarily in drafting the terms of reference of the Commissioner. The department – we wanted him [the Commissioner] to handle anything and everything the Indians would bring forward, his mandate should be very broad, it would encompass aboriginal rights.'

The major argument against including aboriginal land claims as part of the commissioner's mandate was not financial. Officials on all sides of the issue agreed, in recalling the events, that the major opposition to aboriginal rights had been a conceptual one. One department officer claimed, 'The main problem was that it was a new idea. People just couldn't understand it.'

Legal precedents were not available to support the department's position. Even though the Calder case, in which the Nishga Tribal Council sought recognition of their Indian title, had come to trial during April, the judgment was not yet handed down. As Lysyk would note four years later, the concept of aboriginal title suffered from 'obscurity' within the legal profession at that time:

Indeed, so completely had it [the concept of Indian title] faded into history over the last half century that discussion of the subject at this time must contend with a credibility gap, an initial scepticism as to whether the concept of Indian title is one which has any basis at all in our jurisprudence. That this should be so is perhaps not surprising ... While the subject of Indian title attracted discussion in Canadian constitutional law treatises early in this century, references in the standard text-books and casebooks of today are hard to find (1973: 451).

Thus, in the absence of current legislative and executive declarations, and legal precedent, the concept was at best vague, and poorly understood in legal terms. As one opponent of the idea phrased it: 'What did it really mean? Were Indians to really get their land back?' The interpretation of aboriginal rights, developed over the years in the United States, does not appear to have been referred to or discussed in the task force (Cohen 1942: 291-4).

In the end, there were strong formal arguments against accepting the notion of aboriginal title. The chance of the concept's being recognized diminished even further when it became viewed as a special rights measure, and vanished completely when viewed in terms of Trudeau's long-held objection to policies constructed on 'historical might-have-beens.'

It is not surprising, then, that on 10 June, when the terms of reference for the claims commissioner came before the Cabinet Committee on Priorities and Planning, aboriginal land claims were excluded from the mandate. Chrétien described the difficulty as 'a semantic problem,' saying aboriginal title was simply not understood as a concept.[42] DIAND officials had encountered this same difficulty in the task force, but they had also contended with the problem of credibility, of convincing the activists and the cabinet that claims were of vital importance to Indians. As one official summed up the difficulty, 'You know, I don't think they believed us, they didn't really believe what we were saying.'

In the end the legalistic approach, rejecting aboriginal rights, took precedence; the department's political and moral arguments over the previous months were defeated. In the final form of the White Paper, aboriginal claims, treated in a cursory and perfunctory fashion, were dismissed as not being a credible type of claim: 'Other [grievances] relate to aboriginal claims to land. These are so general and undefined that it is not realistic to think of them as specific claims capable of remedy except through *a policy and program* that will end injustice to Indians as members of the Canadian community' (DIAND 1969: 11; my emphasis).

The reference to 'a policy and program ...' alluded to the general commutation proposal that Andras and Jordan had made in the previous months. Somewhat predictably, when the issue of aboriginal rights became a point of contention during the task force, the new activists had not opposed the legalistic argument since it supported their objections to a claims commission and lent a logical consistency to the policy. But on learning of the cabinet's decision, Rudnicki viewed it as a dangerous development, fearing it would 'close off any meaningful communication with Indians [and encourage] a strong reaction.'

The department was more distressed by the exclusion of aboriginal claims from the commissioner's mandate than by its original compromise on a claims commission – which had at least allowed the department to keep the door open for claims settlement. With the most basic feature of claims settlement excised, senior officials feared Indians might reject the policy outright. As one senior official remarked: 'Our policy was inextricably linked to paying off claims. I told them that it would happen in the end and why not do it now with some grace, not with being pushed with swords and backing up all the way. Without claims it would cripple the policy, just kill it.'

The fate of aboriginal claims, the last major issue to engage the policy-makers, was a bitter disappointment to the department.

THE FINAL STAGE OF POLICY-MAKING

The tempo of decision-making increased in early June in time for the House of Commons to receive the final policy before the summer recess. The department sought Treasury Board approval for a very general plan of implementation involving a special consultation and negotiation team within DIAND,[43] but it was obvious that the policy would go forward without the careful planning the Trudeau government had espoused. What was not yet planned would have to be done by the department after the White Paper was released.

The report of the task force's finance group went before the Cabinet Committee on Economic Policy and Programmes on 2 June and its formula for transferring funds to the provinces was approved.[44] For the financial arrangements the cabinet preferred the simplest mode which bypassed the problem of identifying Indians in the transfer of payments to the provinces. There would be no audit to determine how the funds were spent, nor any monitoring procedures to ensure that Indians would receive services comparable with other citizens.

On three other occasions (10, 17 and 18 June) drafts of the White Paper and the claims commissioner's mandate were reviewed by the Cabinet Committee, in which minor changes on the wording of aboriginal claims were made, and a strategy for bargaining with the province was developed.[45] The cabinet is said to have approved the White Paper in principle on 19 June. While it was being translated into French and printed, department officials prepared Chrétien's speech introducing the policy to the House of Commons.[46]

Thus by mid-June the major decisions on the White Paper were made. The arguments were exhausted. Although the task force had rationalized the policy, its main recommendation for a piloting group was repudiated by the cabinet's decisions. Indian priorities, reaffirmed at the last consultation meeting, were soundly rejected by the cabinet less than a week after the conference. Aboriginal rights were ruled out as a basis for claims settlement, and existing treaties were to be dissolved through negotiations between Indians and the government. After the task force's recommendations for a piloting group were rejected, the activists' emphasis on social development programs, rather than on the more narrowly conceived economic development fund, fell by the wayside.

The final compromises produced a policy that was a strange mixture of global termination measures and minor concessions to 'legitimate' Indian grievances. For the most part, the policy was logically consistent within a liberal framework. From the benchmark of formal equality, each proposal was carried forward to its logical conclusion. Because of the PMO's insistence, rationality had overruled political considerations, leaving few policy-makers satisfied with the policy's final form. The language and style of the White Paper, however, generally pleased department officials, who had laboured for weeks over each phrase and word. Even though PCO officials had written and revised parts of the drafts, the White Paper was largely a department product with many authors.

To the extent that either alignment received cabinet approval for its position, it was the department that made the greater gain in that it was given control of policy implementation. In hindsight, the activists did not see this decision as unusual because in their experience, they found that cabinet usually decided in favour of a department's position when it was faced with sharply divided opinion. Within the department, however, there was little optimism about the future of the policy: the general opinion was that if the policy had contained their position on settling claims, the chances for Indian compliance would have been much greater.

THE WHITE PAPER

In its final form, the policy document was entitled 'Statement of the Government of Canada on Indian Policy, 1969,' and on its cover was stamped in bold 'Indian Policy.' It was not titled a White Paper, nor was 'proposal' a prominent part of its language. In its brief ten pages, it described and defended the 'non-discriminatory' policy, and explicitly stated the government's intention to dissolve the department within five years. Despite the editing done on the drafts, the tone of the paper was still one of resoluteness, leaving no doubt of the government's belief that the policy was the right course of action.

Briefly, the White Paper opens with a preamble describing the Indian as a person 'set apart' in law, in government administration, and in society generally. These undesirable conditions are attributed to 'the product of history and have nothing to do with [Indians'] abilities and capacities' (DIAND 1969: 3). The historical direction must change, and the basis of

Indian exclusion and discrimination be eliminated: 'This Government believes in equality. It believes that all men and women have equal rights. It is determined that all shall be treated fairly and that no one shall be shut out of Canadian life, and especially that no one shall be shut out because of his race' (p. 6). After acknowledging that only Indians can set their own goals, the White Paper states that Indians are 'entitled to' a policy of equality which will facilitate their greater participation in society. The government would provide a supportive framework for achieving this goal, and the steps for implementing this framework are spelled out. Legislative equality would be achieved by repealing the Indian Act and by replacing it with an Indian Lands Act: Indians were to 'control' their own lands. Between the full trusteeship for land that presently exists and full title in fee simple as land is normally held, there rests a recognized 'number of intermediate states' of land control and ownership to be explored in the near future. Although placing Indian lands under the provincial taxation systems was seen as inevitable, the transfer might not be undertaken 'immediately.' In addition to the 'enriched services' that Indians were to have during the transitional phase and the 50 million-dollar development fund over a five-year period, Indians were to receive the same services from the same sources as other citizens.

Thus administrative equality required transferring DIAND programs and responsibilities to the provinces and other federal departments. The transfer was set for completion in five years' time, with the exception of reserve lands; it was acknowledged that land transfers might take longer, although no time was specified.

One concession was made to the Indians who wanted to maintain a traditional hunting economy, but this concession was to be temporary, or transitional: 'The Government is prepared to allow such persons transitional freer hunting of migratory birds under the Migratory Birds Convention Act and Regulations' (p. 11).

In terms of claims and treaties, government's responsibilities were limited to 'lawful obligations,' such as are seen to exist in terms of the unfulfilled treaty promises for reserve lands in the Northwest Territories and in some areas of the Prairie provinces. The policy argued that the importance of treaties in serving the broad social and economic needs of Indians had steadily diminished over the years, to the point where 'the anomaly of treaties between groups within society and the government of that society will require that these treaties be reviewed to see how they can be equitably ended' (p. 11). In addition to ending the treaties, aboriginal land title was rejected as a basis for claims. An Indian claims commissioner was to be appointed because the previously proposed Indian claims commission was felt to be a questionable and inappropriate method for settling claims (p. 11).

The final section of the White Paper dealt with the implementation of the policy. Indians were expected to participate in the implementation process through their regional, provincial, and national associations, with the government funding the consultations and compensating Indian leaders for the time involved in the negotiations. Questions of land transference would be determined at the band level, but each band was to specify which Indian association represented its interests in the consultations with government. As well, the provinces and other federal departments would be consulted in working out the details of transferring programs.

The White Paper ended with the caveat, 'A policy can never provide the ultimate solutions to all problems. A policy can achieve no more than is desired by the people it is intended to serve' (p. 13).

In its total cast the White Paper obviously reflected the liberal ideology of the policy-makers in its emphasis on equality, individual choice and responsibility, and freedom. Indians were given the simple option between discrimination or equality, and in discussing this choice, the language of the White Paper, as in other areas, reflected the task force's rationalization of the policy: 'To argue against this right [to equality] is to argue *for* discrimination, isolation and separation. No Canadian should be excluded from participation in community life, and none should expect to withdraw and still enjoy the benefits that flow to those who participate' (p. 8). (Emphasis in original)

More significantly, the White Paper mirrored Trudeau's own ahistorical approach to policy-making, and his strong views on the danger and futility of special legislation for cultural groups such as the French Canadians (see Ch. 2, above). Indian capabilities and needs, for example, were said to have outgrown the government's historical practices, producing anachronisms such as treaties. Hence these practices, ill-suited for coping with the present and the future, had to be set aside. Furthermore, special legislation was no guarantee for cultural survival. Indians, like the French in Trudeau's view, could alone preserve their culture; their language and thought would have vitality to the extent that Indians participated in the wider society, not by remaining in isolation where their cultural heritage would become 'fossils' (p. 9). Implicit in this argument is Trudeau's notion of 'hot house' cultures as artificial isolates, which cause people to turn inwards and backwards, producing the 'wigwam complex' of running from external competition (Trudeau 1968: 211).

THE NEW POLICY IS ANNOUNCED

In mid-June, as the summer recess approached, MPs began pressing for evidence of the new policy. The same day that cabinet approved the White Paper, the fate of the claims commission was questioned by MPs, who obviously doubted the existence of the long-promised bill. Ged Baldwin, MP from Peace River, attacked the department's penchant for secrecy, and warned that if the new policy were released before Indian spokesmen had been consulted, this move would substantiate the government's continued distrust of Indians.[47]

Despite Christie's efforts to open up the policy process in the department, the department's strategy for announcing the policy had not changed since February, when it argued against reviewing the policy with Indian spokesmen.

The night before the White Paper was announced, Indian leaders were flown to Ottawa where they met briefly with Chrétien just before he announced the policy in the House.[48] Dave Courchene, then president of the Manitoba Indian Brotherhood, recalled that the meeting was an informal session, where Chrétien described the policy in such 'vague' terms that its implications were not discernible. Indian spokesmen were then invited to sit in the gallery during the announcement in the House. Courchene recounts that had the Indian leaders known what the policy contained, they would have called an emergency session, as they did immediately after the announcement: 'The shock hit us all and it hit us in the gallery. We had had no preview.'[49]

Before the announcement the provincial governments were briefly informed of the White Paper's general outline, and copies of the statement had been sent to opposition critics.

Chrétien introduced the policy to the House in the early afternoon of 25 June with the remarks: 'Mr. Speaker, I am pleased to place the government's statement on Indian policy before the house. The statement outlines the views the government brings to the consultations which must now be carried on with the Indian people and the provincial governments.'[50] His speech was brief and emphasized that the policy was a response to Indians' demand for a change in the historical relationship between them and government. He referred to the policy as 'a statement' and 'a proposal,' not as a White Paper, and after a cursory description of its contents, he outlined the general steps of implementation: a special unit would be established immediately in the department to consult with Indians, the provinces, and other federal departments on 'the means of implementation and the pace of it.'[51] He expected to meet the provincial premiers during the summer to discuss the policy, and to appoint an Indian claims commissioner very shortly. In the fall, the House would have a chance to examine the policy carefully through the Standing Committee on Indian Affairs. He concluded his remarks by asking for the support of the House and all Canadians in the new policy, and by thanking his department for their loyal support.

While Chrétien was introducing the policy in the House, MacDonald circulated an open letter, with an attached copy of Chrétien's speech, to all department employees, informing them that a copy of the policy would be available in a few days.[52] The letter, clearly intended to allay fears of job insecurity, indicated that the policy would create significant changes in department staffing. Career counselling and job retraining, among other forms of support, would be provided those persons whose jobs would be affected, and future employment might be found with provincial governments which would be handling Indian programs in the future.

In outlining the main features of the new policy, MacDonald explained it as 'an acceleration and extension' of certain existing policies such as those in the field of education. Obviously seized by the importance of the historic moment, he informed the employees that: 'We have the opportunity to participate in one of the most significant acts of social change in the history of our society. Our contribution to making it a success will challenge us all.'[53] MacDonald's assessment of the challenge in implementing the policy was realistic, for his memo was almost immediately seen by Indian spokesmen as a government move to implement the policy without their consultation, belying the status of the new policy as a proposal. In this sense MacDonald had already achieved some degree of credibility for the policy.

CHAPTER SEVEN

Public reaction and government response

The policy process did not end with the announcement of the White Paper on 25 June 1969. The basic issues of the policy are still being debated, and always will be, because these issues reflect the underlying liberal democratic values in Canadian society. The immediate post-White Paper period, however, witnessed an interesting series of responses and counterpoint from Indians and public, alike. More significantly, it witnessed important reversals in Indian policy by the government.

As some of the policy-makers had intended, the White Paper was a powerful shock to Indians. But the response it elicited from them was not one of rational debate and discussion as the policy-makers had hoped. Instead of cutting through the 'emotionalism' of Indian-government relations, as MacDonald had anticipated, the White Paper inflamed Indians who had been led to expect revisions in the Indian Act and some acknowledgment of their priorities. Indian leaders felt duped by the consultation process and were incredulous at the government's assertions that the White Paper was a response to their demands. The White Paper became the single most powerful catalyst of the Indian nationalist movement, launching it into a determined force for nativism – a reaffirmation of a unique cultural heritage and identity. Ironically, the White Paper had precipitated 'new problems' because it gave Indians cause to organize against the government and reassert their separateness, precisely the results Davey had tried to avoid.

The White Paper created an unprecedented interest in Indian affairs on the part of the public, the press, and the MPs in the House of Commons. The shock's current did not stop at Indians. The civil servants in DIAND were equally startled at its contents and understandably concerned about its effect on their careers. The old guard expected a negative reaction from Indians across Canada, with the possible exception of British Columbia where it was felt there might be some support. Nevertheless, there were a few senior officials who felt that if the government remained steadfast, the Indians and the public would eventually accept the new policy.

INITIAL RESPONSE TO THE WHITE PAPER

In the first few days, response to the White Paper from the press and the MPs was generally positive, combining a guarded optimism with a careful wait-and-see attitude until Indian reaction was sensed.

In the hour following the White Paper's release, MPs were cautious, but generally hopeful, that the new policy would bring the long-awaited change in Indian affairs. However, opposition critics took different approaches on how firm and specific the government should be in its commitment to the policy. The PC critic, Ged Baldwin, hoped that the government was putting the policy forward in a serious fashion, 'not merely as a bargaining instrument'[1]; and Frank Howard, the NDP critic, found the policy statement vague but concluded that this was possibly unavoidable since Chrétien was offering it as a basis for discussions with Indians rather than 'dealing with this matter in a unilateral sense.'[2] Parliamentary commentary on the new policy was brief but generally favourable, a fact that Chrétien would remind them of in the weeks ahead.

Press reaction in the first week was supportive, devoted largely to describing the policy statement and speculating about its implications for Indians and both levels of government. The policy was characterized as 'revolutionary,' 'radical,' 'a major breakthrough,' and 'abrupt,' while the policy statement itself was described as 'well written,' 'glossy,' 'eloquent,' or 'vague.'[3] Speculation about the government's real intent arose from the generality of the statement, but only a few journalists attempted to deduce the workings within the policy-making arena that produced the White Paper. The general direction of press commentary was that the prime minister had been the principal force behind the new policy. One article reported that Trudeau had spent more time on Indian policy than on any other issue during his first year of office, and it claimed that Andras 'took charge himself of the cabinet committee refining the new policy.'[4] Another report dissociated both Andras and the department from the policy, claiming that the White Paper had neither the earmarks of Andras' style nor the general thrust of departmental thinking.[5]

Being liberal in its outlook, the press did not question the ultimate correctness of equality as the guiding principle, but it challenged the efficacy of the measures outlined in the policy for achieving equality. More obvious was the press' doubt that the provinces would respond positively to the policy. The history of provincial reluctance to deal with Indians was often stressed both in the press and in the House of Commons, where Stanfield levelled criticism at the lack of consultation with either the Indians or the provinces before the policy was released. There was general scepticism that Indians had any reason to believe the policy would achieve what it was intended to, and for this reason it was felt the government would have a difficult time convincing Indians of the policy's correctness. Significantly, the press did not at first catch the termination of treaties and the denial of aboriginal rights.

First-day reactions from individual Indians interviewed by journalists were also mixed. Walter Deiter, president of the National Indian Brotherhood, was reported to find both acceptable and unacceptable points in the policy,[6] while Harold Cardinal, in keeping with his previous public statements, was said to welcome the demise of the Indian Affairs administration.[7] Varied reactions came from other Indian spokesmen, but by the second day this situation rapidly changed.

Antagonism crystallized by the next day when Indian leaders, who had been been flown to Ottawa for the release of the policy, met in an emergency session to discuss the implications of the White Paper. Their deliberations on 26 June produced a press release, under the aegis of the NIB, which was a tempered but firm repudiation of the White Paper.[8]

Many reasons were cited for the rejection of the policy, but the two basic ones were that the policy had not been developed in good faith in terms of the participation that had been assured Indians, and that the policy was a denial of their special rights, which, Indian leaders reminded the minister, had been recognized and recommended by the government-sponsored Hawthorn Report. The White Paper, the press release noted, had been unilaterally devised by the government without Indian discussion or negotiation, with the result that 'we do not feel we took part in any decision-making process'; either the government had not heard what they had been saying at the consultation meetings, or their statements had been disregarded. This last conclusion was the obvious one because the policy ignored the essential first step Indian spokesmen had proposed for putting Indian-government relations on a new footing; namely, the recognition and resolution of outstanding treaty and aboriginal rights grievances. The press release also noted that the Migratory Birds Convention

Act had received little attention in the policy. Presumably land matters would be negotiated with the provinces, which, the press release emphasized, had benefited from Indian land acquisition in the past. The question posed was whether there would be any consultation with Indians on the appointment of an Indian claims commissioner; it was clear that the NIB did not want a repeat of the Indian Act meetings that had been little more than 'a show of consultation.'

Seeing the White Paper as a government attempt to avoid its constitutional responsibilities, the NIB drew Chrétien's attention to their proposals made at the consultation meetings that asked for recognition of their treaties and rights in the revised BNA Act. They reminded Chrétien they had not asked for the transfer of their affairs to the provinces, but they agreed with the need to improve the living conditions of Indians and to redirect Indian-government relations. Although possibly unintended by the government, the NIB declared that the White Paper would lead to 'the destruction of a Nation of People by legislation and cultural genocide.' The NIB could not be expected to accept such a policy and would not participate in a process that would bring about this end.

On the same day, Dave Courchene denounced the policy far more forcefully and incisively, his personal sense of outrage soon becoming the standard Indian response. Courchene saw the White Paper as an attempt to thwart the development of Indian organizations, which were beginning to articulate Indian goals and objectives. His condemnation of the policy, like that of the NIB, pivoted on the government's broken trust over promised consultations on the policy:

Once again the future of Indian people has been dealt with in a high-handed and arbitrary manner.

We have not been consulted, we have been advised of decisions already taken. I feel like a man who has been told he must die and am now to be consulted on the method of implementing this decision.

The status of Indian people as we know it today is not the result of our decisions in the past. If we are at an impasse, it was government who brought this about. A hundred or more years of acceptance on the part of the Indians, of policies and programs fostered by political experts who at the same time considered themselves amateur sociologists has led us once again up the garden path of false hopes, broken promises, collosal disrespect and monumental bad faith.[9]

Courchene believed the Indian Act consultations had been futile, for the White Paper demonstrated a general disregard for Indian demands. Nor was he impressed with the equating of equality with the removal of special legislation for Indians, and like Cardinal (1969: 142), in the same press release he compared the government's position on French language rights with its new policy on Indians:

Elimination of constitutional distinctions will not bring about equality for Indians any more than the elimination of references to English and French would remove the causes of discontent that presently exist between 'English' and 'French' Canada. We wonder in fact, if this government would have the audacity to suggest that such references to two founding nations and bilingualism should be eliminated so that there would be no distinction between the 'French' and 'English' and the rest of the Canadian ethnic population.

Courchene acknowledged that changes were needed in the Indian Act, but he disagreed with the proposed solution in the White Paper of transferring Indian administration to the provinces.

Indian leaders in Manitoba, Courchene announced, were to discuss the White Paper among themselves in the next few weeks, and would send a brief to the government embodying 'realistic alternatives to social disaster.' This brief was completed by mid-July.[10] By that time, angry Indian spokesmen had uniformly rejected the White Paper, feeling deceived by the consultation process.[11]

In the early weeks, provincial support for the White Paper was limited to Ontario's Premier John Robarts who called it 'a real breakthrough,' and Saskatchewan's Premier Ross Thatcher who welcomed the policy 'because I don't think Ottawa is doing a proper job.'[12] But Manitoba's Premier Ed Schreyer disagreed, referring to the policy as 'unrealistic, discourteous and arrogant.'[13] As Doerr (1973: 293) noted, Indian reaction to the White Paper was so overwhelmingly negative that the provinces were relieved of the necessity of publicly declaring any opposition they may have had to the policy. Subsequent consultations between Chrétien and the provinces were carried on privately, so that the public remained uninformed about the extent of provincial support or opposition.

Indian reaction to the policy rapidly became biting and trenchant. Heated exchanges frequently occurred between Indian spokesmen and Chrétien. In Ontario, in early July, for example, Chrétien was called a liar by angry members of the Union of Ontario Indians, and in Alberta Cardinal informed the press that federal officials who entered reserves to discuss the White Paper risked physical removal.[14] At its mid-July meeting, the NIB passed a resolution asking the provincial premiers not to meet with federal government officials to discuss the White Paper, and Chrétien was instructed not to use the name of the NIB or any provincial Indian organization in statements which might imply Indian compliance with the policy.[15] Furthermore, the NIB considered Chretien's consultations with Indian bands and the provinces an undermining of Indian leadership, and wired the prime minister their 'strong and decisive rejection of the policy.'

The NIB was not the only voice reacting to the policy. Within a few days of the White Paper's release, telegrams and letters were sent by Indian leaders, associations, and bands to MPs issuing terse rejections of the policy. MPs began feeling the initial edge of what became a nation-wide Indian repudiation of the policy. The *Globe and Mail*'s headline the day after the policy was released, 'Opposition Welcomes New Indian Policy,' rapidly became an inappropriate description of the MPs' reaction, who became concerned enough to allude to the possibility of violence. Press reports shifted from being descriptive and neutral to being the voice for angry Indian spokesmen. As the wording and generalities of the White Paper became more fully digested by Indian leaders and the public alike, press coverage became more sceptical and critical. The general criticism of the policy focused on three basic issues: 1/the White Paper's disregard for Indian input during the consultation meetings and the secrecy of its formulation; 2/the possible loss of lands and reserves; and 3/the unpredictable treatment Indians might receive at the hands of the provinces. The question of provincial interest in Indians' well-being was a recurring theme in the press and the Commons, and Indian reaction was well put by one newspaperman who wrote, 'The Indians know a bird in the hand and they are not at all sure about those in the provincial bushes.'[16]

The fundamental question after the first weeks of the White Paper's release was whether the government intended to press forward with its implementation. The policy had been delivered in an ambiguous fashion, although Chrétien denied that it had been, and its status as a proposal had not been emphasized although it would have been easy to do so. Whereas Chrétien claimed that it was just a proposal, both the White Paper document and Chrétien's statement in the House of Commons left a clear impression that the government was committed to its implementation. Both the five-year deadline for the termination of most of DIAND's special services and MacDonald's letter to DIAND employees signalled not only the government's determination to execute the policy, but also the fact that implementation was already in motion.[17] Supporting this aim was DIAND's August announcement that its special consultation and negotiation team was established to proceed with the policy.[18] Finally, there was a tendency for government proposals, despite Indian opposition, to turn into implemented policies.[19]

During this time, Chrétien toured the country, interpreting the policy to provincial officials and attempting to allay Indian fears that the reserves would be dismantled and their lands amalgamated with the provincial land base. As opposition to the policy increased, he began stressing that the White Paper was a proposal for further discussion and negotiation. In defending the ultimate objectives of the policy, he argued that the White Paper was a positive response to public criticism of department paternalism. This was the thrust of his special interview given to *Time Magazine* in early July[20] and of his response, in the *Globe and Mail* a few days later, to Scott Young's criticism of the policy.[21] Where the White Paper had been explicit, such as in the five-year deadline for termination, or where it had been very nebulous, such as in the statements on land holding, the reaction was generally the same – one of alarm and concern about the implications. Chrétien attempted to clarify the meaning of some of the sections of the policy, but as the consequences of the White Paper became clearer to both Indians and MPs, anxiety mounted. Although Chrétien stressed that the policy would not be 'imposed' on Indians, his simultaneous assertions that the government firmly believed in the inherent correctness of the policy simply reinforced doubt. In his 8 July article in the *Globe*, he wrote:

We will not push anything down anyone's throat. We will not abandon anyone or any problem. We will be flexible. We do want to discuss.

The Government believes the proposals are the right ones. It is committed to discussion, negotiating, consulting, to make them the right ones. It wants the chance to do this and it seeks the full and continuing involvement and understanding of those whose decisions will affect its chances.[22]

This was the delivery the department had preferred, but it obviously clouded the issues to the point where the question of implementation became paramount and the substance of the policy was rejected outright. The strategy of delivery was already defeating the intended purpose of discussion.

The explanation and defence of the policy fell to Chrétien who, even though a young and inexperienced minister, proved adept at handling the bitter recriminations and personal attacks he experienced in dealing with the public. Chrétien's tenacity and determination in piloting the White Paper brought him a high degree of respect and empathy in Ottawa, even from opposition MPs in the Commons, who felt that Chrétien had tried sincerely to cope with the Indian problem.

By 11 July, when the first special debate on the White Paper was held in the House of Commons, the Indians' outrage at the policy had reached full tilt. On their part, the MPs sought to determine what the government meant by certain recommendations in the policy, but more particularly, they sought confirmation that the policy was a proposal and that it would not be implemented in the face of Indian opposition. The debate lacked the strident and caustic exchanges that would later characterize parliamentary sessions on Indian policy, but a full range of reservations and criticisms was voiced that day: the policy presumed provincial willingness to take over Indian programs; the policy was a poor example of federal-provincial relations because of the lack of consultation; some provinces would be hard-pressed to take on the additional expenses of Indians; it was too abrupt; it left the question of Indian land-holding arrangements indeterminate, which understandably caused Indians alarm; it was devised without Indian participation; it was tantamount to dumping Indians on the provinces; it was an evasion of federal responsibilities; it presumed that constitutional change was easily managed; it dismissed Indian treaty and aboriginal rights, which Indians considered of major importance; and it set aside an Indian claims commission in favour of a commissioner who would be appointed solely by the federal government.[23] The MPs commentary, however, showed their support in principle for the equality of services for Indians.

During the Commons debate Chrétien defended the policy by arguing that the failure of the traditional system had demanded serious and basic changes in Indian Affairs. His explanation of the problem contained many of the arguments Davey had put forward in the fall of 1968 as the policy was being developed. For example, the Indian problem was 'sometimes ... a problem of regional development rather than a problem of racial development.'[24] But the main thrust of Chrétien's defence was that the policy was a proposal and that he did not intend to rush into its implementation. There was time, he emphasized, and there was flexibility; 'If [Indians] suggest that the present system be retained for a period of years I may agree.'[25] Chrétien's delivery was far more forthright than his introductory statement on the policy on 25 June, and at the end of the debate the MPs seemed reasonably satisfied with his assurances that the policy was to be the subject of extended consultations with Indians.

Outside Parliament, however, ambiguity about the government's intention persisted because the general message reaching the Indians and the public was that although the White Paper was only a proposal, it was 'the right' proposal. The government's firmness was reinforced when the prime minister gave his classic speech in Vancouver on 8 August.[26] The major point of the speech was Trudeau's own concern about the rising expectations among the public of what government could do to cure the problems facing society. Because government had limited resources, it had a duty to throw open the whole range of choices on each issue to the public, thereby educating the public on how the problems could be approached. Public participation, he argued, was not the daily involvement by the public in government, but a process which 'really means explaining our problems to ourselves.' This was the context in which he raised the White Paper on Indian policy.

The government, Trudeau said, had explored the Indian question and came up with two choices: retaining the conventional way of administering to Indians by 'adding bricks of discrimination around the ghetto in which they live'; or discarding the old system by giving Indians full status in society. He acknowledged the difficulty of the choice for both government and Indians, but in his opinion there was basically no choice because the trappings of special rights were incongruous in a modern and just society. On the matter of treaty rights he was adamant:

We will recognize treaty rights – we will recognize forms of contract which have been made with the Indian people by the Crown. And we will try to bring justice in that area. And this will mean that perhaps the treaties shouldn't go on forever. It's inconceivable I think that in a given society, one section of the society have a treaty with the other section of the society. We must be all equal under the laws and we must not sign treaties amongst ourselves and many of these treaties indeed would have less and less significance in the future anyhow.

Regarding aboriginal rights, Trudeau reiterated his ahistorical rationale: 'Our answer may not be the right one and may not be one which is accepted but it will be up to all of you people to make you minds up and to choose for or against it, and to discuss it with the Indians. Our answer is no. We can't recognize aboriginal rights because no society can be built on historical "might-have-beens."' He then repeated an argument that was also familiar to the policy-makers: if aboriginal rights were granted Indians, what then should be done with the related questions of the rights of the French following the defeat on the Plains of Abraham, of the expulsion of the Acadians, as well as of the relocation of the Canadian Japanese during the Second World War?

The prime minister's speech removed any public doubt about his own position on the White Paper. The speech was a personal endorsement that the general direction of the policy, and particularly its stand on treaties and aboriginal rights, was in accord with his own philosophy. The speech echoed the eleventh-hour debates in the policy-making process on the mandate of the claims commissioner, indicating to the public that the department had not been the sole source of thinking behind the policy. However, the public remained unaware that the White Paper did not represent the department's preferred position on aboriginal rights and claims settlement.

Trudeau's speech angered Indian leaders even further. In replying to a letter from Dave Courchene, Trudeau denied he was disavowing the treaties, adding that he had personally supported the policy. Concerning legal protection of ethnic minorities, Trudeau restated his beliefs to Courchene: 'If the Indian character can survive only by the protection of special legislation, then it will disappear of its own account ... But our diversity must continue on its own merits, not artificially, through special legislation or by seeking the protection of history.'[27] Like Chrétien, Trudeau expected that the White Paper would ultimately be accepted: 'We know that the policy proposals must be discussed and that there are many details to be worked out. But we believe in the principles that underlie the policy and in the *inevitability* of their general acceptance. I expect we will all soon see that the conditions of the past will have little relevance to the last part of the twentieth century.' The role of Indians was still seen as assisting in the 'details' of implementation.

FIRM REJECTION SETS IN

By autumn 1969, Chrétien had failed to convince Indians or the public of his intention to discuss the policy. The deception of the Indian Act consultations was still vivid, and Indians had no empirical reason to trust government assertions. Indian spokesmen, band councils, and organizations let it be known through the press and through letters to MPs and editors of newspapers that the policy was unacceptable. Indian organizations had taken the position that they would examine the policy in detail and prepare counter-proposals for government consideration, but until they were ready with their own proposals, they demanded that no steps to implement the White Paper be taken.[28] By September the long-sought-after government funding was finally granted, enabling Indian organizations to research their rights.[29] To this end the organizations in the western provinces moved with firm resolve.

The press continued to carry critical commentary, and academics began to speak out against the White Paper. At a Progressive Conservative policy conference held in October in Niagara Falls, Professor James Duran, a historian from New York State, condemned the policy as a fatal replay of the American termination policy;[30] and Professor Douglas Sanders, a professor of law at the University of Windsor, criticized the policy's treatment of treaty and claims grievances. Sanders was unimpressed with the general argument in the White Paper, noting that 'to a group struggling to assert and protect a special identity, equality is a negative concept.'[31] But the inconsistency in the government's acknowledging treaty grievances at the same time as it ignored aboriginal rights, which were the basis of the treaties, drew his strongest comment:

It is clear that treaties were designed to deal with aboriginal title. Yet today the Federal Government draws an essentially irrational distinction between treaty claims and aboriginal claims. Though the Government wants to terminate the 'inconceivable' treaties it recognizes the legal validity of treaty claims. It does not recognize aboriginal claims although the treaties exist because aboriginal title had to be extinguished.[32]

At the same time, another lawyer, Professor L.C. Green of the University of Alberta, prepared a critical assessment of the White Paper for the provincial government, pointing out that the policy confused the matter of protection with discrimination. Green cautioned that implementation of the policy might lead to serious unrest which 'could make the Riel Rebellion of 1885 look "like a kindergarten picnic." '[33] In late November further criticism came from Peter Cumming, a law professor at Osgoode Hall; at the Liberal Party Thinkers Conference in Harrison Hot Springs, British Columbia, he called for a renewed effort to develop a policy in conjunction with Indian organizations, one possibly along the lines of the Indian Development Institute that the Indian-Eskimo Association had been proposing.[34] He was strongly critical of the government's position on aboriginal rights and treaties, and of its failure to consult Indians during its preparation.

Yet another commentary came from Professor R.W. Dunning, an anthropologist at the University of Toronto, who had been critical of the Hawthorn Report. Dunning felt the policy had correctly recognized the basic problem in Indian Affairs; namely, that the 'system of stewardship' of Indians had failed to achieve its ends (Dunning 1969). However, given the atmosphere of heightened distrust created by the White Paper, Dunning was sceptical of any success in tripartite negotiations between Indians, the provinces, and the federal government. Instead, he proposed a series of procedures requiring the government to break the ties of stewardship in order to launch Indian self-direction (see also Dunning 1971). Like others, Dunning pointed out the incongruity between the government position on Indians and its policies on bilingualism and biculturalism.

In December, Chrétien's repeated affirmations that the White Paper was a proposal were again contradicted by a further step toward implementation. On 19 December, Dr Lloyd Barber, vice-president of the University of Saskatchewan, was appointed Indian Claims Commissioner, and empowered to examine and report on ways of settling treaty and other grievances, but not aboriginal claims.[35] His appointment incited Indian groups to boycott his office. Although Barber eventually succeeded in expanding his mandate to include matters of aboriginal title claims,[36] and in the end gained the personal respect of many Indian leaders, his persistent efforts to get the government to settle claims often met with severe resistance by officials in the Justice Department; because of their legal approach to treaty grievances, few of these claims were ever settled. But Barber was influential in getting the government to adopt a more sympathetic approach to aboriginal claims, which were eventually handled by DIAND through special teams of negotiators.

A further step was taken in early 1970 towards implementation of the policy when the department hired William Wuttunee as a consultant to assist the government in promoting the White Paper. Wuttunee, a successful Calgary lawyer with a Cree background and a liberal philosophy, supported the principles and the plan of the new policy. His book, *Ruffled Feathers* (1971), was highly critical of Indian organizations, especially the Alberta Indian Association headed by Cardinal, and his appointment caused another Indian outburst, resulting in an attempt by his band council to bar him from his own reserve.[37] He resigned his position as consultant in early spring 1970. By that time, Cardinal's critical rejoinder to the White Paper, *The Unjust Society* (1969), was published, rapidly becoming the Indian manifesto of special rights and 'the Indian position' on the White Paper.[38] Pre-dating the Red Paper by six months, its style accurately depicted the general Indian sentiment toward the White Paper.

During the fall of 1969 and winter of 1970, Chrétien and David Munro, the senior official in charge of DIAND's consultation team, continued to defend and promote the White Paper, denying that it was similar in intent or consequence to the American termination policy.[39] Chrétien was frequently required to dodge hostile questions in the House of Commons, promising government would wait for the official responses from the Indian organizations before implementing the policy.

The official Indian response finally came in early June 1970, one year after the White Paper was released. It occurred immediately after Trudeau's return from Australia, where, in answering questions about the White Paper at the Australian National University, he remarked that 'the discussion is raging and this is participation as we never expected it would come' (Trudeau 1970: 224). His next statement foreshadowed his response to the Red Paper: 'If the White people and the Indian people in Canada don't want the proposed policy, we're not going to force it down their throats.'

THE RED PAPER

In the first days of June 1970, Indian leaders gathered in Ottawa, at Carleton University, where they debated whether to adopt the Alberta Indian Association's position paper *Citizens' Plus*[40] as the official National Indian Brotherhood's response to the White Paper. After making certain revisions to the paper, by expanding the section dealing with treaties to include aboriginal rights, they endorsed the Alberta paper on 3 June.[41] The NIB, particularly the Prairie associations, were determined to meet with the prime minister and his cabinet, but they had come to Ottawa without any plans. However, after some carefully executed manoeuvres behind the scenes by the Alberta Indian Association, and some inside help from a few of the activists, including Rudnicki,[42] a meeting with the full cabinet took place on 4 June in the historic Railway Committee Room of the Parliament buildings (see photos).

Senior civil servants have indicated that the government's position before the meeting was for the prime minister to receive the Red Paper, but not to respond in any substantive fashion other than to say that the government would examine the Red Paper seriously and in detail. The outcome of the meeting, however, was uncertain and the atmosphere in the Railway Committee Room was tense.

Traditional Indian regalia was worn by some of the Indian leaders, adding to the drama of the setting.[43] The presentation of the Red Paper was a carefully rehearsed ritual with Chief Adam Soloway and Chief John Snow, both of the Indian Association of Alberta, reading alternately the counterpoints in the White and Red Papers:

Chief Adam Soloway: 'The White Paper states: The legislative and constitutional basis of discrimination should be removed.'
Chief John Snow: 'The Red Paper states: The legislative and constitutional basis for Indian status and rights should be maintained until such times as Indian people are prepared and willing to renegotiate them.'
Chief Soloway: 'The White Paper states: There should be a positive recognition of the unique contribution of Indian culture to Canadian life.'
Chief John Snow: 'Our Red Paper states: These are nice sounding words which are intended to mislead everybody. The only way to maintain our culture is for us to remain as Indians ...'[44]

After the chiefs' delivery, they placed a copy of the White Paper on the table in front of Chrétien, indicating official rejection, and a copy of the

Red Paper was handed to the prime minister, signalling their intent to begin discussing counter proposals.

Cardinal's statement to the cabinet was the standard Indian position that a new Indian-government relationship was contingent upon government recognition of treaty and aboriginal rights. To break the impasse on aboriginal and treaty rights, Cardinal suggested that these claims should be submitted to 'a truly impartial Claims Commission, appointed after consultation with the Indians, with broad terms, wide powers, and whose judgements would be binding on both parties. This, in fact, is the kind of solution proposed by the Liberal Party during the election campaign of 1963.'[45] The thrust of Cardinal's speech was that the negotiations between Indians and the government must continue, but that the government's inflexibility was preventing this process from beginning. In addition to the proposals for a broad approach to claims settlement, he presented a synopsis of the Indian position on the White Paper:

1. We have proposed a review of the Indian Act – not its abolition.
2. We have proposed a new kind of federal agency, different in scope and intention from the present Department of Indian Affairs. This agency would be related to the legal and moral responsibilities of the federal government to the Indian people and would be more attuned and responsive to our needs and aspirations.
3. We have proposed a re-examination of the options open to Indian people for control of their land – without accepting your concepts of property rights.
4. We have also asked for our own Minister of Indian Affairs – a Minister whose sole responsibility would be Indians.

Cardinal went on to stress the need for education and economic development to alleviate the poverty in Indian communities, and that Alberta Indians had specific proposals for self-development. Although he did not expect these changes to take place easily, either for government or for Indians, he called for a mutual respect between both parties as a prerequisite for initial discussions. The implementation of the White Paper, he said, must discontinue, and the department's consultation and negotiation team had to be replaced by a new consultative mechanism acceptable to both the National Indian Brotherhood and the cabinet.

The Red Paper was presented in a forthright and constructive manner, and its text provided detailed criticisms and counter-proposals for government consideration. The prime minister's response, as some senior officials described it, reflected his 'Gallic temperament' more than his normal rational style of operation. Having all the characteristics of an impromptu and candid reply, Trudeau's statements provided the major surprise of the meeting. The government, he said, had sincerely tried to come to grips with the Indians' problems through the White Paper, and although it might have failed, it had been an honest and determined effort by a young, courageous minister. His comments fell short of an apology but they nevertheless made certain admissions that the government failed in its attempt to resolve the issues:

And I'm sure that we were very naive in some of the statements we made in the paper. We had perhaps the prejudices of small 'l' liberals and white men at that who thought that equality meant the same law for everybody, and that's why as a result of this we said, 'well let's abolish the Indian Act and make Indians citizens of Canada like everyone else. And let's let Indians dispose of their lands just like every other Canadian. And let's make sure that Indians can get their rights, education, health and so on, from the governments like every other Canadian.' But we have learnt in the process that perhaps we were a bit too theoretical, we were a bit too abstract, we were not, as Mr Cardinal suggests, perhaps pragmatic enough or understanding enough, and that's fine. We are here to discuss this.[46]

Acknowledging that the policy may have been 'shortsighted or mis-guided,' he stressed that the government's intention had been honest, and that Indians had to believe this; otherwise future discussions would be meaningless. But on the question of special rights, Trudeau maintained his opposition, comparing the Indian problem to the 'case of the French in Canada,' where, in his opinion, 'the way to be strong in Canada is not to be apart but to be equal to the English.' The final arbitration of the matter rested in the Canadian people as a whole because 'you can't convince people just by publishing papers, white or red, nor by making laws.'

As he continued to talk, Trudeau's approach became more informal, and his parting comments shocked the Indian audience:

But let me just say that we will be meeting again and we will be furthering the dialogue, and let me just say, we're in no hurry if you're not. You know, a hundred years has been a long time and if you don't want an answer in another year, we'll take two, three, five, ten, or twenty – the time you people decide to come to grips with this problem. And we won't force any solution on you, because we are not looking for any particular solution.

These remarks were interpreted as the prime minister's assurance that the government would not press the White Paper on Indians.

Trudeau's statements represented the first major political victory for the Indian movement. Cardinal would later write that this had been the moment Indians had worked hard to achieve, but that their inexperienced organizations would fail to capitalize on the political momentum gained by the prime minister's statements (Cardinal 1977: 184). Thordarson, in assessing the conditions under which the prime minister acquiesced to public opposition to White Papers, claimed that Trudeau was not particularly interested in the issue of Indian affairs and this had led him to withdraw the policy (1972: 96). However, this explanation is inconsistent with the opinions of senior officials in DIAND and the PCO who worked under the Trudeau administration both before and after the White Paper. In their view, Trudeau was 'sympathetic' to Indian issues and interested in promoting policies that would improve Indian conditions. The more immediate explanation of Trudeau's remarks on 4 June was probably the emotion of the moment and the obvious effort by Indian spokesmen to develop a constructive response to the White Paper.

Disinterest had certainly not characterized Chrétien's efforts to sell the policy to Indians and the general public; indeed, senior officials claim that briefings went from the department to the PMO before the meeting, advising against any retraction of the policy. Unlike Trudeau's famous remarks on aboriginal rights which reinforced the White Paper, his response to the Red Paper undercut the department's efforts to carry the policy forward. The outcome of the meeting was not welcomed by some department officials who felt, as one of them phrased it, 'the policy could have been carried out with more vigour and courage.' Another official was of the same opinion: 'If we had made it firm, the Indians would have accepted it. They would have had to; they had in the past.' The old guard were the least surprised at the Indian response. Their prediction that British Columbia might be the only receptive area had been at least partially borne out by the Nishga Tribal Council's approval of the policy in principle.[47] Some of the old guard also felt that the provisions for Indian lands in the White Paper were bound to create anxiety among Indians because of their vagueness. This too had been demonstrated in the Indian reaction.

Although some Indian leaders remained highly sceptical that the White Paper was in fact 'dead,'[48] Chrétien's speeches in Parliament showed a redirection in the department's thinking. He began to emphasize a 'new ideology' in Indian Affairs, stressing cooperation between the department and Indian organizations.[49] Joint examination of problems and mutual support would be in order, and if department personnel were unable to adjust their attitudes, they should expect to find new fields of endeavour.

He continued to stress the advantages of consultation and by spring 1971, he made more explicit policy changes along these lines.

On 17 March 1971, at Queen's University in Kingston, Ontario, Chrétien delivered a speech on 'The Unfinished Tapestry – Indian Policy in Canada.' Although most of the speech was devoted to an historical review of Indian policy, his concluding remarks were seen to be his formal retraction of the White Paper:

The Government put forward its proposals for a future Indian Policy a year and a half ago. These stimulated and focused a debate and have served a necessary purpose. They are no longer a factor in the debate. *The Government does not intend to force progress along the directions set out in the policy proposals of June 1969. The future direction will be that which emerges in meetings between Government and Indian representatives and people.* (Emphasis in original)

One of the major demands of the Indian people since the consultation meetings began finally received firmer official acknowledgment; a new policy on Indian-government relations was beginning to emerge.

Despite Trudeau's and Chrétien's retractions of the White Paper, the government's denial of aboriginal rights as a basis for claims settlement remained unchanged. The first case on aboriginal title, the Nishga case, was still before the courts. Chrétien had fought hard to have aboriginal claims accepted in the policy, but cabinet had opposed. In his 'Unfinished Tapestry' speech, Chrétien seemed to be saying, without necessitating too much reading between the lines, that any change in claims policy at this point depended upon Indian initiative. He implied that claims should be settled, dismissing the notion that grievances would easily disappear as a contentious issue.

Indian grievances are legion. Their remedy is a prerequisite for improving their social lot. As long as the grievance persists, the Indian people will be unable to improve their own condition. It is useless to suggest that when social conditions have improved, the grievances will fall away. As long as the grievance persists, the Indian people will not be fully able to come to grips with the problems and will not be able to help themselves to the fullest extent. Unless they do, the problems will remain: for no one but the Indian people can find solutions to many of them.

Acknowledging that the appointment of a claims commissioner had 'been greeted with something less than enthusiasm,' Chrétien attributed Indian reaction to the fact the appointment had been 'proposed in the now defunct policy proposals.'

Although Alberta's Red Paper had set the tone and parameters of the Indian response, other provincial and regional organizations completed their own counter-proposals and presented them to Chrétien. Among these were the Union of British Columbia Indian Chiefs' '*A Declaration of Indian Rights: The B.C. Indian Position Paper*,' November 1970; the Manitoba Indian Brotherhood's paper '*Wahbung: Our Tomorrows*,' October 1971; and the Association of Iroquois and Allied Indians' '*Position Paper*,' November 1971. These counter-proposals reflected regional differences, but they had a common theme in emphasizing special rights and urging the government to improve its educational and economic development programs. Throughout 1970 and 1971, various submissions continued to be sent to the department by Indian groups, but the formal Indian response to the White Paper was basically finished.

In responding to the White Paper, Indians had not used the more routine channel for commenting on government policy, the House of Commons Standing Committee on Indian Affairs. Instead, they withdrew to prepare their own proposals, returning to present them directly to the cabinet in the case of the Red Paper, and to Chrétien in the other instances. The role of the Standing Committee, although more active in the 1970 debates on education, did not become prominent until 1973 during the debate on aboriginal rights.

Although a specific directive was not issued to the department's employees regarding an official retraction of the White Paper, the general understanding was that it had been suspended, if not permanently shelved. The department's brief to the Special Senate Committee on Poverty (DIAND 1970) recognized that much remained to be done in the fields of education, employment, housing, and community development, but by late 1971 the department was experiencing a general policy vacuum. Indian associations were absorbed in historical research and preoccupied with building their organizations. The general climate was conducive to sitting back and digesting the previous year's events, determining how the pieces could be picked up in some systematic fashion. For many senior officials in the department, the aftermath of the White Paper was a demoralizing time; as one official phrased it, 'we went from day to day with *ad hoc* decisions.'

In general, the delivery of the White Paper did not proceed as the policy-makers intended. Chrétien failed to establish credibility with the public that he was bargaining in good faith, and even with the formal retraction of the policy, Indians remained convinced that the White Paper was a hidden agenda within government. The White Paper's disregard for Indian priorities so angered Indian spokesmen, that they foreclosed on the detailed debate Chrétien had hoped for, instead withdrawing to prepare their own proposals which emphasized special rights and historic promises. Nativism, significantly enhanced by the policy, became firmly fixed on special rights, the basic Indian orientation which the White Paper had been designed to change. But the major legacy of the White Paper was the intensification of Indian distrust of government.

CHAPTER EIGHT   Conclusions

The most obvious conclusion about the White Paper is that Trudeau's reforms aimed at centralizing government policy-making had a profound effect on Indian policy. Had the department been able to follow its own wishes, the new policy would not have resembled the White Paper. Instead, as the department proposed in the fall of 1968, it would have expanded the Indian Affairs bureaucracy and amplified the special rights policies under Arthur Laing by establishing an Indian claims commission which might have recognized aboriginal title claims. In February 1969, had the department again been able to implement its proposals, the policy would have been announced publicly in early March, not as a White Paper, but as a partial termination program to be implemented in three years' time, keeping Indian reserve lands free from provincial control. But this version of the policy had not been rationalized, as Trudeau and his advisers insisted, since it still contained 'inconsistencies' in the proposed Indian claims commission. Even though department initiatives were at times acceptable, and contrary to Trudeau's remarks attributing the White Paper to MacDonald (Kernaghan 1976: 453), the guiding framework of values for Indian policy was set by the PMO.

Indian policy-making clearly demonstrated the power of the PMO to shape the course of policy development. Although ministers, not civil servants, were to make the policy decisions according to the reforms Trudeau instituted in the policy-making process, the actual power centre lay in the PMO, not with the individual ministers. Through Davey, the PMO provided the political-partisan perspective for Indian policy by ensuring that the government would not be vulnerable to charges of discrimination against Indians. Thus the PMO set the basic value of equality for the new policy and specified the context for that value in the legal and formal administration of the government. Also in keeping with the reforms, Davey managed the political timetabling of the policy so that it was completed in time to meet the government's deadlines and so that the policy's implications for the next election could be fully considered. Using the technocratic approach to policy-making, Davey pared down the problem to a manageable size, and set forth the procedures for developing the policy, initially with the request for a comprehensive policy review, then with the insistence that policy options be provided for ministerial consideration, and finally with the decision to establish the PCO-based task force to guarantee the systematic rationalization of the policy. As time passed, his mediation between the traditionalist and activist alignments became more pronounced as he sought areas of agreement between the two ministers and the PMO. In the end, however, the compromises between the alignments were made on the basis of the PMO's values of rationality and comprehensive planning for policy-making, and of formal equality for Indians. Above all, Indian policy-making demonstrated the purpose of the recent reforms: to strengthen political and prime-ministerial control over policy-making in general.

Despite election rhetoric on 'participatory democracy,' public participation in the sense of grass roots' influence on policy was not supported by the PMO. At no time did the PMO endorse the activists' proposal of opening up the policy process to Indians, before cabinet approval, in a mutual bargaining and negotiating context. Rather, participation was seen as enhanced public discussion of the policy through the White Paper by which government could gauge public response to its priorities, not to those of Indians.

The reforms in the PCO resulted in a more comprehensive review of department submissions and in a more holistic view of the Indian problem. PCO skills in rationalizing policy far exceeded those of the department, and in the end, the PCO's major contribution to the White Paper was the logical consistency its task force brought to the arguments in the new policy. But the PCO also showed sensitivity towards the social aspects of the Indian problem, reflecting an expertise lacking in both the PMO and the department. Legal definitions of Indians and Inuit, which concerned Davey, did not impress Gordon Robertson and the officials in the Social Policy Secretariat. For this and other reasons the PCO attempted to expand the scope of the problem to include the Inuit and Metis, and to shift the policy-making process away from the department to either a royal commission or a public task force. However, both these attempts failed because Davey felt the proposals would escalate the problem and create undesirable political consequences.

The most prominent characteristic of the PCO was its activism, a feature definitely not a component of Trudeau's reforms. As a philosophy, activism was incongruent with Trudeau's notion of a central political control of policy-making, and as practised by civil servants, it was contrary to Trudeau's desire to shift decision-making from officials to ministers. However, because of Rudnicki's previous experience in DIAND, but more especially because of his skills in conceptualizing issues and promoting the activist ideology, the PCO mounted a strong countervailing force against the department's conventional approach to policy-making. Rudnicki and Andras crafted the role of 'policy minister' into one far more powerful in the public eye than they were able to establish inside government where Chrétien, as senior minister, carried the policy initiative. Without the PCO activists, however, Indian participation in the policy process would not have been advocated. Neither the PMO nor the department shared the view that Indian participation in shaping the policy was important, or that it was a vital precondition for the policy's success. In the end, however, the activists' vantage point in the PCO was not a sufficient power base, and in Rudnicki's case it was not secure. Their ideas lacked effective ministerial support, and conflicted with the hard line preferred in the PMO and the department. In time, the conflict between the two alignments was viewed as counterproductive, and Rudnicki was removed from the policy-making process at the department's insistence.

Even though the department theoretically carried the policy initiative, it was nevertheless forced to work within the guidelines set by the PMO and PCO, as well as within the constraints imposed by the activists. The activists' criticism of the department had placed Chrétien and his senior officials on the defensive early in the policy-making process. Since the department's conceptualizing skills were negligible, it was handicapped in responding with reasoned policy submissions. Instead, the department became increasingly impatient with the policy process and extremely sensitive to public criticism. Excessive public emotionalism was seized on as the immediate problem to which urgent action was proposed as the remedy. As pressures from the PMO and PCO for long-range planning persisted, the department became impulsive, viewing the PCO as an obstruction to be circumvented and arguing for the immediate release of the policy. The department's preference for incremental policies and its penchant for quick solutions made most of its efforts to comply with PMO procedures unacceptable (see Table 10). In the end, however, the department's insistence on reducing public emotionalism was consistent with

TABLE 10 Steps in developing Indian policy

		Cabinet decision to revise the Indian Act (1967)
		Cabinet decision to hold consultation meetings (1968)
		Trudeau government elected
I.	The summer: strategy	1. Indian policy given priority on political agenda of cabinet
		2. PMO and PCO suggest various strategies for formulating policy
		3. PCO mounts holding action against incremental, sectorial, policies
		4. PMO formalizes request for policy review from DIAND
II.	The fall: review and definition of the problem	5. DIAND submits Five Year Plan to test acceptability
		6. DIAND submission found unacceptable
		7. PMO presses for policy review from DIAND
		8. Individuals in PMO, PCO and DIAND respond with various definitions of 'the problem,' and immediate and long-range solutions
		9. PMO reaffirms procedure for developing policy
III.	The winter: options and objective defined	10. PMO presses DIAND for submission on policy options
		11. DIAND responds with brief submission
		12. DIAND submission found unacceptable
		13. Minister without Portfolio circulates his own position paper
		14. PMO stresses urgency to define policy objective
		15. PMO establishes policy objective
		16. Cabinet approves policy objective, and requests plan of implementation and rationalization from DIAND
		17. DIAND responds with submission
		18. DIAND submission found unacceptable
		19. DIAND submits minor revision of submission
		20. DIAND submission found unacceptable and release of policy denied
IV.	The spring: rationalization	21. Cabinet establishes PCO-based task force to prepare implementation plan, rationalization of policy, and White Paper
		22. Task Force submits report on options and preferred positions
		23. Task Force proposals found unacceptable
V.	Early summer: policy approved	24. Cabinet requests DIAND to prepare implementation plan and revise draft of White Paper
		25. Cabinet committees modify and approve various DIAND submissions on specific sections of the policy
		26. Cabinet approves White Paper
		27. White Paper announced in the House of Commons

the political values in the PMO, as well as with Trudeau's own views on the futility of sentiment as a basis for government decisions. The PMO accepted this initiative, and with the exception of the task force interlude, the department retained control of the policy process and its implementation.

As policy-making continued, differences of opinion within the department became sharper. When MacDonald became convinced that emotionalism, as the immediate problem, required the dismantling of the department, the old guard grew increasingly uneasy about the direction of the new policy. More than others in the policy-making arena, they understood Indian demands for special rights and trusteeship, but they were the most marginal actors in the decision-making procedures, and often in the department itself. Their advocacy of special rights was interpreted as self-serving by the activists, who attempted to discredit them at every opportunity. In the end, the department's official stand on Indian policy reflected MacDonald's views, not the old guard's, and certainly not Christie's, the young official, who, like the activists, had tried to open up the policy process to Indian participation before cabinet approval.

As is obvious from the analysis, the most conspicuous feature of the Indian policy-making process was the conflict between the two alignments. Involving more than simply personality differences between the ministers, the conflict reflected two different philosophies of policy-making. The traditional approach, held by the department and reaffirmed by Trudeau's reforms, placed policy-making firmly in the control of the political executive. Policy was to be developed within the secrecy of the cabinet, and public participation, a post-policy development, was intended to inform government of public opinion on government priorities before legislation. The activists, on the other hand, sought to open up the policy-making process before cabinet approval, advocating that policies should be shaped through consultation and negotiation between government and the public. By becoming more informed about the needs of a minority group, ministers would be better able to develop effective and acceptable policies. Although both approaches rested on liberalism and democracy, they differed strongly in the role of public involvement. The values of democratic participation became the key to the conflict. In Bailey's terms, these values were the prize in the competition (1969: 20-3).

As competition between the two alignments increased over the months, the policy-making exercise became essentially one of reaffirming value positions. Rigidity set in and individuals became more quick to reject opposing views and to attribute subversive intentions to the opposite alignment. They typecast each other readily, so that, for example, attempts by department officials to stress the importance of treaties to Indians were interpreted as a department tactic to scuttle the policy. Similarly, when the activists tried to promote some distancing of the department from the policy process, this was seen as a typical activist prejudice against the Indian administration. Stereotyping significantly affected the reception of ideas, and it led to prejudgments and discrediting on both sides. Individuals were required to struggle with greater determination to establish their points as the web of tension and disavowal increased. The exchange of ideas became very difficult early in the policy development, and what were little more than opinions became tenets to be questioned no more. The basic notion, for instance, that the Indian Act was necessarily a barrier to Indian development was never examined. Indeed, revisions to the Indian Act were not even discussed. The fact that the Act made the government vulnerable to charges of discrimination was seized upon and retained by the PMO. Furthermore, when conflict reached a stalemate, Davey's role as mediator became more pronounced, facilitating the establishment of PMO values in the new policy.

A further consequence of the conflict was the increasing insularity of the policy arena, as the policy-makers became preoccupied with their own power struggles. As individuals in each alignment attempted to strengthen their case, they became more selective in interpreting public and Indian demands, a fact clearly illustrated in internal assessments of the final Indian Act consultation meeting. This insularity was reinforced by other factors, such as the negative view of external experts, and the conventional secrecy of policy-making in the federal government; but it was especially encouraged by the fear that Indians might learn of the advanced state of policy development within government before the consultations were finished. Policy-makers became cocooned in self-searching, eventually forgetting about some of the basic problems that the policy had been intended to handle. Even the political implications of the Brophy and Aberle study were not comprehended by the PMO or the department, except for Christie. Indeed, in the last analysis the policy exercise seemed to be carried out for the benefit of the policy-makers while Indian demands grew more remote from their considerations, a condition graphically illustrated in Christie's assessment of the policy in mid-May.

Indian demands were easy to discredit. Because Indians were as yet politically unorganized, their spokesmen could be readily questioned on their representativeness of Indian opinion in general. Furthermore, although the spokesmen remained firm in their demands for special rights and participation in policy-making throughout the consultations, these were undermined by the spokesmen's criticism of the consultation process as an inappropriate mechanism for reflecting Indian feelings. Once Indian demands were taken to the policy-making arena, they met further opposition, the activists believing that Indians were misguided in their insistence on special rights, and the department and the PMO claiming that Indian demands for direct participation in the policy process were unrealistic. Hence, the underlying premise remained unchanged: policy-makers were better able to judge the cause of the problem and its solutions than Indians.

Indian demands were hampered by another equally important obstacle. The simplistic view of ethnic minority survival led some policy-makers to believe that 'the past' could be closed off in some fashion so as to reorient the Indian world view to 'the future.' This attitude was highly compatible with Trudeau's ahistorical position on policy-making. 'The future,' moreover, was envisioned largely as a white world, not one that recognized or accommodated Indian cultural values. Implicit in this thinking was the belief that Indian emphasis on special rights was basically a reaction to their being denied equal status – a defence mechanism based on their exclusion. Indians were viewed as poor 'aspiring whites' who preferred what they did not have. To the extent that Indian cultural systems were recognized, they were cast in the past tense and viewed as outmoded. The importance of these cultural systems to Indians, no matter how acculturated, was simply not understood. In short, Indians were viewed in terms of the socio-economic class structure, not ethnicity.

In its final form, the White Paper responded, or perhaps more accurately corresponded, to white liberal demands from the public, not to Indian demands. At no time, for example, was there an exploration of how special rights could be retained as a basis for Indian self-development. Special rights and special bureaucracies were cemented conceptually, and left unquestioned. In short, the government accepted the public definition of the Indian problem as one of discrimination, and attempts to go beyond this definition by acknowledging special rights, as the department tried to do, and by promoting Indian participation in the policy process, as the activists attempted, were systematically resisted by the PMO in its aim to keep the problem manageable, and its solution logically consistent.

Possibly the greatest irony of the White Paper is that it was not a significant innovation when its individual components are examined. In many ways, it was simply an extention of the policy direction of the Laing era. The transfer of DIAND programs to the provinces, for instance, had begun in the fields of health and education in the 1940s and 1950s and was adopted as a policy in 1964. Consultations with Indians on DIAND's programs had been accepted in principle in 1964, and put into practice in 1965 with the formation of the Indian advisory boards. The principle was carried further in the idea of the Indian Act consultation meetings, but in hindsight, the consultations were simply an attempt to systematize Indian advice. In economic development, the traditional disregard for broadscale socio-economic development programs was carried into the White Paper, social development programs having been set aside with the activists' proposals. Indian claims settlement, in fact, took a retrograde step in the

White Paper, to the post-war position which had come under attack by the special parliamentary committees first in 1947 and later in 1961. Paradoxically, the White Paper stimulated Indian nativism as no claims commission or treaty settlement had ever done.

The White Paper's only innovation was termination, a policy designed to eradicate all special Indian rights in the immediate future. Unlike the American policy which was applied selectively to tribes (LaFarge 1957), the White Paper was to have universal application. The fusion of the liberal ideology with Trudeau's own views against special rights for ethnic groups, especially those rights entrenched in law, made termination the central theme in the new policy. Like the Indian claims commission bills proposed in the mid-1960s, the PMO and DIAND felt the White Paper was the correct approach to the Indian problem, and that it should be implemented. In the end the department's official position was even firmer than the PMO's: implementation should have been pursued resolutely. At the time of its release, the policy-makers did not foresee that the White Paper would eventually be withdrawn.

In the final analysis the White Paper was discredited not because it failed to cater to Indian demands, but because it failed to offer reasonable methods for coping with the problems Indians were experiencing. The policy was a response to values within the policy-making arena, not to the basic problems facing Indians. Although the policy-makers struggled to produce a 'good' policy, the White Paper was basically a self-serving policy designed to free the government from criticism, protecting it from future accusations of discrimination. Had it been otherwise, care would have been taken to ensure that transfer of services to the provinces was scrupulously monitored to protect Indian interests, and that the process of implementation would be open to scrutiny by Indians in order to minimize their distrust and remove their fears of abandonment. Social development programs would have been a central feature for coping with poverty, and funding for Indian organizations would have been offered at the same time. The policy contained none of these provisions.

CHAPTER NINE   Developments after
the White Paper

Within a few years following the retraction of the White Paper, Indian
policy underwent shifts in direction in both aboriginal rights and Indian
participation in policy-making.

Chrétien's retraction of the White Paper did not change the government's denial of aboriginal title as a basis for claims settlement. By 1971
aboriginal claims became the focus of the Indian movement primarily
because enormous energy resource-development schemes, first in
James Bay[1] and then in the Mackenzie Valley,[2] threatened to damage
severely Indian lifestyles. Indians and white supporters organized in an
unprecedented fashion, pressuring the federal government through the
courts and the press to make land claims settlements in Quebec and the
Arctic. Even though Nishga demands for legal recognition of their aboriginal title were rejected before the Supreme Court of Canada in early
1973, a minority dissenting opinion supported the Nishga claim. This
significantly influenced Trudeau's own thinking, leading him to believe
there was greater legitimacy to Indian title than he had thought in 1969.[3]
Public sentiment, strongly supportive of aboriginal claims settlement, was
reflected in the House of Commons Standing Committee on Indian
Affairs which, in a rare instance of disagreement with official government
policy, endorsed the National Indian Brotherhood's demands for recognition of these claims.[4] Combined, these pressures on government from the
public, the courts, and the Standing Committee culminated in a major
policy reversal in August 1973, when Chrétien announced a new policy
on comprehensive claims settlement in non-treaty areas of Canada.[5]

This victory, a more difficult one for the Indian movement than the
retraction of the White Paper had been, represented the last major rever-

sal of the 1969 policy. Between 1970 and 1976, the federal government granted almost $17 million to Indian and Inuit organizations to research their land claims in preparation for submission to the government.[6] Since 1973, the James Bay Agreement has been ratified by Parliament,[7] and claims settlement negotiations have begun in the Yukon[8] and the Western Arctic[9] although they have made limited progress. British Columbia, ironically, has not taken advantage of the government's new claims policy. Pressure from massive resource development, such as occurred in James Bay and the Arctic, were absent in British Columbia, and the collapse of the Union of British Columbia Indian Chiefs in 1975 halted efforts to submit a province-wide claim.[10]

While the Indian movement was preoccupied with aboriginal claims, a second issue arose requiring further defence of Indian rights. Unlike the ecology movement, which supported Indian demands, the womens' rights movement clashed with Indian special rights over the status of Indian women. The basic issue was that the Indian Act penalized Indian women, but not Indian men, who married non-Indians, by abrogating their legal status.[11] Jeannette Lavell, a southern Ontario Ojibwa woman who had married a white man in 1970, and who was influenced by the womens' rights movement, took her case as far as the Supreme Court of Canada, arguing that the membership provisions in the Indian Act were discriminatory on the basis of sex and race.[12] The Drybones decision of 1969, paving the way for Lavell, had eliminated the liquor sections from the Indian Act on the grounds that those provisions were discriminatory on the basis of race and contrary to the Bill of Rights.[13] The broader political implication of the Lavell case was that it threatened to open up the possibility that the entire Indian Act could be considered racist. If the Act were to fall before the courts on racist grounds, the consequence would be the judicial implementation of the White Paper. In a remarkable demonstration of unity, the National Indian Brotherhood and each of its constituent provincial organizations intervened in the Supreme Court case against Lavell, arguing that the proper way to revise the Indian Act was through Parliament, not the courts.[14] Much to the amazement of womens' rights advocates, the Supreme Court judgment in August 1973 went against Lavell, leaving the contentious provisions untouched in the Indian Act. The NIB, and status Indians in general, heralded the judgment as a victory in defending the Indian Act against possible nullification or further erosion, and against the Bill of Rights which was seen to jeopardize their special rights.

Given their recent defence of the Indian Act, Indian organizations were no more interested in revising the Act than they had been during the consultation meetings preceding the White Paper, although the Alberta

Indian Association did propose a series of amendments to the NIB for government consideration (Cardinal 1977). Indeed, Indian distrust of the government was so strong, there was little interest in pursuing a new mechanism for joint Indian-government consultation on policy, as the Red Paper had called for in 1970.

In summer 1970, shortly after the Red Paper's presentation to the cabinet, both the Secretary of State and DIAND submitted policy proposals to the Cabinet Committee on Social Policy which were intended to increase Indian consultation.[15] On receiving the submissions, the committee's prime concern was the political consequences of enhancing public participation because supporting citizens' groups in the past had produced heightened and at times unwelcome demands on the government. The committee felt this issue of public participation had to be faced squarely by the government: 'participation' needed clarification:

The central question which begged an answer was the method through which a democratic government committed to participation could subsidize self-help groups whose action it could not control but the results of which could create unrealistic expectations:

[It was agreed that] Cabinet guidance on the priority problem 'Participation' was urgently needed. Problems would multiply unless government policy on this matter were made clear.[16]

Although an internal government report on public participation was prepared the following year (Doerr 1973: 98), it was not made public, and after the 1972 election the notion of participatory democracy was no longer promoted by the Trudeau administration. However, the policy of consultation continued to be applied to Indians, and the Secretary of State became the source of core funding for Indian organizations while DIAND subsidized the treaty and aboriginal rights research.

In July 1970, as a response to the Red Paper, DIAND proposed to cabinet a new tri-level scheme for Indian-government consultation on general policy. At the top political level, a small committee of ministers from the Cabinet Committee on Social Policy was to set broad policy guidelines, meeting with Indian representatives 'occasionally as required.'[17] At the administrative level, a National Joint Committee on Indian Affairs was to be established, composed of officials from various federal departments and Indian organizations. This latter group, concentrating on programs and services, was to 'provide the national forum in which the Indians could advance their views on policies.'[18] The third level of consultation was a tripartite one involving the federal and provincial governments and

Indian organizations. Ultimately, tripartite committees would be established for each province, although it was felt the provincial-level mechanism might take longer to develop since the provinces, despite agreeing with the White Paper in principle, were withholding any action unless asked by Indians.

DIAND received cabinet committee approval for its proposed consultative machinery, but its officials soon encountered difficulties in informal discussions of the new scheme with Indian representatives.[19] The NIB, and particularly the Alberta Indian Association, objected to the fact that the main channel of communication between Indians and the government was limited to the bureaucracy. Despite Indian displeasure with the proposal, DIAND was authorized to continue informal discussions, and to stress that Indian Affairs was a 'multi-ministerial and multi-departmental' matter, not the responsibility of a single minister as the Red Paper had requested. Furthermore, the advisory nature of the consultation process was to be plainly stated to Indian participants:

It was agreed that:
It be clearly conveyed to the Indian leaders that the consultative structure will not have final decision-making authority; that the conclusions reached at the Review and Recommendation level [the administrative level] must go to the Policy and Negotiation level [ministerial level] and those of that level will be subject to normal processes of government and Parliament.[20]

DIAND's scheme amounted to a negligible gain for Indians in the policy-making process. Even though Indians would have greater contact with civil servants in several departments, this did not link them to the political level as they had sought. The cabinet, however, was not prepared to relax its position. The resulting impasse was evident in July 1972, when the first meeting was held with the executive of the NIB. The meeting proved unsatisfactory for both the government and the NIB, and subsequently there was little desire from either side to continue meeting. Indians' interests lay elsewhere, primarily in James Bay and the Mackenzie Valley, and the government was not prepared at that time to push many policies ahead without Indian support.

But the notion of high-level policy consultation with native peoples did not remain dormant during 1973. Walter Rudnicki had moved to the Ministry of Urban Affairs in June 1969, where he became director of the Canadian Mortgage and Housing Corporation (Shackleton 1977: 155-208). In October 1973 he was fired by the president of CMHC, William Teron, for allegedly showing the Native Council of Canada – the national organization of Metis and non-status Indians – a confidential cabinet document outlining the government's proposed new native housing policy, without the approval to do so (*City Magazine* 1976). Rudnicki, denying that he had violated the Official Secrets Act, argued that he had been instructed to consult with the Native Council on the proposal. In 1976 he was successful in winning his case of wrongful dismissal against the government, but he was not reinstated in the public service. Consultation with Indians *before* cabinet approved a policy had been the activists' goal in 1968, and the Rudnicki judgment brought the issue into the public domain. Pre-cabinet consultation came closer to reality with the increasing political unrest among Indians in 1973–74 and because of lobbying behind the scene by Clive Linklater, then the executive director of NIB, and Lloyd Barber, Indian Claims Commissioner.

DIAND offices in Ottawa were occupied by Indian youth in summer 1973, and the following year a more militant demonstration of Indian disaffection occurred when Indians occupied DIAND's Calgary office (Ryan 1978). The Anishinabe Park occupation in Kenora followed, with Indian protest reaching a peak in Ottawa in the fall of 1974, after the Native Caravan's trek from Vancouver to Ottawa and demonstration on Parliament Hill.[21]

Indians were 'in motion,' as they were in the United States (e.g. Deloria 1969, Witt 1968), where the violence of Wounded Knee had inspired more militant uprisings. In an apparent effort to quell the agitation in Canada, the Trudeau government reconsidered its efforts to establish a new consultative mechanism with Indians in 1975. Thus, in late 1974 and early 1975, under pressure from the NIB, the government took unprecedented action by creating a Joint Cabinet-National Indian Brotherhood Committee which, unlike the 1970 proposals, linked the executive of the NIB directly to a special group of cabinet ministers in the Social Policy Cabinet Committee (Price 1977: 61-132). The intent was 'to establish a process designed to yield agreements between government and the representatives of the Indian people on major policy issues.'[22] In summer 1976 further refinements were announced in a cabinet-approved policy entitled 'New Federal Government-Indian Relationship.' The new policy recognized the continuing special status of Indians, which it described as 'a concept of Indian identity within Canadian society rather than separation from Canadian society or assimilation into it.'[23] The global policy approach, as used in the White Paper, was judged unsuitable for meeting the different needs of Indian communities; it was set aside in favour of developing more flexible policies and systematic joint planning between Indians and the government at the national, provincial, and band levels.

Indian participation took yet another form when Indian leaders such as Fred Kelly in Ontario, Elijah Smith in the Yukon, Ahab Spence in Manitoba, and Harold Cardinal in Alberta were hired to take on senior positions in DIAND. But with the exception of Ahab Spence, their tenure was short-lived, with Cardinal's dismissal becoming a *cause célèbre* when he pursued his investigations of financial mismanagement among certain bands in Alberta.[24] Increased native employment in government was generally espoused,[25] but by 1977 the climate of public opinion, becoming more conservative under the economic recession, was less sympathetic to government sponsorship of social programs. The turnover of ministers of Indian Affairs began to pick up speed, much as it had in the mid-1960s, with Judd Buchanan succeeding Chrétien in 1974, and Warren Allmand following shortly after for a tenure of one year before Hugh Faulkner was appointed in September of 1977 (see Table 2).

Initially both the government and the NIB were cautiously optimistic about the prospects of the Joint Cabinet-NIB Committee. The link between the NIB and the cabinet was a unique structure for the federal government, and there was hope that it would optimize the chances of developing mutually acceptable policies. However, by winter 1978, relations within the joint committee deteriorated. The government perceived the joint committee as an 'advisory' body, whereas the NIB understood that it would be a 'negotiating' forum; the NIB resented the limited powers it felt it had in the arrangement, as well as the continued reluctance of the government to declare its views to Indian participants; the government, in turn, found many of the NIB demands unreasonable and unrealistic. Whatever the circumstances behind the breakdown of relations in the joint committee, the NIB abruptly pulled out in April 1978. Among the reasons cited by Noel Starblanket, NIB President, were the government's implementation of the White Paper and its failure to move ahead on any NIB proposals.[26] After three years of operation, the joint committee had failed to produce any new policies of mutual acceptance. Although there are complex factors undoubtedly behind this failure, it demonstrates that the basic issue of Indian participation, raised during the preparation of the White Paper, remains problematic for both the government and Indian organizations.

The White Paper forged Indian associations into a defensive stance, but the skills necessary to counter the 1969 policy are understandably different from those needed to sustain high-level policy negotiations and compromises. Indians had organized *against* the White Paper out of fear of losing their special rights, but when they organized *for* specific policies, such as education, housing, and economic development, government compliance was negligible.[27] When the government opened the door to the cabinet for consultation, the legacy of Indian distrust from the White Paper was continually encountered, feeding back into the joint committee the suspicion that the government had powerfully fostered in 1969.

Although there is sound empirical reason for this distrust, the pervading atmosphere of suspicion cannot help but affect Indian leaders and government officials who are seriously trying to improve the services and policies for Indians. Although there is good reason for cynicism, given the ill-conceived policies, indiscriminant suspicion saps energies and resources that are badly needed to cope with issues facing Indians at the community level. It hinders effective Indian lobbying in Ottawa, especially under conditions of economic cutbacks and political conservatism, and it diverts attention to debates on whether the White Paper is still being implemented. Indeed, the White Paper has become a symbol of any unpopular and unapproved government initiative. In the sense that the White Paper is the embodiment of the liberal ideology, it will inevitably be in a state of perpetual implementation whenever the liberal ideology predominates in the government.

When we look back and assess it more fully, the decade of 'Indian participatory democracy' may turn out to be a period in which Indians became politically organized and the government experimented with policies. Yet little progress was made in alleviating most of the problems facing Indians in their communities.[28] As Trudeau acknowledged in assessing his own administration in 1978, 'the Indian question is still with us.'[29] The decade has proven that an experiment like the White Paper is a costly and unwise *strategy*, particularly for minority groups which are economically and politically marginal in society. The White Paper was an experiment for which both Indians and government will pay for many years to come.

Notes

PREFACE

1 Sally M. Weaver, 'A Case Study of the Role of Social Science in Policy Formulation: The White Paper on Indian Policy 1969,' paper read at the National Social Science Conference sponsored by the Social Science Research Council of Canada, Ottawa, 20–22 November 1975.

INTRODUCTION

1 These were contained in: *Citizens Plus* [The Red Paper], Indian Chiefs of Alberta (Edmonton 1970); *Wahbung: Our Tomorrows*, Manitoba Indian Brotherhood (Winnipeg 1971); *A Declaration of Indian Rights: The B.C. Indian Position Paper*, Union of British Columbia Indian Chiefs (Victoria 1970); *Position Paper*, Association of Iroquois and Allied Indians (Brantford 1971).

2 'Statement by the Prime Minister at a Meeting with the Indian Association of Alberta and the National Indian Brotherhood, Ottawa, June 4, 1970,' printed by the Indian-Eskimo Association (Toronto 1970).

3 Jean Chrétien, 'The Unfinished Tapestry – Indian Policy in Canada,' speech given at Queen's University, Kingston, Ontario, 17 March 1971 (Ottawa: DIAND Press Release).

4 National Indian Brotherhood, 'Indians Withdraw from Cabinet Discussions,' press release, 13 April 1978 (Ottawa); Theresa Nahanee, 'The '69 White Paper Is Being Implemented: Anthony Francis,' *Indian News* (DIAND) 17/9 (1976): 5, 'New Minister Tells NIB Assembly "You're the Boss,"' *Indian News* 17/9 (1976): 2, 'Indian Leaders Cannot Afford to Sit on the Fence Any Longer: Dave Ahenakew,' *Indian News* 17/1 (1976): 3,6, 'White Paper of '69 Not Being Pursued Minister Tells Alberta Chiefs,' *Indian News* 18/1 (1977): 1; and Brass (1977).

5 See Watkins (1957), LaFarge (1957), Lurie (1972), Edgerton (1962), Hood (1972), Menominee (1972), Orfield (1966), Stern (1965), Tyler (1964), and Ames and Fisher (1959).

6 Pierre Elliott Trudeau, 'Notes and Remarks by the Prime Minister at the Harrison Liberal Conference,' Harrison Hot Springs, British Columbia, 21 November 1969. See also Hockin (1971b), Doern (1971, 1971a), and Szablowski (1971).

7 Confidential interviews with PCO officials. See also Thordarson (1972).
8 Pierre Elliott Trudeau, 'Statement by the Prime Minister on the "Just Society,"'
Liberal Party of Canada, Ottawa, May 1968.

CHAPTER 1

1 The Indian Act, Revised Statutes of Canada, 1951, Ch. 149. For a summary of
Indian Affairs programs in this decade see 'A Review of Activities, 1948–58,'
Department of Citizenship and Immigration 1959.
2 One of the earliest reports demonstrating this was R.M. Vanderburgh's 'The Canadian Indian in Ontario's School Texts: A Study of Social Studies Textbooks, Grades 1
through 8,' prepared for the University Women's Club of Port Credit, Ontario, 1968.
3 See the following briefs by the Indian-Eskimo Association of Canada: 'An Economic
Development Plan for Indian Reserve Communities in Canada,' 1964; 'Indian Hunting Rights and the Migratory Birds Convention Act: A Brief to the Government of
Canada from the Indian-Eskimo Association of Canada,' July 1967; 'An Action Project to Encourage and Support Indian and Metis Community Action for Improved
Housing through the Development and Use of Appropriate Programs of Assistance:
For Presentation to the Honourable Arthur Laing, Minister of Indian Affairs and
Northern Development,' September 1967; 'Trappers Assistance Program: A Brief to
the Government of the Northwest Territories from the Indian-Eskimo Association of
Canada, Northwest Territories Division,' November 1967; 'An Action Research Pro-
ject on "Indians and the City" for Presentation to the Honourable Arthur Laing,
Minister, Indian Affairs and Northern Development,' September 1967. See also
O'Connell (1968) and McEwen (1968).
4 Arthur Laing's speeches, 'The Indian People and the Indian Act,' given to the
Ryerson's Men's Club, Vancouver, British Columbia, 16 October 1967, and 'The
Conflicting Heritage,' given to the Vancouver Institute at the University of British
Columbia, 23 March 1968 (Ottawa: DIAND press releases).
5 Interviews with senior and retired Indian Affairs Branch officials.
6 IODE, 'Re. A Proposal for a Research Programme to Assist Canadian Citizens of
Indian Origin' and letter, H.M. Jones to Hon. R. Bell, 7 January 1963, both found in
Public Archives of Canada, Record Group 10, Vol. 7983.
7 Interviews with Harry Hawthorn, Alan Cairns and Stuart Jamieson, February 1976,
Vancouver.
8 George E. Mortimore, 'Vast Aid Urged to Enable Indians to Move from Depressed
Reserves,' Toronto Globe and Mail, 22 February 1967. See also Mortimore (1967)
for a journal review of the report.
9 Interviews with Harry Hawthorn, February 1976, Vancouver.
10 The 1949 figure comes from 'The Big Picture: Indian Affairs Branch Statement for
Federal-Provincial Conference on Poverty,' by Walter Rudnicki, November 1965,
p. 4; the 1968 figure comes from 'Facts and Figures, 1968,' DIAND.
11 Annual Report of the Department of Health and Welfare for 1961/62, p. 98.
12 'The Big Picture: Indian Affairs Branch Statement for Federal-Provincial Conference
on Poverty,' by Walter Rudnicki, November 1965.
13 Confidential interviews with DIAND and PCO officials.
14 'Federal-Provincial Conference Coordinating Committee Report on Indian Affairs
Administration,' DIAND, 11 September 1963.
15 Cabinet memorandum, 'Community Development – Indian Affairs Branch,'
17 March 1964; and cabinet decision, 'Proposals for Indian Development and Integration,' 1 June 1964.
16 Cabinet decision, 'Proposals,' p. 2.
17 'Report of Proceedings of the Federal-Provincial Conference on Indian Affairs,'
29–30 October 1964, Department of Citizenship and Immigration.

18 Annual Report of the Department of Citizenship and Immigration for 1964/65, pp. 25-7; and for 1965/66, p. 46.

19 'Minutes of Fourth Meeting, National Indian Advisory Board, Ottawa, May 1–5, 1967,' DIAND, pp. 30-5; and interviews with senior DIAND officials.

20 Interviews with Walter Rudnicki, June 1976, Ottawa.

21 Personal communication, Victor Valentine, April 1977; interviews with Harry Hawthorn, Alan Cairns, and Stuart Jamieson, February 1976, Vancouver.

22 'Summary of Discussions and Recommendations of the Regional Indian Advisory Councils on the Indian Act,' DIAND 1967; 'Minutes of First Meeting, National Indian Advisory Board, Ottawa, January 10–12, 1966'; 'Minutes of Second Meeting, National Indian Advisory Board, Ottawa, September 19–23, 1966'; 'Minutes of Third Meeting, National Indian Advisory Board, Winnipeg, December 5–9, 1966'; and 'Minutes of Fourth Meeting, National Indian Advisory Board, Ottawa, May 1–5, 1967,' DIAND: Arthur Laing, press release, 21 September 1967.

23 'Minutes of Fourth Meeting,' p. 5.

24 'Minutes of Fourth Meeting,' pp. 6-14.

25 'Minutes of Fourth Meeting,' Appendix 2, 'Revision of the Indian Act.'

26 George Manuel, personal communication, 29 March 1977.

27 Jameson J. Bond, 'A Report on the Pilot Relocation Project at Elliot Lake, Ontario,' submitted to DIAND, December 1967, and 'An Evaluation Study of a Pilot Relocation Project for Indians at Elliot Lake, Ontario,' DIAND Education Branch, Employment and Related Services Division, June 1970. See also the National Film Board's 'Elliot Lake Relocation.'

28 Sources for Canadian treaties are Cumming and Mickenberg (1972), Lysyk (1968, 1969, 1973), Sanders (1973, 1974, 1974a, 1974b, 1974e), McInnes (1969), Canada (1912), DIAND (1966), McGilp (1963:299-301).

29 For a thorough discussion of aboriginal title see Lysyk (1973) and Sanders (1974). See also Mickenberg (1971), Indian Claims Commission (1975, 1977), Cumming and Mickenberg (1972).

30 Sanders (1973a, 1976), Beth Van Dyke and Douglas Sanders, 'The Indian Land Claim Struggle in British Columbia: A Brief History,' unpublished paper, 1975; Douglas Sanders, 'The Politicians and the Land Claims,' a talk given to the First Annual Assembly of the Haida Nation Organization, Skidegate, Queen Charlotte Islands, 6 December 1975.

31 'Brief Prepared by the Aboriginal Native Rights Regional Committee of the Interior Tribes of British Columbia,' and 'Supplemental Brief,' published in Joint Committee of the Senate and House of Commons on Indian Affairs, Minutes of Proceedings and Evidence, 26–27 May 1960, No. 7, pp. 592-621. See also Manuel and Posluns (1974: 27-32, 86-98).

32 Sources for the USA Claims Commission are Lysyk (1972), Lurie (1955, 1957), Barney (1955, 1960), Barker (1960), Vance (1974).

33 Minutes of Proceedings and Evidence, Special Committee of the House of Commons Appointed to Consider Bill No. 79, An Act Respecting Indians, 1951, No. 1, pp. 15-16.

34 'Bill [not numbered], An Act to Provide for the Establishment of an Indian Claims Commission,' 1st session, 25th Parliament, 1962; House of Commons Debates, 27 September 1962, p. 8, and 18 October 1962, p. 654; interviews with senior DIAND officials.

35 Interviews with senior DIAND officials.

36 'Bill C-130, An Act to Provide for the Disposition of Indian Claims,' 1st session, 26th Parliament, 1963.

37 'Summary of Submissions on the Indian Claims Bill C-130: 1964–65,' Indian Affairs Branch, Department of Citizenship and Immigration.

38 Letter, T.R. Berger to R. Williams of Indian Affairs Branch, 20 July 1965 (DIAND file 1/3-11-21).
39 'Bill 123, An Act to Provide for the Disposition of Indian Claims,' 3rd session, 26th Parliament, 1965; House of Commons Debates, 22 June 1965, pp. 2749-63.
40 House of Commons Debates, 22 June 1965, pp. 2760-3.
41 'Indian Claims Commission,' DIAND memo, 30 May 1963.
42 Arthur Laing's speeches 'The Indian People and the Indian Act,' 16 October 1967, and 'The Conflicting Heritage,' 23 March 1968.
43 Indians were not allowed land as compensation in any of the claims commission bills.
44 'Indian Claims Commission,' DIAND memo, 30 May 1963, p. 3.
45 Quebec (1976), CASNP (1975).
46 B.Van Dyke and Douglas Sanders, 'The Indian Land Claim Struggle in British Columbia: A Brief History,' unpublished paper, 1975.
47 'National Indian Brotherhood, Canadian Metis Society, Indian-Eskimo Association: Report of a Joint Meeting of the Boards of Directors of the Above Organizations for Purpose of Reviewing and Re-directing the Role of the Indian-Eskimo Association,' 26 September 1968; 'Joint Meeting Works Out Important Policy Changes,' Indian-Eskimo Association *Bulletin* 1968, 9(4); letter, K. Goodwill to J. Lagasse, 9 February 1968 (DIAND file 1/24-2-38, Vol. 2).
48 Gordon Lee, 'Indian-Eskimo Association; Canadian Association in Support of the Native Peoples: Historical Summary and Analysis,' Canadian Association in Support of the Native Peoples, Ottawa, 1976.
49 George Manuel, personal communication, 29 March 1977.
50 Records of the National Liberal Party Conferences for 1966 and 1968. Public Archives of Canada, Vol. 896 and 897.
51 Interviews with senior DIAND officials.
52 Interviews with senior DIAND officials. See also A.G. Leslie, 'Policies, Programs and New Directions in Indian Affairs,' address to the Department of Sociology and Anthropology at the University of Calgary, 10 March 1967 (DIAND Press Release).
53 Memo, R. Battle to the Minister, 8 June 1967, pp. 21-2 (DIAND file 1/19-2-10-1).
54 Arthur Laing's speech 'The Indian People and the Indian Act,' 16 October 1967.
55 Letter, Arthur Laing to Gordon Robertson, 19 October 1963.
56 See note 54.
57 House of Commons Debates, 11 December 1967, p. 5264.

CHAPTER 2

1 Interviews with senior DIAND officials.
2 Memo, Head of the Special Planning Secretariat to Gordon Robertson, 14 February 1967.
3 Ibid.
4 Letter, E. Manning, W.R. Thatcher, and D. Roblin to Prime Minister Pearson, 8 March 1967.
5 'Briefing Paper, PM, Indian Affairs,' 1 April 1968, prepared in the Social Policy Secretariat of the PCO; and confidential interviews with PCO officials.
6 Arthur Laing, press release, 18 March 1968.
7 Arthur Laing, press release, 1 May and 18 March 1968; and letter, R.F. Battle to the Minister, 7 March 1966 (DIAND file 6/15-2, Vol. 1).
8 Pierre Elliott Trudeau, 'Transcript of the Prime Minister's Remarks at the Vancouver Liberal Association Dinner, Seaforth Armories, Vancouver, British Columbia,' 8 August 1969, and 'Statement by the Prime Minister at a Meeting with the Indian Association of Alberta and the National Indian Brotherhood, Ottawa, June 4, 1970,' printed by the Indian-Eskimo Association, Toronto.
9 Quote on back cover of Trudeau (1968).

10 'PM: No Ready Answer to Indian-Eskimo problems,' Winnipeg *Tribune*, 13 June
    1968; 'Trudeau: Handling of Indians Blot on Record,' Ottawa *Citizen*, 13 June 1968;
    'Let's Treat Indians More Like Canadians,' Calgary *Albertan*, 14 May 1968; 'Trudeau
    Promises to Help Indians,' Winnipeg *Free Press*, 13 June 1968.
11 Pierre Elliott Trudeau, 'Transcript,' 8 August 1969.
12 Christian and Campbell (1974: 33-75), Marchak (1975: 12-26).
13 Christian and Campbell (1974: 65).
14 Ibid., 61-2.
15 Sources on general government reform are Doern (1971, 1971a, 1974), Hockin
    (1970, 1971, 1971a, 1971b), Aucoin (1975), Szablowski (1971, 1973), Kernaghan
    (1968), Robertson (1968), Sharp (1976), Abel (1968), Lamontagne (1968), Smith
    (1971), Jackson and Atkinson (1974), Stewart (1971).
16 Sources on the PMO are Lalonde (1971), Robertson (1971), Smith (1971), Doern
    (1971a), Wearing (1971), Hockin (1971a), Schindeler (1971), Doerr (1973), and
    'The Brains around Trudeau,' *Weekend Magazine*, 31 August 1968.
17 Doern (1971a: 57,67), Doerr (1973: 84-6).
18 Hockin (1971a, 1971b), Robertson (1971), Szablowski (1971), Doern (1971).
19 Sources on the PCO are Robertson (1968, 1971, 1976), Schindeler (1971), Doern
    (1971a), Ward (1972), Prefontaine (1973).
20 Sources on the general role of the deputy minister are Hodgetts (1974: 207-11),
    Johnson (1961), Pickersgill (1972), Balls (1976).
21 *Parliamentary Guide*, ed. Normandin (Ottawa: Intertask Ltd. 1974), p. 216; *Canada's
    28th Parliament: A Guide to the Members, Their Constituencies and Their Government*
    (Toronto: Methuen, 1971), p. 249.
22 *Canada's 28th Parliament* (Toronto: Methuen, 1971), p. 103.
23 'Chretien Living Proof of Point: French Can Get Top Portfolios,' Ottawa *Journal*,
    3 September 1968; 'Choice of Cabinet Based on Potential,' Ottawa *Journal*, 6 July
    1968; 'Ottawa Keeps Eye on Indian Affairs,' Montreal *Star*, 20 July 1968; CP Wire,
    'Trudeau-Responsibilities,' 19 July 1968; 'Job Challenging: Chretien,' Winnipeg
    Tribune, 10 August 1968.
24 'Consultations with the Indian People,' DIAND 1968.
25 Interviews with senior DIAND officials.
26 Standing Committee on Indian Affairs and Northern Development, 13 May 1969,
    Minutes of Proceedings and Evidence, p. 753; Consultation Report, Yellowknife,
    25–27 July 1968 (DIAND 1968–69 [1]: 1).
27 Quote is from Consultation Report, Moncton, 29–31 July 1968 (DIAND 1968–69 [2]:
    12). See also Consultation Report, Sudbury, 21–23 August 1968 (DIAND 1968–69 [5]:
    31); Quebec City 30 September to 4 October 1968 (DIAND 1968–69 [7]: 7); and
    Whitehorse, 21–23 October 1968 (DIAND 1968–69 [10]: 2).
28 See Consultation Report, Moncton, 29–31 July 1968 (DIAND 1968–69 [2]: 24) and
    Sudbury, 21–23 August 1968 (DIAND 1968–69 [5]: 31).
29 Consultation Report, Moncton, 29–31 July 1968 (DIAND 1968–69 [2]: 14); and
    Quebec City, 30 September to 4 October 1968 (DIAND 1968–69 [7]:8).
30 Consultation Report, Fort William, 16–19 August 1968 (DIAND 1968–69 [4]: 2);
    Sudbury, 21–23 August 1968 (DIAND 1968–69 [5]: 1-3); Toronto, 12–14 August
    1968 (DIAND 1968–69 [3]: 25); and letter , R. Andras to Prime Minister Trudeau,
    4 September 1968.
31 Consultation Report, Yellowknife, 25–27 July 1968 (DIAND 1968–69 [1]: 2-3).
32 Consultation Report, Toronto 12–14 August 1968 (DIAND 1968–69 [3]: 3-4).
33 Robert K. Andras, 'Notes for Address to the Third Annual National Citizenship
    Seminar of the Canadian Council of Christians and Jews, Halifax, Nova Scotia,
    August 30, 1968' (Ottawa: DIAND Press Release).
34 Consultation Report, Quebec City, 30 September to 4 October 1968 (DIAND 1968–69
    [7]: 8-9).

35 Interviews with John A. MacDonald, 8 June and 27 July 1976.
36 'Indian Issue Creates Split in Cabinet,' Toronto *Globe and Mail*, 1 October 1968; 'White Feather Getting Generous,' Calgary *Albertan*, 27 January 1969.
37 Interview with Robert Andras, 6 December 1976; interviews with Walter Rudnicki, summer 1976.
38 Interview with Jean Chrétien, 10 June 1976.
39 Interview with Robert Andras, 6 December 1976; 'Ottawa Keeps Eye on Indian Affairs,' Montreal *Star*, 20 July 1968.
40 Memo, Gordon Robertson to the Prime Minister, 15 July 1968; interview with Jean Chrétien, 10 June 1976.
41 Confidential interviews with DIAND and PCO officials.
42 Interview with Robert Andras, 6 December 1976, and with Jean Chrétien, 10 June 1976.
43 'Liberal Calls Indian Plight Nation's Shame,' Toronto *Globe and Mail*, 31 August 1968; 'Rebel in Office,' Red Deer *Advocate*, Alberta, 3 September 1968; 'New Hope for Canada's Indians?' Kingston *Whig-Standard*, 3 September 1968; 'Indians Seek Claims Board Not Promises, Says Minister,' Quebec *Chronicle Telegraph*, 30 September 1968; 'Rift within the Lute,' Charlottetown *Guardian*, 3 October 1968; 'Chretien, Andras Patch Up Split,' Toronto *Star*, 3 October 1968; DIAND Press Release, 'Notes for an Address by the Honourable Robert K. Andras to the Indian Consultation Meetings, Regina, Saskatchewan, September 17, 1968' in which Andras refers to himself as 'the Minister responsible for the development of new policies and programs' (p. 3).
44 'Indian Issue Creates Split in Cabinet,' Toronto *Globe and Mail*, 1 October 1968.
45 Memo, Jordan to Deputy Secretary in PCO, 29 July 1968; memo, Rudnicki to Deputy Secretary in PCO, 13 August 1968; memo, Rudnicki to Robert Andras, 8 August 1968; memo, Jordan to Deputy Secretary in PCO, 13 August 1968.
46 Memo, Jordan to Deputy Secretary in PCO, 29 July 1968; memo, Rudnicki to Deputy Secretary in PCO, 23 August 1968.
47 Memo, Rudnicki to the Prime Minister, 9 September 1968.
48 Memo, Rudnicki to Deputy Secretary in PCO, 14 August 1968.
49 House of Commons Debates, 12 September 1968, p. 8.
50 Ibid., p. 7.
51 Letter, Robert Andras to the Prime Minister, 4 September 1968.
52 Robert Andras, 'Notes for Address,' 30 August 1968, p. 11 (see note 33).
53 Memo, Gordon Robertson to Jordan, 18 September 1968.
54 Memo, Gordon Robertson to the Prime Minister, 19 September 1968; memo, Jordan to Gordon Robertson, 16 September 1968; letter, Prime Minister to Robert Andras, 23 September 1968.
55 Memo, Gordon Robertson to the Prime Minister, 19 September 1968.
56 Letter, the Prime Minister to Jean Chrétien, 23 September 1968; letter, the Prime Minister to Robert Andras, 23 September 1968.
57 'Indian Issue Creates Split in Cabinet,' Toronto *Globe and Mail*, 1 October 1968; 'Rift within the Lute,' Charlottetown *Guardian*, 3 October 1968; 'Andras Quitting Rumors "Untrue,"' Calgary *Albertan*, 4 October 1968; 'Chretien, Andras Patch Up Split,' Toronto *Star*, 3 October 1968; 'Indians May Revolt – Andras,' Winnipeg *Free Press*, 4 January 1969; 'Andras Says Violence Possible over Indian Grievances,' Toronto *Globe and Mail*, 4 January 1969; column by Fred Kennedy 'I Write as I Please,' Calgary *Albertan*, 22 February 1969.
58 Interview with Robert Andras, 6 December 1976; House of Commons Debates, 1 October 1968, pp. 623-4. See also 'Backs Minister: Trudeau Settles Indian Rift,' Toronto *Globe and Mail*, 2 October 1968.
59 House of Commons Debates, 2 October 1968, p. 690; 'Stanfield Charges Indian Affairs with Bureaucratic Indifference,' Ottawa *Citizen*, 3 October 1968.

60 1 October 1968.
61 3 October 1968.
62 Ibid.
63 'Indian Issue Creates Split in Cabinet,' Toronto *Globe and Mail*, 1 October 1968.
64 Annual Report of DIAND for 1968/69, p. 153.
65 House of Commons Debates, 1 October 1968, p. 624.
66 House of Commons Debates, 2 October 1968, p. 690.
67 Ibid., 691.
68 Ibid., 692.
69 Ibid., 689; see also Jean Chrétien's statements to the Standing Committee on Indian Affairs and Northern Development, 19 November 1968, Minutes of Proceedings and Evidence, p. 86.
70 Confidential interviews with DIAND and PCO officials.
71 'Chretien, Andras Patch Up Split,' Toronto *Star*, 3 October 1968.
72 Confidential interviews with PCO officials.
73 'Andras Says Violence Possible over Indian Grievances,' Toronto *Globe and Mail*, 4 January 1969.
74 Memo, Jim Davey to Marc Lalonde, 24 September 1968; memo, Gordon Robertson to Marc Lalonde, 24 September 1968; House of Commons Debates, 2 October 1968, p. 689; memo, Gordon Robertson to Rudnicki, 1 October 1968.

CHAPTER 3

1 Memo, Gordon Robertson to the Prime Minister, 23 October 1968.
2 Memo, Director of Policy and Planning in DIAND, 'Indian Affairs Policy and Planning Program Task Force,' 6 September 1968 (DIAND file 1/44-1, Vol. 1).
3 Interview with John A. MacDonald, 8 June 1976; covering memo, John A. MacDonald to Gordon Robertson, 30 October 1968; draft cabinet memorandum 'Canadian Indian and Eskimo Affairs,' dated October 1968, and background document 'Policy and Program Proposals for Indian and Eskimo Affairs; Brief to Cabinet Committee on Social Policy,' October 1968.
4 Memo, John A. MacDonald to Gordon Robertson, 30 October 1968.
5 Ibid.; Draft cabinet memorandum p. 1.
6 Draft cabinet memorandum, p. 1.
7 Ibid., 4-5.
8 Ibid., 6.
9 Ibid., 15.
10 Ibid., 72.
11 Ibid., 72.
12 Ibid., 67.
13 Ibid., 19.
14 Cabinet memorandum 'Canada Assistance Plan: Indian Welfare Agreements,' 25 October 1968.
15 'Angry Indians Cry MacDonald, Quit Job!' Toronto *The Ryersonian*, 29 October 1968.
16 Quoted in Bowles et al. (1972: 1).
17 See Cardinal (1969a) for his published speech.
18 Interview with John A. MacDonald, 8 June 1976.
19 Memo, 'Indian and Eskimo Policy,' Rudnicki to Gordon Robertson, 1 November 1968; memo, 'Policy for Native Peoples,' Rudnicki to Gordon Robertson, 13 November 1968.
20 Memo, 1 November (see note 18).
21 Ibid.
22 Memo, Rudnicki to Gordon Robertson, 13 November 1968.

23 Ibid., p. 24.
24 Memo, Gordon Robertson to Rudnicki, 7 November 1968.
25 Memo, Gordon Robertson to the Prime Minister, 23 November 1968.
26 Confidential interviews with PCO officials.
27 Confidential notes of PCO official, 27 October 1968.
28 Memo, Jim Davey to Marc Lalonde, 21 November 1968.
29 Confidential notes of PCO official, 27 October and 18 November 1968; memo, Jordan to Gordon Robertson, 8 November 1968.
30 Cabinet memorandum, 'Indian Treaties 8 and 11, Mackenzie District, Northwest Territories,' 19 November 1968.
31 House of Commons Debates, 23 September 1968, p. 325.
32 Standing Committee on Indian Affairs and Northern Development, 28 November 1968, Minutes of Proceedings and Evidence, pp. 116-17.
33 Andras' address to the Indian delegates in Consultation Report, Chilliwack, British Columbia, 18-22 November 1968 (DIAND 1968-69 [14]: 94]; see also 'Summary of Submission on the Indian Claims Bill C-130,' Department of Citizenship and Immigration, 1965.
34 Kenneth Lysyk, 'Resource Paper on Human Rights and Canada's Native People,' paper read at the Ninth Annual Meeting and Conference of the Indian-Eskimo Association of Canada, Toronto, September 1968. Printed by the Indian-Eskimo Association, Toronto.
35 Memo, Gordon Robertson to Rudnicki, 20 November 1968; memo, Rudnicki to Gordon Robertson, 20 November 1968; memo, Gordon Robertson to the Prime Minister, 23 November 1968.
36 Memo, Executive Assistant of Andras to Jim Davey, 29 November 1968.
37 Memo, Jim Davey to the Prime Minister, 25 November 1968; confidential interviews with PCO and DIAND officials. See also Thordarson for an evaluation of academic influence on foreign policy-making (1972: 118, 129, 148).
38 For Indian suspicion that the government was already taking decisions see, e.g. Consultation Report, Kelowna, British Columbia, 12-16 November 1968 (DIAND 1968-69 [13]: 64) and Consultation Report, Toronto, 20-24 January 1969 (DIAND 1968-69 [17]: 11). Also, memo, PCO Deputy Secretary to the Prime Minister, 11 October 1968; and House of Commons Debates, 14 November 1968, p. 2724.
39 John A. MacDonald, 'The Indian and His Future,' speech delivered to the Kiwanis Club, Ottawa, 13 September 1968. Ottawa: DIAND Press Release.
40 Memo, John A. MacDonald to Gordon Robertson, 9 December 1968.
41 Ibid.
42 Confidential interviews with PCO officials.
43 Memo, Gordon Robertson to the Prime Minister, 23 November 1968.
44 Confidential notes of a PCO official, 27 October 1968; memo, Gordon Robertson to the Prime Minister, 23 November 1968.
45 Memo, Gordon Robertson to Marc Lalonde, 24 September 1968.
46 Ibid., and memo, Gordon Robertson to the Prime Minister, 23 November 1968.
47 Memo, Jim Davey to the Prime Minister, 25 November 1968.
48 Ibid.
49 Ibid.
50 Confidential interviews with DIAND and PCO officials.
51 Memo, Jim Davey to Marc Lalonde, 6 December 1968.
52 George Manuel, personal communication, 29 March 1977.
53 Ibid.
54 'PM Refuses Indians Seat at Constitutional Talks,' Toronto Globe and Mail, 7 December 1968; 'Indians Dine with PM,' Winnipeg Free Press, 7 December 1968.
55 'Indian Delegates Happy with Trudeau Meeting,' Ottawa Citizen, 7 December 1968.
56 'PM Rejects Indian Bid for Ottawa Talks Role,' Montreal Star, 7 December 1968.

57 National Indian Brotherhood, Brief to Prime Minister Trudeau, 5 December 1968.
58 House of Commons Debates, 11 December 1968, p. 3811.
59 Letter, Prime Minister to Robert Andras and to Jean Chrétien, 10 December 1968.
60 Consultation Report, Winnipeg, 18-20 December (DIAND 1968–69 [16]: 26-7).
61 Consultation Report, Edmonton, 12-13 December (DIAND 1968–69 [15]: 7).

CHAPTER 4

1   'Minister's Arrival Ends Indian Boycott,' Calgary *Herald*, 12 December 1968.
2   'Indians Keep Trumps Hidden from Andras,' Edmonton *Journal*, 12 December 1968.
3   'Indian Policy Rift in Ottawa,' Calgary *Albertan*, 14 December 1968.
4   'Minister's Arrival Ends Indian Boycott.'
5   'Indian Policy Rift in Ottawa.'
6   'Early Ottawa Action Urged/Andras Says Violence Possible over Indian Grievances,' Toronto *Globe and Mail* 4 January 1969.
7   'Will Investigate Death,' Montreal *Star*, 18 December 1968; 'Indians Say Ottawa Careless in Death of Woman 22,' Toronto *Star*, 18 December 1968.
8   House of Commons Debates, 16 December 1968, p. 3969.
9   'Indian's Death Accident – Chretien,' Ottawa *Citizen*, 18 December 1968.
10 Memo, PCO Deputy Secretary to Jordan, 20 December 1968; letter, Prime Minister to Jean Chrétien, 23 December 1968.
11 Confidential interviews with senior DIAND officials.
12 Summary of Marshall Plan, John A. MacDonald, 9 December 1968.
13 Letter, Jean Chrétien to the Prime Minister, 15 January 1969.
14 'Intellectual Seeks Truth, Politician Seeks Possible,' Toronto *Star*, 13 January 1969.
15 House of Commons Debates, 16 December 1968, p. 3969.
16 Letter, Jean Chrétien to the Prime Minister, 15 January 1969.
17 Ibid.
18 Memo, Jim Davey to Marc Lalonde, 13 January 1969 and 17 January 1969.
19 Interview with John A. MacDonald, 8 June 1976.
20 Ibid.
21 Draft cabinet memorandum, 'Indian Program,' 14 January 1969.
22 Confidential interviews; memo, Jim Davey to Marc Lalonde, 13 January 1969.
23 House of Commons Debates, 10 December 1968, p. 4232.
24 House of Commons Debates, 14 January 1969, p. 4237.
25 Ibid.
26 Ibid., 4238.
27 Letter, Jean Chrétien to the Prime Minister, 15 January 1969.
28 Letter, Robert Andras to the Prime Minister, 13 January 1969; 'Draft of Policy,' a working paper prepared for Andras by one of his executive assistants, 17 January 1969.
29 Minutes of the Cabinet Committee on Social Policy and Cultural Affairs, 15 January 1969.
30 Ibid.
31 Memo, Jim Davey to Marc Lalonde, 17 January 1969.
32 Memo, Jim Davey to Marc Lalonde, 13 January 1969.
33 'He Opts for Ottawa: What Makes Up-Front Jean Chretien Run?' Philip Teasdale, *Financial Post*, 24 September 1977.
34 Memo, Jim Davey to Marc Lalonde, 17 January 1969.
35 Ibid., and confidential notes of PCO official on discussion with Jim Davey, 21 January 1969.
36 'Working Paper on Indian Policy,' Robert Andras, 28 January 1969.

37 'Policy Options – Indian Affairs,' Rudnicki, 10 January 1969, forwarded to Gordon Robertson by memo, 21 January.
38 'Working Paper,' p. 7.
39 Ibid., 2-3, 16, 25.
40 Ibid., 28-9.
41 Ibid., 20.
42 Memo, 'Indian Policy,' Secretary of the Cabinet Committee on Priorities and Planning to the Prime Minister (CCPP), 28 February 1969; letter, Robert Andras to Gordon Robertson, 4 February 1969; interviews with PCO officials.
43 Memo, 'Indian Policy,' Secretary of the CCPP to the Prime Minister, 28 February 1969; memo, Rudnicki to Jordan, 7 February 1969.
44 Memo, Jordan to Deputy Secretary in PCO, 'Notes for the PM, Cabinet Meeting, 13 February 1969.'
45 Memorandum, 13 February 1969.
46 Draft cabinet memorandum, 'Indian Policy,' 19 February 1969.
47 Memo, Secretary of the CCPP to the Prime Minister, 28 February 1969.
48 Jean Chrétien, 'The Indian People and Government – Toward a New Relationship,' speech given to the annual dinner of the Cornwall Board of Trade, Cornwall, Ontario, 29 January 1969 (Ottawa: DIAND Press Release).
49 Cabinet memorandum, 'Indian Policy,' 25 February 1969.
50 Ibid., 3.
51 Chrétien (1969: 10-11), and 'Playing Politics with the Indians,' Edmonton *Journal*, 3 February 1969.
52 Interview with Jean Chrétien, 10 June 1976.
53 Interviews with senior DIAND officials.
54 Memo, Secretary of the CCPP to the Prime Minister, 28 February 1969.
55 'Canada's Indians and the Unjust Society,' Toronto *Star*, 22 February 1969.
56 'A New Deal Outlined for Indians,' Toronto *Star*, 20 February 1969.
57 'Chretien Postpones March Pow-wow,' Ottawa *Citizen*, 26 February 1969.

CHAPTER 5

1 Memo, Secretary of CCPP to the Prime Minister, 28 February 1969.
2 Cabinet memorandum, 'Indian Program' 5 March 1969.
3 Interviews with senior DIAND officials.
4 Interviews with DIAND and PCO officials.
5 Memo, Jordan to Secretary of CCPP, 5 March 1969; memos from Rudnicki to Jordan 5 and 6 March 1969; confidential notes of PCO official, 4 March 1969.
6 Confidential notes of PCO official, 12 March 1969; memo, Gordon Robertson to Secretary of CCPP, 6 March 1969; memo, Chairman of Task Force to the Prime Minister, 1 April 1969; 'Composition of Working Groups on Indian Policy,' Appendix 3 to cabinet memorandum 'Report of the Interdepartmental Committee on Non-discriminatory Participation by Indians in the Economic, Social and Political Life of Canada,' 5 May 1969; and confidential interviews.
7 The following are the titles of the background papers prepared for the task force, from mid-March to the end of April 1969: Comparative Policies of Five Nations in Native Affairs Administration (DIAND); Study of Health Services for Canadian Indians by the Department of Health and Welfare; Alternatives for Senior Governments in the Development of Indian Local Government (DIAND); Indian Rights: Implications of the Policy in Respect to Rights (DIAND); Indian Rights (DIAND); Indian Claims (DIAND); Indian Lands (DIAND); Welfare: Principal Problems: Considerations for the Future (DIAND? DNH&W?); Economic Development of the Indians (DIAND?); Education Program by Program Areas (DIAND); Educational Services for Indians (DIAND); Indian Housing: Policy and Suggested Alternatives (DIAND);

Position Paper: Economic Development (DIAND?); Activities Related to Persons of Indian Ancestry (DREE); Community Services and Structures; Position Paper (DIAND?).
8 Interviews with senior DIAND officials.
9 Confidential interviews with core group officials.
10 First Drafting group report, 20 March 1969.
11 Fourth Drafting group report, 21 March 1969.
12 Memo, 'Policy Options – Indian Affairs,' by Rudnicki, 10 January 1969.
13 Cabinet memorandum, 'Report of the Interdepartmental Committee on Non-discriminatory Participation by Indians in the Economic, Social and Political Life of Canada,' Chairman of the Task Force, 5 May 1969, p. 2.
14 Memo, Jordan to Chairman of the Task Force, 2 May 1969, p. 9.
15 Ibid., 10.
16 Ibid., 5-6.
17 Ibid., 7.
18 Memo, Jordan to Chairman of the Task Force, 5 May 1969, pp. 3-4.
19 Confidential interviews.
20 Cabinet memorandum, Chairman of the Task Force, 2 May 1969, p. 10.
21 'Background Paper on the Financial and Certain Federal-Provincial Implications of the Proposal to Seek Provincial Cooperation in Extending a Full Range of Provincial Services to Indians,' appended to Cabinet memorandum, 'Formula for Financial Compensation to Provinces in Proposed Policy for Indian Canadians,' from finance group to Jordan, 5 May 1969.
22 Ibid., 3-7.
23 Ibid., 10.
24 Ibid., 6; and confidential interviews.
25 Ibid., 2; and memo from finance-group official to Jordan, 5 May 1969, p. 1.
26 Ibid., memo p. 3.
27 Ibid., memo, p. 1; and 'Background Paper,' p. 12. It is interesting to note that no reference was made to the Hawthorn Report's proposal for an Indian Progress Agency, which was to have had the same watchdog function. I am grateful to Dr Alan Cairns for this observation.
28 Ibid., memo p. 2.
29 Memo, Jim Davey to Marc Lalonde and the Prime Minister, 17 January 1969.

CHAPTER 6

1 'Verbatim Report of the National Conference on Indian Act, April 28–May 2, 1969,' Holiday Inn, Ottawa,' DIAND, p. 4.
2 Ibid., 279-98.
3 'Verbatim Report,' and 'Rapporteur's Account of National Conference on Indian Act, Holiday Inn, Ottawa, April 28–May 2, 1969,' DIAND. See also 'Resumé of Reports of the Indian Act Consultation Meetings,' March 1969, DIAND.
4 'Verbatim Report,' pp. 1-2.
5 House of Commons Debates, 5 May 1969, pp. 8292, 8307-8; 'Changes "a la King".' Toronto Telegram, 6 May 1969; 'Indians, Metis Sorry Andras Was Moved,' Toronto Star, 7 May 1969.
6 'Verbatim Report,' pp. 151-2.
7 Ibid., 260.
8 Consultation Report, Edmonton, 12–13 December 1968 (DIAND 1968–69 [15]: 7); Consultation Report, Winnipeg, 18–20 December 1968 (DIAND 1968–69 [16]: 26-7).
9 'Verbatim Report,' p. 352.
10 Ibid., 374.
11 Ibid., 242-96.

12 Ibid., 321-2.
13 Ibid., 327.
14 Colin Tatz, personal communication. Dr Tatz, a political scientist from Melbourne University, Australia, was on sabbatical leave at Queen's University, Kingston, and during the period from May to July 1969 he travelled throughout Canada interviewing Indian spokesmen on the consultation process. He attended the national consultation meeting and later wrote a report on consultation for DIAND which has not been released.
15 'An End to Isolation: New Day for Indians,' Ottawa *Citizen*, 3 May 1969; 'New "Partnership Era" for Indians Promised by Government,' Ottawa *Citizen*, 3 May 1969.
16 'Chretien Capitulates to Indians Demands, Backs Panel to Probe Treaty, Related Rights,' Toronto *Globe and Mail*, 3 May 1969.
17 Cabinet memorandum, 'Report on the Interdepartmental Committee on Non-discriminatory Participation by Indians in the Economic, Social and Political Life of Canada,' Chairman of the Task Force, 5 May 1969.
18 Draft of White Paper, April–May 1969 (Task Force document), pp. 5-6.
19 'Statement of the Government of Canada on Indian Policy, 1969,' prepared by DIAND officials, April 1969.
20 House of Commons Debates, 2 May 1969, p. 8260.
21 Memo, Gordon Robertson to the Prime Minister, 7 May 1969.
22 'Andras Transfer Displeases Saskatchewan Native Leaders,' Regina *Leader Post*, 8 May 1969; 'Indians, Metis Sorry Andras Was Moved,' Toronto *Star*, 7 May 1969; "Hellyer Gap Filled without Pain,' London *Free Press*, 6 May 1969.
23 Confidential interviews with DIAND and PCO officials.
24 Cabinet memorandum, 'Indian Policy,' 14 May 1969.
25 Ibid.
26 Hellyer's resignation from cabinet, when his task force proposals on housing were not accepted (Axworthy 1971), may well have influenced cabinet in a negative way regarding the idea of a task force in Indian policy. I have some evidence to suggest this, but nothing concrete enough to confirm it.
27 Interview with Jean Chrétien, 10 June 1976; interview with MacDonald, 27 July 1976.
28 Cabinet memorandum, 'Indian Policy,' 14 May 1969.
29 Ibid.
30 Ibid.
31 Letter, Robert Andras to the Prime Minister, 21 May 1969.
32 Confidential interviews with senior DIAND officials.
33 Memo, 'Policy Objectives and Tactics of Implementation,' by Christie, prepared in early May 1969 (dated by DIAND officials).
34 Ibid., 2.
35 Ibid., 2.
36 Ibid., 4-6.
37 Confidential interviews.
38 'Statement of the Government of Canada on Indian Policy, 1969,' prepared by DIAND officials, mid-May 1969.
39 Confidential interviews.
40 Confidential interviews.
41 Pierre Elliott Trudeau, 'Transcript,' 8 August 1969.
42 Interview with Jean Chrétien, 10 June 1976; interviews with senior DIAND officials.
43 Letter, John A. MacDonald to Secretary of the Treasury Board, 10 June 1969 (DIAND file 20-3-20).
44 Cabinet memorandum, 'Formula for Financial Compensation to Provinces in Proposed Policy for Indian Canadians,' Secretary of the Cabinet Committee on Economic Policy and Programmes, 4 June 1969 (reporting decisions meeting of 2 June).

45   Confidential notes of PCO official, 10 June 1969; and Cabinet memorandum, 'Indian Policy,' 17 June 1969.
46   Confidential interviews.
47   House of Commons Debates, 19 June 1969, p. 10414.
48   Confidential interviews: Manitoba Indian Brotherhood, 'Position Paper with Respect to Statement of the Government of Canada on Indian Policy – 1969,' 16 July 1969. Winnipeg.
49   Personal communication, Dave Courchene, 15 May 1978.
50   House of Commons Debates, 25 June 1969, p. 10581.
51   Ibid., 10582.
52   Memo, John A. MacDonald to DIAND employees, 25 June 1969 (DIAND file 20-3-20).
53   Ibid., 2.

CHAPTER 7

1   House of Commons Debates, 25 June 1969, p. 10583.
2   Ibid., 10584.
3   'Indian Policy Heralds Just Society,' Toronto Star, 26 June 1969; 'New Start for Indians,' Montreal Star, 26 June 1969; 'Full Equality for Indian Set,' Ottawa Citizen, 26 June 1969; 'Ottawa Plans to Treat Indians as Full Citizens,' Toronto Star, 26 June 1969; 'End Special Status of Canada's Indians, Ottawa's Decision,' Toronto Globe and Mail, 26 June 1969; 'Indians Cautious, Sceptical on Chretien Equality Plan,' Toronto Star, 26 June 1969.
4   'Indian Policy Heralds Just Society,' Toronto Star, 26 June 1969.
5   'Does Trudeau Care about Our Indians?' Ottawa Citizen, 27 June 1969.
6   'Indians Remaining Cautious – They've Heard it all before,' Ottawa Citizen, 26 June 1969; 'Full Equality for Indian Set,' Ottawa Citizen, 26 June 1969.
7   'Reactions of Indian Leaders Vary from Anger to Cautious Silence,' Toronto Globe and Mail, 26 June 1969.
8   National Indian Brotherhood, 'Statement on the Proposed New Indian Policy,' Ottawa, 26 June 1969.
9   Dave Courchene, Press Release, Manitoba Indian Brotherhood, Winnipeg, 26 June 1969.
10   Manitoba Indian Brotherhood, 'Position Paper with Respect to Statement of the Government of Canada on Indian Policy – 1969,' Winnipeg, 16 July 1969.
11   Ibid.; 'Indians Fearful: Federal Proposals Rejected as "Unacceptable,"' Ottawa Citizen, 29 June 1969; 'Indians Press Ottawa for Policy Change,' Toronto Globe and Mail, 27 June 1969; 'Indians Angry: Federal Officials May be Ejected,' Canadian Press Wire, 8 July 1969.
12   'Robarts Praises New Indian Policy,' Toronto Star, 26 June 1969; 'Robarts Calls New Policy Breakthrough,' Toronto Globe and Mail, 26 June 1969; 'Full Equality for Indian Set,' Ottawa Citizen, 26 June 1969.
13   'Indian Act Plans Are Arrogant, Schreyer Tells NIB Meeting,' Winnipeg Tribune, 18 July 1969.
14   'Indians Call Chretien a Liar,' Toronto Weekend Telegram, 5 July 1969; 'Alberta Indians Ready to Fight Federal Policy,' Toronto Globe and Mail, 8 July 1969.
15   National Indian Brotherhood, Press Release, 18 July 1969. See also 'Government Statement on Indian Policy June 25, 1969: Comparison with Remarks Recorded at Consultation Meetings on the Indian Act,' March 1970, DIAND.
16   'Do Indians Dare Buy Chretien's Dream?' Ottawa Citizen, 8 July 1969.
17   National Indian Brotherhood, Press Release, 26 June 1969; Manitoba Indian Brotherhood, 'Position Paper,' 16 July 1969.
18   DIAND, Press Release, 'Assistant Deputy Minister Appointed,' 27 August 1969.
19   Personal communication, George Manuel, 29 March 1977.

20 'Indians to End Bitter Heritage,' *Time Magazine*, 4 July 1969, pp. 15-18.
21 'A Big Flaw in Plans for Indian Equality,' Toronto *Globe and Mail*, 1 July 1969; 'Why an Old Indian Pattern Was Broken,' Toronto *Globe and Mail*, 8 July 1969.
22 Ibid.
23 Special Debate on Indian Policy, House of Commons Debates, 11 July 1969, pp. 11123-48.
24 Ibid., 11145.
25 Ibid.
26 This and the following quotations are from 'Transcript of the Prime Minister's Remarks at the Vancouver Liberal Association Dinner, Seaforth Armories, Vancouver, British Columbia,' 8 August 1969.
27 Letter, the Prime Minister to Dave Courchene, 25 September 1969 (DIAND file 1/44-1, Vol. 5).
28 National Indian Brotherhood, 'Press Release,' 18 July 1969.
29 DIAND Press Release, 16 September 1969.
30 'Indian Policy Like "Big U.S. Failure",' Ottawa *Citizen*, 11 October 1969; Duran (1970).
31 Douglas Sanders, 'A Critical Review of the New Indian Policy and Native Claims,' prepared for the Progressive Conservative's Thinkers' Conference, Niagara Falls, Ontario. October 1970 (Toronto: Indian-Eskimo Association).
32 Ibid., 4.
33 'Chretien's Hard Sell Finding Few Buyers,' Toronto *Globe and Mail*, 11 October 1969; Green (1970, 1976).
34 'Rewrite Indian Policy, Liberal Thinkers Told,' Toronto *Globe and Mail*, 22 November 1969; Peter Cumming, 'The State and the Individual (Indian Affairs): The "New Policy" – "Panacea" or "Put-On?"' paper prepared for the Task Force on the Individual for presentation at the Harrison Liberal Conference, December 1969.
35 Order in Council, PC 1969-2405, 19 December 1969; 'Red Paper: Indian Raps Govt. White Paper,' Ottawa *Citizen*, 13 January 1970.
36 Indian Claims Commission (1975: 231; 1977), Barber (1974, 1976).
37 'Wuttunee Termed "Traitorous"; Barred from his Home Reserve,' Toronto *Globe and Mail*, 4 May 1970; 'Indian Policy Loses Support of Wuttunee,' Toronto *Globe and Mail*, 7 May 1970.
38 For press commentary on Cardinal's *The Unjust Society* see 'The Unjust Society: New Crisis for Gov't Indian Policy,' Ottawa *Journal*, 3 December 1969; 'Stark Warning to Ottawa; Canada's Indians Rise in Anger,' December 1969; 'Red Paper: Indian Raps Govt. White Paper,' Ottawa *Citizen*, 13 January 1970; 'Indian Visions,' Ottawa *Citizen*, 15 January 1970; see also Duran (1970).
39 Jean Chrétien's speeches, 'Why an Old Indian Pattern Was Broken,' 8 July 1969; 'The Government of Canada's Indian Policy Proposals: A Discussion Paper for the Saskatchewan Young Liberal Conference,' Regina, Saskatchewan, 13 September 1969; 'Statement by the Honourable Jean Chretien Minister of Indian Affairs and Northern Development Based on a Speech Delivered in Regina,' 2 October 1969; and 'Indian Policy – Where Does It Stand?,' given to the Empire Club, Toronto 16 October 1969; David A. Munro, 'The Indian Policy – A Flexible Approach,' speech delivered to Lethbridge Chamber of Commerce, Lethbridge, 19 November 1969 (DIAND Press Releases).
40 Indian Chiefs of Alberta (1970).
41 National Indian Brotherhood, 'Amendments to the Red Paper Suggested and Agreed to by the Meeting of the National Indian Brotherhood June 3, 1970.'
42 Information on arranging the cabinet meeting comes from Clive Linklater, a staff member of the Indian Association of Alberta in 1970, and Walter Rudnicki.
43 'Indians Set to Present a Red Paper,' Toronto *Globe and Mail*, 4 June 1970; 'The Pow-wow on the Hill,' Toronto *Telegram*, 5 June 1970; 'PM Promises Indians, "No

Forced Solutions,"' Montreal *Star*, 5 June 1970; 'PM to Indians: We Won't Force Policy on You,' Toronto *Star*, 5 June 1970; 'Special Rights to Indians Depends on Electorate – PM,' Toronto *Telegram*, 5 June 1970; 'Naive but Honest,' Winnipeg *Tribune*, 6 June 1970.

44 Standing Committee on Indian Affairs and Northern Development, Minutes of Proceedings and Evidence, 4 June 1970, p. 8.

45 Harold Cardinal, 'Address by Harold Cardinal, President, Indian Association of Alberta, During Presentation by the Indian Chiefs of Alberta to the Prime Minister and the Government of Canada, June 4, 1970.' Toronto: Indian-Eskimo Association.

46 'Statement by the Prime Minister at a Meeting with the Indian Association of Alberta and the National Indian Brotherhood, Ottawa, June 4, 1970.' Toronto: Indian-Eskimo Association.

47 Resolutions of the 12th Annual Convention of the Nishga Tribal Council in letter from Frank Calder (president) to Jean Chrétien, 10 November 1969 (DIAND file 1/24-2-16, Vol. 2).

48 'Indians are Skeptical of PM's Assurances,' Toronto *Globe and Mail*, 6 June 1970; 'The Indians' Answer,' Toronto *Globe and Mail*, 9 June 1970. For more recent expressions of scepticism, see 'Provinces Upset by Indian Policy,' Ottawa *Journal*, 20 October 1976; Brass (1977).

49 Jean Chrétien, 'Notes for the Honourable Jean Chretien, Minister of Indian Affairs and Northern Development to the Alberta Indian Socio-Economic and Cultural Development Conference, Edmonton, Alberta,' 5 November 1970.

CHAPTER 9

1 Quebec (1976), Richardson (1972, 1975), Spence (1972), James Bay Committee (1973), Bourassa (1973), Salisbury et al. (1972), CASNP (1975), Indian Claims Commission (1975: 175-82), *Recherches amérindiennes au Quebec*, Vol. 1, 1971 and Vol. 1, 1972.

2 Indian Brotherhood of the NWT position paper presented to NIB at Regina, July 1971; and 1975; Cumming and Aalto (1974), Rea (1976), Keith et al. (1976), DIAND (1975), Dosman (1975).

3 Lysyk (1973); Manuel and Posluns (1974: 225); CASNP (1976d).

4 Standing Committee of the House of Commons on Indian Affairs and Northern Development, Minutes of Proceedings and Evidence, Numbers 11-14, April 1973; Bauer (1973, 1974); Gibbins and Ponting (1976); CASNP (1976, 1976c); Yabsley (1976, 1976a).

5 Jean Chretien, 'Statement by the Honourable Jean Chretien, on Claims of Indians and Inuit People,' 8 August 1973 (Ottawa: DIAND Press Release), Indian Claims Commission (1977), Doerr (1975).

6 DIAND, Annual Report for 1975, p. 43.

7 James Bay and Northern Quebec Native Claims Settlement Act, *Canada Gazette*, 1976–77, ch. 32, Part 3; Quebec (1975); Gardner (1976); DIAND Press Release, 'James Bay Settlement Act Proclaimed, Faulkner Announces,' 31 October 1977.

8 Yukon Native Brotherhood, 'Together Today for Our Children Tomorrow: A Statement of Grievances and an Approach to Settlement by the Yukon Indian People,' prepared for the Commissioner for Indian Claims and the Government of Canada (Whitehorse: Council for Yukon Indians, 1977); J.K. Naysmith, 'A Statement to the Alaska Highway Pipeline Inquiry by Dr. J.K. Naysmith, Federal Government's Special Claims Representative (Yukon),' 20 May 1977 (DIAND); CASNP (1976a); Lysyk, Bohmer, and Phelps (1977).

9 Pimlott et al. (1973); Freeman and Hackman (1975); Indian Brotherhood of the Northwest Territories (1975), 1976, 1976a); McCallums (1975); O'Malley (1976); Inuit Tapirisat of Canada (1976, 1976a, 1976b); *The Canadian Forum* (1976); Nelson

(1976); CASNP (1976b, 1976e, 1976f, 1976g); Gribbons (1976); Berger (1977); Timson (1977); Erasmus (1977); Watkins (1977); 'Government, Western Arctic Eskimos Reach Tentative Land-Settlement Pact,' Toronto *Globe and Mail*, 15 July 1978.

10 *Bulletin*, Union of BC Indian Chiefs, 30 April, 2 May, 5 May 1975; Joy Hall, 'George Manuel Speaks with the Editor,' *The National Indian* (NIB) 1 (6): 5-7; CASNP (1976d).

11 Indian Act, Revised Statutes of Canada, 1970, Ch. 149, section 12(1)(b).

12 Sanders (1974d, 1974f, 1975); Whyte (1974); Royal Commission on the Status of Women (1970); Weaver (1974, in press); Jamieson (1978).

13 Lysyk (1968); Sanders (1972); Sinclair (1970); Tarnopolsky (1975).

14 National Indian Brotherhood, 'Resolution on the Lavell Case, Indian Status and the Indian Act,' press release, 27 September 1976.

15 Cabinet memorandum, 'Financial Assistance to Native Associations,' 13 July 1970; Cabinet memorandum, 'Consultation Mechanism – Indian Policy Proposals,' 22 July 1970.

16 Cabinet memorandum, 'Financial Assistance to Native Associations,' 29 July 1970.

17 Cabinet memorandum, 'Consultative Mechanism – Indian Policy Proposals,' 22 July 1970.

18 Ibid.

19 Cabinet memorandum, 'Consultation Mechanism – Indian Policy Proposals,' 29 July 1970.

20 Cabinet memorandum, 'Interim Report: Consultative Mechanism – Indian Affairs,' 12 November 1970.

21 Carmen Maracle, '150 Indian Youth Seize Indian Affairs Offices,' *Indian News* 16/6 (1973): 1, 14; 'The Native Caravan: A Call for Justice,' *Inuit Monthly*, 3/9 (1974): 22-7, 97-8; Whiteside (1973a); Jack (1970); Castellano (1970); Waubageshig (1970).

22 Joint Cabinet–National Indian Brotherhood Committee, 'Press Release: Issued Jointly by Mr. George Manuel, President of the National Indian Brotherhood, and the Honourable Marc Lalonde, President of the Joint Committee,' 14 April 1976, and 'Interview with Noel Starblanket,' *Indian News*, 18/2 (1977): 1-2, 12-14; *The National Indian* (1977, 1977a, 1977b).

23 'New Federal Government – Indian Relationship,' DIAND, July 1976.

24 'Interview with Harold Cardinal,' *Indian News*, 18/2 (1977): 1, 6; 'Statement by Harold Cardinal, Regional Director-General, Alberta,' *Indian News*, 18/2 (1977): 1; DIAND Press Release, 22 November 1977; DIAND Press Release, 'Minister Regrets Kelly Resignation,' 1 June 1978.

25 'Increased Indian, Metis and Non-Status Indian and Inuit Participation in the Public Service of Canada,' Minutes of the Treasury Board, Ottawa, 21 June 1977; 'Native People and Employment in the Public Service of Canada,' Impact Research, Ottawa, 1976 (DIAND).

26 National Indian Brotherhood, 'Indians Withdraw from Cabinet Discussions,' press release, 13 April 1978; 'Indians Leave Cabinet Committee,' Ottawa *Citizen*, 14 April 1978; 'Indians Quit Role with Gov't,' Ottawa *Journal*, 14 April 1978; House of Commons Debates, 20 March 1978, pp. 3921-2.

27 National Indian Brotherhood, 'Indian Control of Indian Education: Policy Paper Presented to the Minister of Indian Affairs and Northern Development,' 1972; 'Housing Policy Development,' *The National Indian*, 1/6 (1977): 10-12; National Indian Brotherhood, 'Indians: Lands and Resources,' November 1973; Weitz (1974); Gill (1975).

28 While this book was in press, DIAND published a report, *Indian Conditions: A Survey* (1980), which substantiates this statement.

29 'Interview with Pierre Elliott Trudeau,' *Maclean's Magazine*, 3 April 1978, pp. 4-12.

Bibliography

Abel, Albert S. 1968. Administrative Secrecy. *Canadian Public Administration* 11: 440-8
Abler, T.S., and S. Weaver. 1974. *A Canadian Indian Bibliography, 1960–1970.* Toronto: University of Toronto Press
Ames, D., and B.R. Fisher. 1959. The Menominee Termination Crisis: Barriers in the Way of Rapid Cultural Transition. *Human Organization* 18: 101-11
Aucoin, Peter. 1971. Theory and Research in the Study of Policy-Making. In *The Structures of Policy-Making in Canada*, ed. G. Bruce Doern and Peter Aucoin, pp. 10-29. Toronto: Macmillan
— 1975. Pressure Groups and Recent Changes in the Policy-Making Process. In *Pressure Group Behaviour in Canadian Politics*, ed. A. Paul Pross, pp. 172-92. Toronto: McGraw-Hill Ryerson
Axworthy, Lloyd. 1971. The Housing Task Force: A Case Study. In *The Structures of Policy-Making in Canada*, ed. G. Bruce Doern and Peter Aucoin, pp. 130-53. Toronto: Macmillan
Baetz, Reuben. 1967. The Citizens' Organization. *Canadian Welfare* 43 (July-Aug): 4-9
Bailey, F.G. 1969. *Stratagems and Spoils.* Toronto: Copp Clark
Balls, Herbert. 1976. Decision-making: The role of the Deputy Minister. *Canadian Public Administration* 19: 417-31
Barber, Lloyd I. 1974. Indian Claims Mechanisms. *Saskatchewan Law Review* 38: 11-15
— 1976. The Basis for Native Claims in Canada. *The Western Canadian Journal of Anthropology* 6(2): 5-12
Barker, Robert W. 1960. The Indian Claims Commission – The Conscience of the Nation in Its Dealings with the Original American. *Federal Bar Journal* 20: 240-7
Barney, Ralph A. 1955. Legal Problems Peculiar to Indian Claims Litigation. *Ethnohistory* 2: 315-25
— 1960. Some Legal Problems under the Indian Claims Commission Act. *Federal Bar Journal* 20: 235-9
Bauer, George W. 1973. Aboriginal Rights in Canada. *The Canadian Forum* May: 15-20
— 1974. Aboriginal Rights: The Continuing Debate. *The Canadian Forum* April: 10-14
Berger, Thomas. 1977. *Northern Frontier, Northern Homeland: The Report of the Mackenzie Valley Pipeline Inquiry.* 2 vols. Ottawa: Department of Supply and Services
Borovoy, A.A. 1966. Indian Poverty in Canada. *Canadian Labour* 12: 13-15
Bourassa, H. 1973. *James Bay.* Montreal: Harvest House

Bowker, W.F. 1970. The Canadian Bill of Rights – S94(b) Indian Act – Irreconcilable Conflict – Equality before the Law – Regina v. Drybones. *Alberta Law Review* 8: 409-18

Bowles, R.P., J.L. Hanley, B.W. Hodgins, and G.A. Rawlyk. 1972. *The Indian: Assimilation, Integration or Separation?* Scarborough, Prentice-Hall

Brass, Lloyd. 1977. Starblanket Presses for Indian Involvement in BNA Act Talks. *The Saskatchewan Indian* 7(4): 17

Bregha, Francis J. 1971. Community Development in Canada: Problems and Strategies. In *Citizen Participation: Canada*, ed. James A. Draper, pp. 72-83. Toronto: New Press

Brophy, William A., and Sophie D. Aberle. 1966. *The Indian: America's Unfinished Business: Report of the Commission on the Rights, Liberties, and Responsibilities of the American Indian.* Norman, OK: University of Oklahoma Press

Canada. 1912. *Indian Treaties and Surrenders from 1680-1902.* Ottawa: King's Printer (reprinted in 1971 by Coles Publishing Co., Toronto)

— 1959. *Report of the Royal Commission Appointed to Investigate the Unfulfilled Provisions of Treaties 8 and 11 as They Apply to the Indians of the Mackenzie District* [Nelson Commission]. Ottawa

Canada. Senate. 1971. *Poverty in Canada.* Report of the Special Senate Committee on Poverty. Ottawa: Queen's Printer

Canada. Senate and House of Commons. 1927. Report of the Special Committee of the Senate and the House of Commons to Inquire into the Claims of the Allied Indian Tribes of British Columbia. Ottawa.

— 1946-48. Special Joint Committee of the Senate and House of Commons on the Indian Act. Minutes of Proceedings and Evidence

— 1959-61. Joint Committee of the Senate and House of Commons on Indian Affairs. Second and Final Report to Parliament, Minutes of Proceedings and Evidence, 1961, No. 16

Canada. Statutes. 1951. The Indian Act. Chapter 149

— 1970. The Indian Act. Chapter 149. Revised Statutes of Canada 1970

— 1977. James Bay and Northern Quebec Native Claims Settlement Act. *Canada Gazette* 1976-77, Ch. 32, Part 3

Canadian Corrections Association. 1967. *Indians and the Law.* Ottawa: The Canadian Welfare Council

Canadian Forum. 1976. Special Issue on the Mackenzie Pipeline. *The Canadian Forum*, November 1976

Canadian Welfare. 1967. The Emerging Indian Crisis. Special Issue of *Canadian Welfare*, 43 (July-August): 1, 10-32

Cardinal, Harold. 1969. *The Unjust Society.* Edmonton: Hurtig

— 1969a. Canadian Indians and the Federal Government. *The Western Canadian Journal of Anthropology* 1(1): 90-7

— 1977. *The Rebirth of Canada's Indians.* Edmonton: Hurtig

CASNP (Canadian Association in Support of the Native Peoples). 1975. Native People in Quebec. Special Issue of the CASNP *Bulletin*, Vol. 16, No. 4, December 1975

— 1976. Aboriginal Rights. Special Issue of the CASNP *Bulletin*, Vol. 17, No. 3, December 1976

— 1976a. The Yukon Settlement. CASNP *Bulletin* 17(3): 23

— 1976b. Making a Case for the Inuit. CASNP *Bulletin* 17(1): 9-12

— 1976c. Native Land Settlements. Special Issue of the CASNP *Bulletin*, Vol. 17, No. 1, March 1976

— 1976d. 'Nishga Land Is Not for Sale.' CASNP *Bulletin* 17(3): 25

— 1976e. 'Nunavut – Our Land.' CASNP *Bulletin* 17(1): 19-20

— 1976f. Update: The Dene Present Their Case ... And Hope. CASNP *Bulletin* 17(3): 45-6

— 1976g. The Theft of Our Humanity: A Case for the Dene. CASNP *Bulletin* 17(3): 6-11

Castellano, Marlene. 1970. Vocation or Identity: The Dilemma of Indian Youth. In *The Only Good Indian*, ed. Waubageshig, pp. 52-60. Toronto: New Press

Chrétien, Jean. 1970. Indian Policy: A Reply. *The Canadian Forum* (March): 279-81

Christian, W., and C. Campbell. 1974. *Political Parties and Ideologies in Canada.* Toronto: McGraw-Hill Ryerson

City Magazine, 1976. William Teron vs. Walter Rudnicki: How Ottawa Does its Business. *City Magazine* 2(5): 14-24

Council for Yukon Indians. 1977. *Together Today For Our Children Tomorrow.* Brampton, Ont: Charters Publishing Co

Cumming, Peter, and Kevin Aalto. 1974. Inuit Hunting Rights in the Northwest Territories. *Saskatchewan Law Review* 38(2): 251-324

Cumming, Peter A., and N.H. Mickenberg (eds.). 1972. *Native Rights in Canada.* Toronto: Indian-Eskimo Association, and General Publishing Co., second edition

Currie, Walter. 1968. The Hidden World of Legislated Discrimination. *The Northian* 5(3): 24-6

Deloria, Vine Jr. 1969. *Custer Died for Your Sins.* London: Collier-Macmillan

Department of Citizenship and Immigration. 1961/66. *Annual Reports.* Ottawa: Queen's Printer

Department of Health and Welfare. 1961/62. *Annual Report.* Ottawa: Queen's Printer

DIAND (Department of Indian Affairs and Northern Development). 1966. *The Canadian Indian: A Reference Paper.* Ottawa: DIAND

— 1967-78. *Annual Reports.* Ottawa: Queen's Printer

— 1968. *Choosing a Path.* Ottawa: Queen's Printer

— 1968-69. Reports of the Indian Act Consultation Meetings. Ottawa: DIAND. 1. Yellowknife, NWT, 25-27 July 1968. 2. Moncton, NB, 29-31 July 1968. 3. Toronto, Ont, 12-14 August 1968. 4. Fort William, Ont, 16-19 August 1968. 5. Sudbury, Ont, 21-23 August 1968. 6. Regina, Sask, 16-20 September 1968. 7. Quebec City, Que, 30 September-4 October 1968. 8. Montmorency, Que, 1-4 October 1968. 9. Prince George, BC, 14-18 October 1968. 10. Whitehorse, Yukon, 21-23 October 1968. 11. Terrace, BC, 24-28 October 1968. 12. Nanaimo, BC, 30 October-1 November 1968. 13. Kelowna, BC, 12-16 November 1968. 14. Chilliwack, BC, 18-22 November 1968. 15. Edmonton, Alta, 12-13 December 1968. 16. Winnipeg, Man, 18-20 December 1968. 17. Toronto, Ont, 20-24 January 1969. 18. Terrace, BC, 17-18 January 1969.

— 1969. [*The White Paper*] *Statement of the Government of Canada on Indian Policy 1969.* Ottawa: Queen's Printer

— 1970. Brief Submitted to the Special Senate Committee on Poverty. Special Senate Committee on Poverty, Minutes of Proceedings and Evidence, No. 14, 20 January 1970, pp. 40-191

Dimock, Hedley G. 1971. Social Intervention: Philosophy and Failure. In *Citizen Participation: Canada*, ed. James A. Draper, pp. 106-14. Toronto: New Press

Doern, G. Bruce. 1971. Recent Changes in the Philosophy of Policy-Making in Canada. *Canadian Journal of Political Science* 4: 243-64

— 1971a. The Development of Policy Organizations in the Executive Arena. In *The Structures of Policy-Making in Canada*, ed. G. Bruce Doern and Peter Aucoin, pp. 39-78. Toronto: Macmillan

— 1974. Horizontal and Vertical Portfolios in Government. In *Issues in Canadian Public Policy*, ed. G. Bruce Doern and V. Seymour Wilson, pp. 310-36. Toronto: Macmillan

Doern, G. Bruce, and Peter Aucoin (eds.). 1971. *The Structures of Policy-Making in Canada.* Toronto: Macmillan

Doern, G. Bruce, and V. Seymour Wilson (eds.). 1974. *Issues in Canadian Public Policy.* Toronto: Macmillan

Doerr, Audrey D. 1973. The Role of White Papers in the Policy-Making Process: The Experience of the Government of Canada. Unpublished PhD dissertation, Department of Political Science, Carleton University

— 1975. The Dilemma of Indian Policy in Canada. *Quarterly of Canadian Studies for the Secondary School* 3(4): 198-207

Dosman, Edgar J. 1975. *The National Interest: The Politics of Northern Development 1968-75*. Toronto: McClelland and Stewart

Draper, James A. (ed.). 1971. *Citizen Participation: Canada*. Toronto: New Press

Dunning, R.W. 1959. Ethnic Relations and the Marginal Man. *Human Organization* 18: 117-22

— 1967. The Hawthorn Report. *The Canadian Forum* 1967: (June) 52-3

— 1969. Indian Policy – A Proposal for Autonomy. *The Canadian Forum* 1969: (Dec) 206-107

— 1971. The Indian Situation: A Canadian Governmental Dilemma. *International Journal of Comparative Sociology* 12: 128-34

Duran, James A. 1970. The Unjust Society. *The Canadian Forum* (Feb): 252-4

Economic Council of Canada. 1968. *The Fifth Annual Review: The Challenge of Growth and Change*. Ottawa

Edgerton, R.B. 1962. Menominee Termination: Observations on the End of a Tribe. *Human Organization* 21: 10-16

Erasmus, Georges. 1977. We the Dene. In *Dene Nation – The Colony Within*, ed. Mel Watkins, pp. 177-81. Toronto: University of Toronto Press

Freeman, Milton M.R., and Linda Hackman. 1975. Bathurst Island NWT: A Test Case of Canada's Northern Policy. *Canadian Public Policy* 1: 402-14

Fumoleau, Rene. 1975. *As Long as This Land Shall Last*. Toronto: McClelland and Stewart

Gardner, Eddie. 1976. James Bay One Year After. CASNP *Bulletin* 17(3): 17-20

Gibbins, Roger, and J. Rick Ponting. 1976. Indians and Indian Issues: What Do Canadians Think? Part I. CASNP *Bulletin* 17(3): 38-43

Gill, A. 1975. Indian Concern in Indian Education Management. *The Northian* 2(2): 20-5

Graham-Cumming, G. 1967. Health of the Original Canadians, 1867–1967. *Medical Services Journal of Canada* 13 (Feb): 115-66

Green, L.C. 1970. Canada's Indians: Federal Policy, International and Constitutional Law. *Ottawa Law Review* 4(1): 101-31

— 1976. Trusteeship and Canada's Indians, *Dalhousie Law Journal* 3: 104-35

Gribbons, Collin. 1976. Important Changes to the 'Nunavut' Claim. CASNP *Bulletin* 17(3): 13-15

Harding, James. 1965. Canada's Indians: A Powerless Minority. The Student Union for Peace Action. Published later in *Poverty in Canada*, ed. J. Harp and J. Hofley, pp. 239-52. Scarborough, Ont: Prentice-Hall 1971

Hawthorn, H.B. 1966–67. *A Survey of the Contemporary Indians of Canada: Economic, Political, Educational Needs and Policies*, 2 vols. Ottawa: Queen's Printer

Hawthorn, H.B., C.S. Belshaw, and S.M. Jamieson. 1958. *The Indians of British Columbia*. Toronto: University of Toronto Press

Haycock, Ronald G. 1971. *The Image of the Indian*. Waterloo: Waterloo Lutheran University Press

Hockin, Thomas A. 1970. The Advance of Standing Committees in Canada's House of Commons: 1965 to 1970. *Canadian Public Administration* 13: 185-202

— 1971. *Apex of Power: The Prime Minister and Political Leadership in Canada*. Scarborough, Ont: Prentice-Hall

— 1971a. The Prime Minister and Political Leadership: An Introduction to Some Restraints and Imperatives. In *Apex of Power*, ed. Thomas Hockin, pp. 2-21. Scarborough, Ont: Prentice-Hall

— 1971b. Pierre Trudeau on the Prime Minister and the participant Party. In *Apex of Power*, ed. Thomas Hockin, pp. 96-102. Scarborough, Ont: Prentice-Hall

Hodgetts, J.E. 1974. *The Canadian Public Service: A Physiology of Government 1867–1970*. Toronto: University of Toronto Press

Hodgson, J.S. 1976. The Impact of Minority Government on the Senior Civil Servant. *Canadian Public Administration* 19: 227-37

Hood, Susan. 1972. Termination of the Klamath Indian Tribe of Oregon. *Ethnohistory* 19: 379-92

Indian Brotherhood of the Northwest Territories. 1975. *The Dene Declaration.* 19 July 1975. Reprinted in M. Watkins (1977: 3-4)

— 1976. A Proposal to the Government and People of Canada: Agreement in Principle between the Dene Nation and Her Majesty the Queen, in Right of Canada. 25 October 1976. Reprinted in M. Watkins (1977: 182-7)

— 1976. *The Dene: Land and Unity for the Native People of the Mackenzie Valley: A Statement of Rights.* Brampton, Ont: Charters Publishing Co

Indian Chiefs of Alberta. 1970. *Citizens Plus.* [The Red Paper] Presented to Prime Minister Pierre Trudeau, June 1970. First part published in *The Only Good Indian,* ed. Waubageshig, pp. 5-40. Toronto: New Press

Indian Claims Commission. 1975. *Indian Claims in Canada: An Introductory Essay and Selected List of Library Holdings.* Ottawa: Research Resource Centre, Indian Claims Commission. Queen's Printer

— 1977. *Commissioner on Indian Claims: A Report, Statement and Submissions.* Ottawa: Department of Supply and Services

Indian-Eskimo Association of Canada. 1970. *Native Rights in Canada.* Toronto: General Publishing

Innis, Hugh R. 1973. *Bilingualism and Biculturalism: An Abridged Version of the Royal Commission Report.* Toronto: McClelland and Stewart

Inuit Tapirisat of Canada. 1976. *Inuit Land Use and Occupancy Study.* 3 vols. Ottawa: Department of Supply and Services

— 1976a. *Nunavut: A Proposal for the Settlement of Inuit Lands in the Northwest Territories.* Ottawa: Inuit Tapirisat of Canada

— 1976b. *Inuit Tapirisat of Canada: An Introduction to the Eskimo People of Canada and their National Organization.* Ottawa: Inuit Tapirisat of Canada

Jack, Henry. 1970. Native Alliance for Red Power. In *The Only Good Indian,* ed. Waubageshig, pp. 162-80. Toronto: New Press

Jackson, Robert J., and Michael M. Atkinson. 1974. *The Canadian Legislative System.* Toronto: Macmillan

James Bay Committee, ed. Fikret Berkes. 1973. *James Bay Forum: Public Hearing on the James Bay Project Held in Montreal, April 1973.* Comité pour la défense de la Baie James, Montreal

Jamieson, Kathleen. 1978. *Indian Women and the Law in Canada: Citizens Minus.* Ottawa: Department of Supply and Services. Published for the Advisory Council on the Status of Women and Indian Rights for Indian Women

Jenness, Diamond. 1942. Canada's Indian Problems. *America Indigena* 2(1): 29-38

— 1947. Plan for Liquidating Canada's Indian Problem within 25 Years. Published in the Special Joint Committee of the Senate and the House of Commons on the Indian Act, Minutes of Proceedings and Evidence, 25 March 1947. No. 7, pp. 310-11

Johnson, A.W. 1961. The Role of the Deputy Minister. *Canadian Public Administration* 4: 363-73

Josephy, Alvin M. 1971. *Red Power.* New York: American Heritage Press

Keith, R.F., et al. 1976. *Northern Development and Technology Assessment Systems.* Science Council of Canada, Background Study No. 34. Ottawa: Information Canada

Kernaghan, W.D.K. 1968. An Overview of Public Administration in Canada Today. *Canadian Public Administration* 11: 291-308

— 1976. Politics, Policy and Public Servants: Political Neutrality Revisited. *Canadian Public Administration* 19: 432-56

Koolage, W.W. 1972. Relocation and Culture Change: A Canadian Sub-arctic Case Study. *Proceedings of the International Congress of Americanists,* pp. 613-17. Geneva: Tilgher

Labour Gazette. 1969. The Divine Right to be Human. *The Labour Gazette* 69: 66-71
LaFarge, Oliver. 1957. Termination of Federal Supervision: Disintegration and the American Indians. In *The Annals of the American Academy of Political and Social Science.* 311(May): 41-6
Lagasse, Jean H. 1961. Community Development in Manitoba. *Human Organization* 20: 232-7
Lalonde, Marc. 1971. The Changing Role of the Prime Minister's Office. *Canadian Public Administration* 14: 509-37
Lamontagne, Maurice. 1968. The Influence of the Politician. *Canadian Public Administration* 11: 264-71
Lindblom, C.E. 1968. *The Policy-Making Process.* Englewood Cliffs, NJ: Prentice-Hall
Lloyd, Anthony John. 1967. *Community Development in Canada.* Ottawa: Canadian Research Centre for Anthropology. St Paul University
Loram, C.T., and T.F. McIlwraith (eds.). 1943. *The North American Indian Today.* Toronto: University of Toronto Press
Lotz, Jim. 1977. *Understanding Canada: Regional and Community Development in a New Nation.* Toronto: NC *Nation*
Lueger, Richard. 1977. A History of Indian Associations in Canada (1870–1970). Unpublished MA thesis, Institute of Canadian Studies, Carleton University
Lurie, Nancy O. 1955. [Indian Claims Commission]: Problems, Opportunities, and Recommendations. *Ethnohistory* 2: 357-75
— 1957. The Indian Claims Commission Act. In *The Annals of the American Academy of Political and Social Science* 311(May): 56-70
— 1972. Menominee Termination: From Reservation to Colony. *Human Organization* 31: 257-70
Lysyk, Kenneth. 1967. The Unique Constitutional Position of the Canadian Indian. *Canadian Bar Review* 45: 514-53
— 1968. Human Rights and the Native Peoples of Canada. *Canadian Bar Review* 46: 695-705
— 1968a. Canadian Bill of Rights – Irreconcilable Conflict with Another Federal Enactment – 'Equality before the Law' and the Liquor Provisions of the Indian Act. *Canadian Bar Review* 46: 141-9
— 1969. Canada's Native People – Their Rights Have Been Denied. *Human Relations* (Ontario Human Rights Commission) 9(17): 13-15
— 1972. The United States Indian Claims Commission. In *Native Rights in Canada*, eds. P.A. Cumming and N.H. Mickenberg, pp. 243-64. Toronto: General Publishing
— 1973. The Indian Title Question in Canada: An Appraisal in the Light of Calder. *Canadian Bar Review* 51: 450-80
Lysyk, Kenneth, Edith E. Bohmer, and Willard L. Phelps. 1977. *Alaska Highway Pipeline Inquiry.* Ottawa: Department of Supply and Services
Manuel, George, and M. Posluns. 1974. *The Fourth World: An Indian Reality.* Toronto: Collier-Macmillan
Marchak, M. Patricia. 1975. *Ideological Perspectives on Canada.* Toronto: McGraw-Hill Ryerson
McCallum, Hugh and Karmel. 1975. *This Land Is Not for Sale: Canada's Original People and Their Land.* Toronto: Anglican Book Centre
McConnell, W.H. 1974. The Calder Case in Historical Perspective. *Saskatchewan Law Review* 38: 88-122
McDiarmid, Garnet, and D. Pratt. 1971. *Teaching Prejudice.* Toronto: Ontario Institute for Studies in Education
McEwen, E.R. 1968. *Community Development Services for Canadian Indian and Metis Communities.* Toronto: Indian-Eskimo Association
McGilp, J.G. 1963. The Relations of Canadian Indians and Canadian Governments. *Canadian Public Administration* 6: 299-308

McInnes, R.W. 1969. Indian Treaties and Related Disputes. *University of Toronto Faculty of Law Review* 27: 52-72

Melling, John. 1966. Recent Developments in Official Policy towards Canadian Indians and Eskimos. *Race* 7: 379-99

Menominee. National Committee to Save the Menominee People and Forests. 1972. *Freedom with Reservation: The Menominee Struggle to Save Their Land and People.* Madison, WI: Impressions, Inc.

Methuen Ltd. 1971. *Canada's 28th Parliament.* Toronto: Methuen

Mickenberg, Neil H. 1971. Aboriginal Rights in Canada and the United States. *Osgoode Hall Law Journal* 9: 119-56

Mortimore, George E. 1967. The Indians Were Here First: Treat Them as 'Citizens Plus.' *Human Relations* (Ontario Human Rights Commission) 7(15): 4-6

National Indian Brotherhood. 1977. Briefs and Beefs: Another NIB – Cabinet Committee. *The National Indian* (NIB) 1(3): 5

Native Voice. 1963. *The Native Voice.* Vancouver, BC

Nelson, J. Gordon (ed.). 1976. Arctic Land Use Issues. *Contact: Journal of Urban and Environmental Affairs.* 8(4). Waterloo: University of Waterloo

Normandin, P.G. (ed.). 1974. *Parliamentary Guide.* Ottawa: Intertask Ltd

O'Connell, Martin. 1968. Confrontation: IEA and Lester Pearson. *The Northian* 5(3): 20-1

O'Malley, Martin. 1976. *The Past and Future Land: An Account of the Berger Inquiry into the Mackenzie Valley Pipeline.* Toronto: Peter Martin Associates

Orfield, Gary. 1966. *A Study of the Termination Policy:* National Congress of American Indians, Denver, CO

Pickersgill, J.W. 1972. Bureaucrats and Politicians. *Canadian Public Administration* 5: 418-27

Pimlott, D.H., K. Vincent, and C. McKnight (eds.). 1973. *Arctic Alternatives.* Ottawa: Canadian Arctic Resources Committee

Porter, John. 1965. *The Vertical Mosaic: An Analysis of Social Class and Power in Canada.* Toronto: University of Toronto Press

Prefontaine, Norbert. 1973. What I Think I See: Reflections on the Foundations of Social Policy. *Canadian Public Administration* 16: 298-306

Price, Richard T. 1977. Indian Land Claims in Alberta: Politics and Policy-Making (1968–77). Unpublished MA thesis, Department of Political Science, University of Alberta

Quebec. 1976. *The James-Bay Agreement: Agreement between the Government of Quebec, the Grand Council of the Crees, the Northern Quebec Inuit Association and the Government of Canada.* Quebec: Government Printer

Rea, K.J. 1976. *The Political Economy of Northern Development.* Science Council of Canada Background Study No. 36. Ottawa

Recherches Amérindiennes au Québec. 1971. *La Baie James des Amérindiens.* Vol. 1

– 1972. *La Baie James des Amérindiens: Bibliographie.* Vol. 2, Special Issue, No. 1

Richardson, Boyce, 1972. *James Bay: The Plot to Drown the North Woods.* Toronto: Clarke, Irwin

– 1975. *Strangers Devour Their Land.* New York: A. Knopf

Robertson, Gordon. 1968. The Canadian Parliament and Cabinet in the Face of Modern Demands. *Canadian Public Administration* 11: 272-9

– 1971. The Changing Role of the Privy Council Office. *Canadian Public Administration* 14: 487-508

Royal Commission on the Status of Women. 1970. Report of the Royal Commission on the Status of Women in Canada. Ottawa: Queen's Printer

Ryan, Joan. 1978. *Wall of Words.* Toronto: Peter Martin Associates

Salisbury, Richard F., et al. 1972. *Development and James Bay: Socio-economic Implications of the Hydro-electric Project.* Montreal: McGill University Press

Sanders, Douglas E. 1972. The Bill of Rights and Indian Status. *UBC Law Review* 7: 81-105

— 1973. Native People in Areas of Internal National Expansion: Indians and Inuit in Canada. *International Work Group for Indigenous Affairs.* Document 14. Copenhagen
— 1973a. The Nishga Case. *BC Studies* 19 (Autumn): 3-20
— 1974. Canadian Courts and the Concept of Indian Title. In *Proceedings of the First Congress, Canadian Ethnology Society.* Ottawa: National Museum of Man, Mercury Series, No. 17, pp. 4-34
— 1974a. *Cases and Materials on Native Law.* Privately printed by D. Sanders
— 1974b. Indian Hunting and Fishing Rights. *Saskatchewan Law Review* 38: 45-62
— 1974c. Case Law Digest. In *A Canadian Indian Bibliography, 1960–1970,* eds. T.S. Abler, D. Sanders and S. Weaver, pp. 306-61. Toronto: University of Toronto Press
— 1974d. Indian Act – Status of Indian Woman on Marriage to Person without Indian Status. *Saskatchewan Law Review* 38: 243-9
— 1974e. Hunting Rights – Provincial Laws – Application on Indian Reserves. *Saskatchewan Law Review* 38: 234-42
— 1974f. The Indian Act and the Bill of Rights. *Ottawa Law Review* 6: 397-415
— 1975. Indian Women: A Brief History of Their Roles and Rights. *McGill Law Journal* 21: 656-72
— 1975a. Land Claims: A Legal History of the Land Claims. (Series of articles) *Nesika* Union of BC Indian Chiefs, 3(11)
— 1976. *The History We Live with: Indian Land Claims in British Columbia,* Victoria, BC: Victoria Indian Cultural Centre
Schindeler, Fred. 1971. The Prime Minister and the Cabinet: History and Development. In *Apex of Power,* ed. Thomas A. Hockin, pp. 22-48. Scarborough, Ont: Prentice-Hall
Shackleton, Doris. 1977. *Power Town: Democracy Discarded.* Toronto: McClelland and Stewart
Sharp, Mitchell. 1976. Decision-Making in the Federal Cabinet. *Canadian Public Administration* 19: 1-7
Simeon, Richard. 1972. *Federal-Provincial Diplomacy: The Making of Recent Policy in Canada.* Toronto: University of Toronto Press
Sinclair, J.G. 1970. The Queen vs. Drybones: The Supreme Court of Canada and the Canadian Bill of Rights. *Osgoode Hall Law Journal* 8: 599-619
Smith, Denis. 1971. President and Parliament: The Transformation of Parliamentary Government in Canada. In *The Apex of Power,* ed. Thomas A. Hockin, pp. 224-41. Scarborough, Ont: Prentice-Hall
Spence, John A. (ed.).1972. *Not by Bread Alone.* Prepared for the James Bay Task Force of the Indians of Quebec Association and the Northern Quebec Inuit Association
Staats, Howard. 1964. Some Aspects of the Legal Status of Canadian Indians. *Osgoode Hall Law Journal* 3: 36-51
Stern, Theodore. 1965. *The Klamath Tribe: A People and Their Reservation.* Seattle: University of Washington Press
Stevenson, David S. 1968. Problems of Eskimo Relocation for Industrial Employment. Ottawa: DIAND, Northern Science Research Group
Stewart, Walter. 1971. *Shrug: Trudeau in Power.* Toronto: New Press
Szablowski, George F. 1971. The Optimal Policy-Making System: Implications for the Canadian Political Process. In *Apex of Power,* ed. Thomas A. Hockin, pp. 135-45. Scarborough, Ont: Prentice-Hall
— 1973. The Prime Minister as Symbol: A Rejoinder. *Canadian Journal of Political Science* 6: 516-17
Thompson, P. 1965. The Reserve Tomorrow. *The Northian* 2(3): 11-15
Tarnopolsky, W.S. 1975. The Supreme Court and the Canadian Bill of Rights. *Canadian Bar Review* 53: 649-74
Thordarson, Bruce. 1972. *Trudeau and Foreign Policy.* Toronto: Oxford University Press
Timson, Judith. 1977. Berger of the North. *Maclean's Magazine* (10 January 1977), pp. 30-6

Tobias, John L. 1976. Protection, Civilization, Assimilation: An Outline History of Canada's Indian Policy. *The Western Canadian Journal of Anthropology* 6(2): 13-30
Trudeau, Pierre Elliott. 1968. *Pierre Elliott Trudeau: Federalism and the French Canadians.* Toronto: Macmillan
— 1970. Excerpts from Prime Minister Trudeau's Remarks on his Visit to the Australian National University, May 18, 1970. In *The Indian: Assimilation, Integration or Separation*, eds. R.P. Bowles, et al. pp. 223-4. Scarborough, Ont: Prentice-Hall 1972
Tyler, Samuel L. 1964. *Indian Affairs: A Work Paper on Termination, with an Attempt to Show Its Antecedents.* Provo, Utah: Institute of American Indian Studies
Vance, John. 1974. Indian Claims: The US Experience. *Saskatchewan Law Review* 38: 1-10
Ward, Norman. 1972. The Changing Role of the Privy Council Office and Prime Minister's Office: A Commentary. *Canadian Public Administration* 15: 375-7
Watkins, Arthur V. 1957. Termination of Federal Supervision: The Removal of Restrictions over Indian Property and Person. In *The Annals of the American Academy of Political and Social Science* 311(May): 47-55
Watkins, Mel (ed.). 1977. *Dene Nation: The Colony within.* Toronto: University of Toronto Press
Waubageshig (ed.). 1970. *The Only Good Indian.* Toronto: New Press
Wearing, Joseph. 1971. President or Prime Minister. In *The Apex of Power*, ed. Thomas A. Hockin, pp. 242-60. Scarborough, Ont: Prentice-Hall
Weaver, Sally M. 1972. *Medicine and Politics among the Grand River Iroquois: A Study of the Non-conservatives.* Ottawa: National Museum of Canada, Publications in Ethnology, No. 4
— 1974. Judicial Preservation of Ethnic Group Boundaries: The Iroquois Case. In *Proceedings of the First Congress, Canadian Ethnology Society.* Ottawa: National Museum of Man, Mercury Series, Canadian Ethnology Service, Paper No. 17, pp. 48-66
— 1976. The Role of Social Science in Formulating Canadian Indian Policy: A Preliminary History of the Hawthorn-Tremblay Report. In *The History of Canadian Anthropology, Proceedings No. 3, Canadian Ethnology Society*, ed. J. Freedman, pp. 50-97. Hamilton: McMaster University, Department of Anthropology
— in press. Indian Women, Marriage and Legal Status. In *Marriage and Divorce in Canada*, ed. K. Ishwaran. Toronto: McGraw-Hill Ryerson
Weitz, J.M. 1974. A Look at Indian Control of Indian Education. *The Northian* 10(1): 11-15
Whiteside, Don. 1973. *Historical Development of Aboriginal Political Associations in Canada: Documentation.* Ottawa: National Indian Brotherhood
— 1973a. *Contemporary Indian Protests: Reference Aids – Bibliographies.* 3 vols. Ottawa: National Indian Brotherhood
Whyte, John D. 1974. The Lavell Case and Equality in Canada. *Queen's Quarterly* 81: 28-42
Witt, Shirley Hill. 1968. Nationalist Trends among American Indians. In *The American Indian Today*, ed. S. Levine and N. Lurie, pp. 53-76. Deland, FL: Everett/Edwards
Wilson, V. Seymour. 1971. The Role of Royal Commissions and Task Forces. In *Structures of Policy-Making in Canada*, eds. G. Bruce Doern and Peter Aucoin, pp. 113-29. Toronto: Macmillan
Wuttunee, William. 1971. *Ruffled Feathers: Indians in Canadian Society.* Calgary: Bell
Yabsley, Gary. 1976. Aboriginal Rights. *Inuit Today* 5(9): 20-3
— 1976a. An Historic View: Aboriginal Rights. *Inuit Today* 5(10): 32-5

Index